本书为 2018 年教育部人文社会科学研究一般项目"中国英语学习者工作记忆对二语句子加工影响的 ERP 研究"（项目批准号：18YJA740060）的成果

工作记忆与二语学习

徐方　著

中国海洋大学出版社

·青岛·

图书在版编目(CIP)数据

工作记忆与二语学习 / 徐方著 . -- 青岛:中国海
洋大学出版社,2023.6
　ISBN 978-7-5670-3521-8

　Ⅰ. ①工…　Ⅱ. ①徐…　Ⅲ. ①第二语言－语言学习－
研究　Ⅳ. ①H09

　中国国家版本馆 CIP 数据核字(2023)第 094203 号

出版发行	中国海洋大学出版社		
社　　址	青岛市香港东路 23 号	**邮政编码**	266071
出 版 人	刘文菁		
网　　址	http://pub.ouc.edu.cn		
订购电话	0532-82032573(传真)		
责任编辑	林婷婷	**电　　话**	0532-85901092
印　　制	青岛国彩印刷股份有限公司		
版　　次	2023 年 6 月第 1 版		
印　　次	2023 年 6 月第 1 次印刷		
成品尺寸	170 mm ×230 mm		
印　　张	13.25		
字　　数	204 千		
印　　数	1～1 000		
定　　价	50.00 元		

简　介

大量证据表明,工作记忆与读写和计算这些必不可少的学习有关。二语学习尤其与工作记忆密切相关。

本书首先阐述了工作记忆的历史、理论和成分以及学者们对工作记忆容量的研究,介绍了与工作记忆密切相关的前额皮层,并探讨了提高工作记忆的方法。

本书第二章论述了短时记忆与二语学习的关系。短时记忆在外语学习中起着十分重要的作用。第二章详述了短时记忆的特点以及短时记忆与长时记忆、工作记忆的关系,探讨了短时记忆与外语学习的关系,最后提出了提高外语学习效率的一些方法。

第三章述评了国内二语习得中对于短时记忆的研究。短时记忆是近年来二语习得研究领域的重点课题。本章分析了短时记忆和工作记忆的关系、短时记忆的特点和短时记忆的信息提取;同时,从输入和输出两个方面回顾了国内短时记忆教学研究的成果,并在此基础上探讨了国内短时记忆研究领域的新发现和未来研究的发展趋势。

第四章综述了二语习得视域下句子理解中工作记忆的研究。工作记忆是近年来二语习得研究领域的重点课题。本章讨论了工作记忆与短时记忆的区别和联系,介绍了工作记忆的理论模型,阐述了工作记忆与句子理解的测量工具,总结评论了国内外二语习得中的工作记忆与句子理解和加工的研究现状,并分析了未来二语习得视域下句子理解中的工作记忆研究的发展趋势。

第五章述评了神经机制下工作记忆和二语句子理解的研究。本章从神经认知学角度，探讨神经机制下工作记忆和二语句子理解的关系；阐述了来自神经成像研究的工作记忆的功能以及工作记忆各成分在二语学习中的角色；分析了习得年龄、一语向二语迁移以及内容熟悉度是如何与工作记忆相联系来制约和促进二语句子理解；回顾了神经机制下工作记忆和二语句子理解的实验研究；最后总结了此领域的新发现和未来研究的发展趋势。

　　第六章探讨了工作记忆容量差异对二语歧义句加工的影响。本章总结评论了国内外近年来二语习得中的工作记忆与歧义句的研究现状，并分析了未来二语习得视域下歧义句与工作记忆研究的发展趋势。

　　第七章通过理论探索与实证研究，评估了短时记忆对于以英语为外语学习的中国学生听力理解的影响，探讨了改善短时记忆是否对提高可理解性输入起到重要作用。笔者对实验数据进行皮尔逊积矩相关分析和多元回归分析，得出的结论是：短时记忆是听力理解的一个重要组成部分；对句法的短时记忆在提供可理解性输入方面起重要作用。

　　第八章通过ERP实证研究证明了工作记忆容量对二语句子加工中的生命性有影响，而对世界知识没有影响。

　　第九章探讨了任务复杂度和工作记忆容量对二语写作表现的影响。二语写作受诸多因素的影响，其中包括任务因素和学习者因素。任务复杂度是一项重要的认知因素，其相关研究大多以"认知假说"和"竞争假说"为理论指导。由于对注意力资源分配的理解不同，两者关于任务复杂度对语言产出的影响做出了不同的预设。写作涉及多个过程相互作用，会对有限的工作记忆容量造成压力，其运行情况会影响写作的质量。除此之外，二语写作的动机、焦虑和自信心等也是影响二语写作表现的情感因子。事实上，任务因素和学习者因素可以相互结合，为二语写作任务提供多元化的指导。

目 录

第一章

工作记忆

1.1　工作记忆（working memory）

工作记忆是一个核心的执行功能且容量有限的认知系统，负责短暂存储和加工信息（Diamond，2013）。工作记忆在推理和指导决策和行为时至关重要。研究者们经常把工作记忆与短时记忆（short-term memory）按同义词来对待，但是神经心理学家认为两种形式的记忆截然不同：工作记忆操纵存储的信息，而短时记忆仅仅涉及短时存储信息（Nelson，2008）；它们分别与不同的神经子系统相联系，工作记忆更多依赖于背侧前额叶皮层（dorsolateral prefrontal cortex），而在大脑中维持信息并不需要涉及背侧前额叶皮层。成像研究表明，前额激活对不超阈值的记忆维持仅仅存在于腹外侧前额叶皮层（ventrolateral prefrontal cortex）中。工作记忆和短时记忆也显示出不同的发展进程，后者发展得更早、更快些。工作记忆是认知心理学、神经心理学和认知科学中至关重要的理论概念。

1.1.1　历史

词语"工作记忆"由 Pribram, Miller & Galanter 创造（Pribram et al.，1960；Baddeley，2003），在 20 世纪 60 年代把思想比作一台计算机的理论语境中得到应用。Atkinson & Shiffrin（1968）使用这个词语来描述"短时存储"。我们现在所称的工作记忆，以前分别以各种不同的形式被称为短时存储（short-term store）、短时记忆、初级记忆（primary memory）、即时记忆（immediate

memory)、操作记忆(operant memory)和临时记忆(provisional memory)
(Fuster, 1997)。短时记忆是短暂时间内(按秒的顺序)记忆信息的能力。如
今大多数理论学家使用工作记忆概念来代替或包括短时记忆这个更老的概
念,更强调操纵信息而不是被动地保存的概念。

最早提及以工作记忆为神经基础的实验可以追溯到一百多年前,Hitzig
和 Ferrier 描述了前额皮层的切除实验,并总结出前额皮层(frontal cortex)对
认知加工过程的重要性(Fuster, 2008)。Jacobsen(1935)首次表明前额叶切除
对延迟反应的有害影响。

1.1.2 理论

探讨工作记忆是如何在解剖和认知方面运作的各种模式纷纷涌现,最著
名的工作记忆模式有以下三种。

1.1.2.1 Baddeley 和 Hitch 提出的模式

Baddeley & Hitch(1974)提出了工作记忆模式,试图推出一个更准确的
初级记忆模式(经常被称作短时记忆)。工作记忆把初级记忆分成多个成分,
而不是一个单一的、统一的概念。Baddeley 和 Hitch 的最初模式由三个主要
成分组成:中央执行系统(central executive)、语音环(phonological loop)和视
觉空间模板(visuospatial sketchpad)。Baddeley 和 Hitch 对于更老模式中两个
类别特异性(domain-specific)从属系统区别的论点来自双任务范式(dual-task
paradigms)的实验发现:被试使用两个独立的感知域(视觉和口头任务)来执
行两个同时发生的任务,几乎和单独执行任务一样有效率;相反,被试努力使
用相同的感知域同时执行两项任务,比单独执行任务更没有效率。

(1)成分

① 中央执行

中央执行系统有控制中心的功能,在语音和视觉空间成分中指导信息
(Levin, 2011)。中央执行系统尤其负责指导注意力与相关信息、压制不相
关信息和不适当的行为,并且同时执行多项任务来协调认知过程。中央执
行系统是负责监督信息的组合和协调负责短时维持信息的从属系统(slave
system)。中央执行系统是一个灵活的系统,负责控制和调节认知加工过程,
具有以下功能:

• 把来自信息源的信息综合成连贯的情节；

• 协调从属系统；

• 在任务或提取策略间转换；

• 选择性地注意和抑制。

中央执行系统被看作监督体系，它控制认知过程，并在迷失方向时进行干预。Miyake et al.（2000）对中央功能研究表明，中央执行成分并不如Baddeley和Hitch模式中构想的那样是中枢成分，而似乎存在着分开的执行功能；它能很大程度上在个体间独立地变化，并能选择性地受到或免除大脑损伤的影响。

② 语音环

语言环是一个从属系统，负责储存语音信息（语言的声音），并且通过在复述环（rehearsal loop）中不断更新来阻止衰退。例如，一个人只要反复复述七位数字的电话号码就可以记住它（Weiten，2013）。语音环（或发音循环，articulatory loop）总的来说涉及声音或者语音信息，它由两部分组成：对易于迅速衰退的听觉记忆痕迹的短时语音储存成分和能使记忆痕迹恢复的发音练习成分（有时称为发音环）。

任何听觉言语信息都被认为是自动进入语音储存的。视觉上呈现的语言能通过沉默发音（silent articulation）转换成语音代码，从而被编码进语音储存。发音控制过程促进了这种转变。语音储存充当内耳（inner ear），按时间顺序记忆言语声音，而发音过程充当内在声音（inner voice），重复回路上的单词（或其他的言语要素）来阻止它们的衰退。语音回路可以在二语者习得词语时扮演重要角色，尤其是二语者的幼年期（Baddeley et al.，1998），它也对二语学习至关重要。

③ 视觉空间工作记忆

Baddeley的工作记忆理论还有另一个从属系统，即视觉空间模板。视觉空间模板储存视觉和空间信息，它可以用来构建和操纵视觉图像，并且表征心理地图。模板可进一步分成视觉子系统（涉及形状、颜色和结构）和空间子系统（涉及位置）。视觉空间模板被认为是自己储存工作记忆，因为它并不干涉语音回路的短时加工过程。研究发现，视觉空间模板可以与语音回路同时加工听觉和视觉刺激语料，而不会彼此影响。

Baddeley et al.（2009）将短时记忆重新定义为工作记忆来解释这种现象。在短时记忆最初的理论中，一个人只有一种即时信息的存储，在很短时间内仅仅容纳总共 7±2 个项目，有时只要几秒钟。数字广度测试是一个对经典短时记忆测量的最完美例证。基本上，如果一个人不能在几分钟内，通过发现即将转换成长时记忆信息所存在的联系而对 7±2 个项目进行编码，那么此信息便会消失并永不被编码。人们对短暂记忆（例如，视觉感觉记忆）间的差异也可能存在着误解。因此，当视觉感觉记忆是一种表征或感觉记忆，信息会被储存，但储存只持续大约一秒。一个视觉感觉记忆的常见情况是个体可以记忆并看见并不真实存在的事物，或者并不能记忆存在于他们视线中的特定事物。记忆仅仅是短暂的，如果它在几秒内不被注意，便会消失（Gluck et al.，2008）。

在工作记忆的视觉空间模板中，大脑有两个控制不同功能的路径。模板包含空间短时记忆（spatial short-term memory）和物体记忆（object memory）。对视觉空间模板的物体记忆主要是学习并记忆物体是什么（Baddeley et al.，2009）。应当注意的是，这两种不同视觉能力间的差异，很大程度上是因为大脑中每种能力的不同路径：探测一个人环境内外的空间表征的大脑视觉路径是背侧通路（dorsal stream）；而决定物体形状、尺寸、颜色和其他决定性特征的视觉通道是腹侧通路（ventral stream）。这两条通路中的任何一条都不依赖于对方，独立运行，所以如果一条通道在执行操作，另一条通道依然可以传递信息。

下面三个主要发现为视觉空间模板中的视觉和空间成分间的差异提供了证据：

（a）视觉和空间任务间的干扰比两个视觉任务或两个空间任务间的干扰更小（Klauer & Zhao，2004）；

（b）脑损伤只影响两个成分中的一个成分而不影响另一个成分；

（c）脑成像结果表明对视觉物体的工作记忆任务激活左半球的大部分区域，而对空间信息的任务激活右半球的更多区域（Smith & Jonides，1997）。

语音环储存口头内容，而视觉空间模板满足视觉空间数据的需要，两个从属系统只充当短时储存中心。

④ 情景缓冲器

Baddeley（2000，2001）增添了第四个成分，即第三个从属系统，由此扩展了此模式——情景缓冲器（episodic buffer）。情景缓冲器保存各种表征，例如，综合语音、视觉和空间信息以及可能没有被从属系统包含的信息（例如，语义信息、音乐信息）。情景缓冲器也是联系工作记忆和长时记忆的纽带（Weiten，2013）。此成分是情节的，因为是它把信息结合成一种统一的情节表征。情景缓冲器与 Tulving（2002）的情节记忆（episodic memory）概念相似，但不同的是情景缓冲器是一个短暂的存储。情景缓冲器把跨领域的信息联系起来，以便形成按时间排序的视觉、空间和言语信息的综合单元，例如，记忆一个故事或一段电影场景。Baddeley（2000）也认为情景缓冲器与长时记忆和语义意思相联系。Baddeley & Wilson（2002）介绍这一成分的主要动机是他们观察到一些患遗忘症（尤其是高智商）的病人在长时记忆中没有编码新信息的能力，然而他们却对故事有很好的短时记忆，可以比在语言回路中回忆更多的信息。

（2）生物学／神经科学

与长时存储不同的是，更多的证据支持短暂的记忆缓冲。语音回路似乎与左半球的激活相联系，尤其是颞叶（temporal lobe）。视觉空间模板激活依赖于任务难度的不同区域：不强烈的任务似乎激活枕叶（occipital lobe），而更复杂的任务出现在顶叶（parietal lobe）。中央执行器依然是一个谜，它似乎位于大脑的额叶；而情景缓冲器似乎位于两个半球（双侧），激活大脑额叶和颞叶，甚至海马区的左边部分（Rudner et al.，2007）。

1.1.2.2 Cowan 提出的模式

Cowan（1995）认为工作记忆不是一个分开的体系，而是短时记忆的一部分。工作记忆的表征是长时记忆表征的子集。工作记忆可以组织成两个嵌入的层次：第一个层次由被激活的长时记忆表征组成，理论上，对长时记忆表征的激活没有限制；第二个层次称为注意焦点，焦点被认为容量有限，可容纳至多四个被激活的表征。Oberauer（2002）通过增加第三个成分扩展了 Cowan 的模式，此成分是一个更狭窄的注意焦点，一次只能保存一个语块。一要素焦点嵌入在四要素焦点中，以便选择单一的语块来加工。例如，实验把数字 2 加到每一个数字中，要求被试对每一个数字进行独立的加工，因为大多数被试不能同时执行几个数字的加工（Schweppe, 2014）。Oberauer 的注意成分选择其中的一个数字进行加工，然后转换注意焦点到下一个数字，持续此过程直到完成所有数字的加工。

1.1.2.3　Ericsson 和 Kintsch 提出的模式

Ericsson & Kintsch（1995）认为在大多数日常任务中，我们都使用熟练记忆（skilled memory）。例如，阅读任务要求我们在记忆中保存多于七个的语块，而我们的大脑只有七个语块的容量，此理论由 Miller 于 1956 年提出。在记忆几个句子后，我们的工作记忆会被装满，我们将不能理解在小说或科学文本中表达的复杂关系。我们通过在长时记忆储存所阅读的大多数内容，并且通过提取结构把它们联系起来。我们需要在工作记忆中保存一些概念，这些概念充当线索，通过提取结构来提取与它们相联系的每一件事情。Ericsson 和 Kintsch 把这组加工过程称为长时工作记忆（long-term working memory），因此提取结构依据专门技能领域而变化。Gobet（2000）认为，它们可以分为三类：类属提取结构、领域知识提取结构和情节文本结构。第一种类型与 Ericsson 和 Kintsch 的"经典"提取结构相对应；领域知识提取结构与模式和图式相似；情节文本结构在文本理解中享有独特功能。对于最后的类型，Kintsch et al.（1999）认为如果文本写得好，并且内容对于读者来说熟悉，每位阅读者都能在文本理解中形成情节文本结构，并运用最后的特征。Guida & Tardieu（2005）和 Guida et al.（2009）提出"个性化方法"作为实施长时工作记忆的一种方式。回顾神经影像学文献，Guida et al.（2012）提供了生理学的证据来支持长时工作记忆理论。

1.2　工作记忆容量

1.2.1　测量和相关事物

工作记忆容量可以由多种任务来测量。一个被广泛使用的测量方式是双任务范式（dual-task paradigm），它把记忆广度测量与一个并存的任务处理相结合，有时被称为"复杂广度"。Daneman & Carpenter（1980）创造了这种任务的第一个版本——阅读广度（reading span），即被试阅读一些句子（通常为二到六个句子），努力记住每个句子的最后一个单词，在一串句子的最后，他们按照正确的顺序复述出该单词。没有这种双任务特点的其他任务也显示出对工作记忆容量很好的测量(Oberauer et al.,2000)。一项任务必须具备何种特征才能很好地测量工作记忆容量,这一直是研究者们的研究课题。

工作记忆容量的测量与个体其他复杂认知任务(例如,阅读理解、问题解决)中的表现密切相关,也与智商测量密切相关(Conway et al.,2003)。一些研究者认为,工作记忆容量反映了个体执行功能的效率(Engle et al.,1999),尤其是面对令人分心的不相关信息时个体维持多重与任务相关的表征的能力。这些任务似乎反映了个体集中和维持注意能力的差异,尤其是当出现其他事件吸引个体的注意时,这些效应似乎是脑额区域的职责(Kane & Engle,2002)。

一些研究者提出了工作记忆容量以在心理上形成元素间关系的能力为特征,或者是以在已知信息中获取关系的能力为特征。

1.2.1.1　工作记忆广度:先前学习效果

工作记忆容量广泛被认为是可以同时加工和储存信息的心理工作空间(Baddeley,1986;Danemnan & Carpenter,1980;Just & Carpenter,1992)。Daneman & Merikle(1996)认为可以通过测量各种工作记忆广度评估工作记忆容量(相对于由传统广度测量的简单、被动存储的容量)。个体和小组都被认为在基本认知容量方面存在差异。与此观点一致的是,工作记忆广度任务预测包括阅读理解、文本回述和推理的一系列技能的表现(Daneman & Merikle,1996)。然而,工作记忆广度测量是复杂的,因而它很难决定认知成分,因为认知成分影响了广度分数的多少,并且负责预测(Baddeley et al.,1985;Tirre & Pena,1992;Waters & Caplan,1996)。

Greenberg & Underwood(1950)调查了被试参与先前记忆实验对工作记忆广度的影响,先前的经历对其他记忆任务有很大的不利的影响。例如,被试连续几天学习一连串词语,由于5小时和48小时记忆间隔所学习的先前一连串词语,造成了当天对词语的记忆力下降。同样地,延迟24小时后回忆一个单一的、实验室中学习的词语明显地受到先前实验室学习的一连串词语的影响。随着先前学习的词语数量的增加,甚至当目标词使用了不同于以往的单词时,回忆一连串目标词也会从75%下降到25%(Underwood,1957;Keppel et al.,1968;Zechmeister & Nyberg,1982)。

随着词语的增加而表现力下降通常是由于前摄干扰(proactive interference)，即被试的先前学习对提取更多近来所学信息的破坏性影响。一些研究表明，前摄干扰对工作记忆广度分数起着决定性作用。首先，个体和小组(例如，差的阅读者、小孩子、老年人)特别易受到前摄干扰的影响，与不易受到前摄干扰影响的青年人相比，他们在广度任务中表现得更差(Chiappe et al.,2000；Dempster,1992)。同样，具有高工作记忆广度的青年人比低工作记忆广度的青年人在前摄干扰任务中表现得更好(Dempster & Cooney,1982；Rosen & Engle,1998)。一项任务分析表明，许多工作记忆广度任务无意间在任务中鼓励了前摄干扰的发展，因为工作记忆广度任务由一系列学习—回忆试次组成，这些试次都是由最短的词语开始，到最长的词语结束(Dempster,1992；May et al.,1999；Whitney et al.,2001)。Keppel & Underwood（1962)认为前摄干扰可以在一项任务的几个测试中迅速增强，即被试对工作记忆广度任务中早期试次项目的研究和记忆会破坏后面测试中对项目的回忆。大多数工作记忆广度任务中，对于被试获得高广度分数必不可少的长试次也出现在测试的后面，因而也最容易受到前摄干扰的破坏。前摄干扰是在这些时间最长、最近和最重要试次中对被试造成破坏性表现的可能性因素，意味着工作记忆广度测量很大程度上取决于被试是否易受到前摄干扰的影响。

1.2.1.2　工作记忆容量的实验研究——不同的方法

关于容量限制的特性存在几种假设：一种假设是有限的认知资源被用来保持表征活跃，因此可以用来执行各个加工过程(Just & Carpenter,1992)；另一种假设则是工作记忆中的记忆痕迹会在几秒内衰退，除非通过复述来更新，因为练习的速度是有限的，我们只能维持有限的信息(Towse et al.,2000)。然而，另一种观点支持保存在工作记忆容量中的表征彼此相互干扰(Waugh & Norman,1965)。

理论家已讨论过一些形式的干扰。① 一个最古老的观点是工作记忆中的新项目会替代旧项目。② 另一种形式的干扰是提取竞争。例如，当任务是要求被试按顺序记忆七个单词时，需要被试从第一个单词开始回忆。当被试努力提取第一个单词时，由于第二个单词在表征上与第一个单词临近，也意外被提取，这样就会造成回忆时两个单词的互相竞争。在回忆任务中的错误经常是记忆中相邻项目的混乱(所谓的移项 transpositions)，表明了提取竞争在限制被试按顺序回忆单词时所起的作用,可能也存在于其他工作记忆任务中。③ 第三种形式的干扰是覆盖特征(Oberauer & Kliegl, 2006; Bancroft & Servos, 2011):工作记忆中的每一个单词、数字或其他项目都按一些特征来表征;当两个项目共享一些特征时,其中的一个项目会从另一个项目中夺取一些特征;工作记忆保留的项目越多,重叠的特征就会越多,更多的项目会因为失去一些特征而退化。

1.2.1.3　基于时间的资源共享模型(time-based resource sharing model)

Barrouillet et al.(2004)提出,解释工作记忆中维持和加工相互作用的实验数据的最成功理论是基于时间的资源共享模型。此理论认为,除非更新工作记忆中的表征,否则它们会衰退;而更新工作记忆中的表征需要注意机制,此机制也适用于任何同时发生的加工任务。当加工任务不需要注意的短暂时间间隔时,时间便可用来更新记忆痕迹。因此,此理论预测忘记加工的程度依赖于对加工任务注意需求的时间密度——此密度被称为认知负荷(cognitive load)。认知负荷依赖于两个变量:加工任务要求个体按单独步骤来执行的速度和每个步骤持续的时间。例如,如果加工任务包括正在增加的数字,那么每半秒增加一个数字比每两秒增加一个数字会给系统带来更高的认知负荷。干扰假设预测加工步骤耗尽了被试的记忆空位(memory slot),但是简单衰退假设预测递增的加工时间会造成被试的记忆衰退。在一系列实验中,被试对一系列字母的记忆既不依赖于加工步骤的数量,也不依赖于加工的总时间,而是依赖于认知负荷。被试增加大数字比增加小数字需要花费更多的时间,因此如果必须增加更大的数字,被试的认知负荷会变得更高。然而,对于基于时间的资源共享模型的难题是,记忆语料和被加工的语料之间的相似性也同样影响着被试的记忆准确性。

1.2.2　注意力(attention)

Fukuda & Vogel(2009)的研究表明,个体的工作记忆容量和他/她控制来自环境的信息的能力有着密切联系。环境对他们来说,可以选择性地改善或忽视。这样的注意力涉及一个人对空间位置或物体的信息加工目标的自发转换,而不是由于感觉的突显(sensory saliency)(例如,救护车汽笛)而吸引注意的目标自发转换。对注意的目标指导受到来自大脑前额叶皮层自上而下（top-down）信号的驱使，因为前额叶皮层倾向于后皮层区域的加工（Desimone & Duncan, 1995）；也受到来自下皮层结构（subcortical structure）和初级感官皮层（primary sensory cortices）的"自下而上"的控制（Yantis & Jonides, 1990）。忽视感官获取注意（sensory capture of attention）的能力在个体间存在很大差异，这种差异与工作记忆容量密切相关。一个人工作记忆容量越大，他／她抵制感觉获取的能力也越强。无视注意获取的有限能力可能导致工作记忆中不必要的信息存储，这说明较差的工作记忆不仅影响注意，而且也会更进一步地限制工作记忆容量。

1.3　前额皮层

前额皮层包含布罗德曼区（brodmann area）8、9、10、11、12、13、14、24、25、32、44、45、46、47（Murray et al., 2016）。前额皮层是覆盖大脑额叶前部的大脑皮层（cerebral cortex）。有研究者指出，一个人的性格与前额皮层功能之间有着不可缺少的联系（DeYoung et al., 2010）。脑区涉及的是计划复杂认知行为、个性表达、决策制定和调节社会行为（Yang & Raine, 2009）。脑区的基本活动是按照内在目标把思想和行为协调地结合起来。对于前额皮层区执行的功能，用最典型的心理学词汇来描述是执行功能（executive function）。执行功能涉及各种能力，诸如辨别相矛盾的思想，决定好与坏、稍好和更好、相同和不同、当前活动的未来结果，朝着一个既定目标努力来预测结果，以及根据行动和社会"控制"（抑制冲动的能力，如果不抑制，会在社会上造成不可接受的结果）来展望。额皮层帮助学习者按规则学习。Badre et al.（2010）认为，沿着额皮层吻尾轴（rostro-caudal axis）的更多脑前区支持高层次提取的规则学习。

1.3.1　结构

1.3.1.1　定义

研究中存在三种可能的方式来定义前额皮层：

• 颗粒状的额皮层；

• 丘脑背内侧核的突出区；

• 电刺激并不会引起运动的额皮层的一部分。

基于细胞结构学，前额皮层由于皮层颗粒层Ⅳ的存在而被定义。研究者并不清楚是谁第一个使用了此标准，许多早期细胞结构学研究者把词语 prefrontal 的使用限制在一个更小的皮层区域。Jacobsen（1935）使用词语 prefrontal 来区别颗粒状的前额区及无颗粒的运动区和前运动区。

根据布罗德曼区域，前额皮层传统意义上包括区域 8、9、10、11、44、45、46、47。严格来说，这些区域不都是颗粒状的，因为 44 是不正常颗粒的（dysgranular），而尾部（caudal）11 和眼眶（orbital）47 是无颗粒的（Preuss，1995）。此定义的主要问题是，它只适用于灵长目动物而不是非灵长目动物，因为后者缺少颗粒层Ⅳ（Uylings et al.，2003）。把前额皮层定义为皮层区，因为皮层区与内侧背核（mediodorsal nucleus）与任何其他的丘脑核（thalamic nucleus）都有着更强的相互联系（Uylings et al.，2003）。对前额皮层的第三个定义是电刺激并不能引起看得见的运动的额皮层区域。例如，Ferrier（1890）按这个意义使用了这个词语，此定义的一个复杂化问题是电沉默（silent）额皮层包括颗粒区域和无颗粒区域。

1.3.1.2 相互联系

前额皮层与大部分脑区紧密联系，包括与其他脑皮层、下皮层和脑干区域的广泛联系（Alvarez & Emory，2006）。背侧前额叶皮层尤其与涉及注意、认知和行动的脑区相联系（Goldman-Rakic，1988），而腹侧前额叶皮层主要与涉及情感的脑区紧密联系（Price，1999）。前额皮层也接受来自脑干觉醒系统（brainstem arousal system）的输入信息，其功能尤其依赖于神经化学环境（Robbins & Arnsten，2009）。因此，Arnsten et al.（2010）提出加工者的觉醒状态和心理状态之间存在着协调。

1.3.2 功能

1.3.2.1 执行功能

Fuster et al.（2000）和 Goldman-Rakic（1996）的早期研究强调了前额皮层可以表征非当前环境中信息的基本能力，以及此功能在创造大脑速写本（mental sketch pad）中的核心作用。Glodman-Rakic 谈论了如何使用这种表征知识来明智地指导思想、行动和情感，包括抑制不恰当的想法、分散注意的事物、行为和情感。因此，工作记忆被认为对注意和行为抑制有至关重要的作用。Fuster 研究了这种前额能力如何把过去与将来结合起来，同时在创造有明确目标导向的知觉—行动循环周期中建立交互时间（cross-temporal）和交互模式（cross-modal）间的联系。这种表征能力构成所有其他更高的执行功能的基础。Shimamura（2000）提出动态过滤理论（dynamic filter theory）来描述执行功能中前额皮层的角色，前额皮层被认为是提高有目标导向的激活和抑制不相关激活的高层面门控（high-level gating）。

前额皮层功能的综合理论（integrative theory of prefrontal cortex function）起源于 Goldman-Rakic 和 Fuster 的早期成果，从本质上说，两者都认为前额皮层指导输入信息和联系，从而允许认知控制加工者的行为。当加工者需要自上而下加工时，前额皮层起着重要作用。依据定义，加工者自上而下的加工是当行为受到内在状态或意图指导时而产生的。他们的理论含义能够解释在指导控制认知行为时，前额皮层扮演着重要的角色。

近年来，研究者使用了神经影像技术，发现前额皮层与基底神经节共同涉及学习实例（learning exemplar）。学习实例是实例理论（exemplar theory）的一部分，是加工者大脑把事物分类所使用的三个主要方式之一。实例理论提出加工者通过把它与储存的记忆内相似的以往经验进行比较来分类判断（Schacter et al., 2011）。Yuan & Raz（2014）的元分析发现，前额皮层容量越大、皮层越厚，与更好的执行表现联系越密切。

1.3.2.2　注意和记忆

一个涉及大脑前额皮层功能并被广泛接受的理论是前额皮层具有短时记忆存储的功能。此观点由 Jacobsen（1936）提出，他报道了灵长目动物前额皮层的损伤造成了短时记忆的缺陷。Pribram et al.（1952）认为对这个缺陷负责的前额皮层区域部分是区域 46，也被称为背侧前额叶区。

Funahashi et al.（1993）通过暂时使背侧前额叶部分区域不活跃来引起局部区域短时记忆丧失。工作记忆概念在神经科学领域由 Baddeley（1986）建立，神经心理学总结出前额皮层执行工作记忆。工作记忆概念主要集中于短时维持信息，而不是集中于操纵或监督信息或使用信息来决策。与此观点一致的是，前额皮层的主要功能是维持记忆，前额中的延期活动（delay-period activity）常被解释为记忆痕迹（memory trace），在延期中的前额活动更有助于进行注意选择的加工而不是记忆存储。

1.3.3　神经系统维持(neural maintenance)

在过去的二十多年中,研究者已更多地了解到工作记忆功能是在大脑哪个区域执行任务的,但对大脑如何完成短时维持信息和有目标导向的操纵信息还是了解得甚少。在工作记忆任务延迟阶段,持续激活某些神经元表明大脑具备没有外在输入而维持表征活跃的机制。然而,如果任务需要维持超过一个语块的信息时,工作记忆就不足以保持表征活跃。同时,每个语块的成分和特征必须被联系在一起才能阻止被混淆。Raffone & Wolters（2001)的实验要求必须同时记忆一个红色三角形和一个绿色正方形,且必须确保红色是"三角形"、绿色是"正方形"。建立这样联系的一种方式是同时激活代表相同语块特征的神经元,并且不同步激活那些代表属于不同语块特征的神经元。例如,代表红色的神经元会与代表三角形的神经元同步激活,但与代表正方形的神经元不同步激活。到目前为止,并没有直接的证据表明工作记忆使用这种联系机制。Klimesch（2006)已推测出涉及的工作记忆同步激活的神经元会产生 theta 波段(4～8 赫兹)的频率震荡。事实上,EEG 中波段的功率会随着工作记忆负荷的增加而增加,当人们竭力记忆信息中两个成分间的联系时,在头骨的不同部分测量到的 theta 波段的震荡变得更协调（Wu et al.,2007)。解释前额叶皮层基底神经节工作记忆（prefrontal cortex basal ganglia working memory)可以解释大脑中的工作记忆,由 Barbey et al.（2013)进行的一个人类损伤研究提供了支持背侧前额叶皮层在工作记忆中扮演角色的证据。

1.4　回声记忆(echoic memory)

1.4.1　早期工作

Baddeley et al.（2009)的工作记忆模式由视觉空间模板和语音环组成。视觉空间模板与图像记忆（iconic memory)相关。语音环以两种方式进行听觉信息加工:第一种方式是语音储存,它在衰退前有着保留信息 3～4 秒的容量,在时间上比图像记忆(少于 1 000 毫秒)更持久些;第二种方式是默读复述加工过程（sub-vocal rehearsal process),即通过使用自己的内在声音而使记忆痕迹保持更新。然而,这种模式并没有对初始感觉输入和随后的记忆加工过程间的关系提供一个详细的描述。Cowan（2008）提出的短时记忆模式试图通过更详细地描述言语感觉记忆输入和储存来解决这个问题。短时记忆模式表明,前注意感觉储存系统(pre-attentive sensory storage system)能在短期内保留大量正确信息并且由两个阶段组成：第一个阶段是 200～400 毫秒初始阶段输入；第二个阶段是把信息转换成更长时记忆的储存,以便能融进 10～20 秒后就开始衰退的工作记忆中(Glass et al.,2008)。

1.4.2　测试方法——非匹配负波(mismatch negativity)

Näätänen & Escera（2000）认为,更客观和独立的任务是非匹配负波任务(mismatch negativity tasks),它不需集中注意便能测量听觉感觉记忆(auditory sensory memory)。非匹配负波任务通过使用 EEG（electroencephalography)来记录大脑中激活的各种变化。EEG 记录了刺激后 150～200 毫秒时引发的大脑活动的听觉事件相关电位(even-related potentials)的各要素,此刺激语料是在一系列标准刺激语料中呈现的无意识的、偶然的、怪异的或反常的刺激语料,因此把异常的刺激语料比作记忆痕迹(Sabri et al.,2004)。

1.4.3　神经学基础(neurological basis)

Alain et al.（1998）认为,听觉感觉记忆被储存在所呈现信息的耳朵对侧(contralateral)的初级听觉皮层(primary auditory cortex)。由于涉及不同的加工过程,图像记忆存储影响到几个不同的大脑区域。涉及的主要大脑区域位于前额皮层；中央控制也位于此处,负责注意控制。语音存储和练习系统似乎是基于左半球的记忆系统,因为在这些区域已观察到了增强的大脑活动。143 涉及的主要区域是左腹侧前额叶皮层后部(left posterior ventrolateral prefrontal cortex)、左前运动皮层(left premotor cortex)和左侧顶叶皮层后部(left posterior parietal cortex)。在腹外侧前额叶皮层中,布罗卡区(Broca's area)是负责言语练习和发音加工的主要区域；背侧前运动皮层是负责有节奏地组织和练习的区域；后顶叶皮层在空间确定物体位置时扮演着角色。研究还没有涉及由非匹配负波反应的听觉感觉记忆的大脑皮层区找出确切的位置,然而一些研究已在颞上回(superior temporal gyrus)和颞下回(inferior temporal gyrus)发现了被试脑区的相对激活(Schonwiesner et al.,2007)。

1.5 神奇的数字 7±2

"The Magical Number Seven, Plus or Minus Two: Some Limits on Our Capacity for Processing Information"是心理学引用次数最多的论文之一,此论文由普林斯顿大学心理学系的认知心理学家 George A. Miller 于 1956 年发表在期刊 *Psychological Review* 上,它提出平均每个人工作记忆中所能保留信息的数量是 7±2,经常被称作 Miller 定律(Miller's Law)。

1.5.1 Miller 的文章

在文章中,Miller 讨论了一维绝对判断(one-dimensional absolute judgement)限度和短时记忆限度的巧合。在一维绝对判断任务中,被试被呈现一系列在一维中变化的刺激语料(例如,只在音高上变化的 10 种不同音调)并且用相对应的回应(以前学习过)来回复每一个刺激语料。被试在实验开始时表现得近乎完美,可以达到 5 或 6 个不同的刺激语料,但随着不同刺激语料数量的增加,他们的表现也逐渐下降。任务可以被描述为一种信息传送:输入由 n 个可能的刺激语料中的一个刺激语料组成,输出则由 n 个回应中的一个回应组成。输入中包含的信息可以由二元决策的数量来决定,需要做出二元决策来获得可选的刺激语料,同样也适用于回应。因此,人们在一维绝对判断的最佳表现可描述为具有容纳 2～3 个比特信息的信息通道容量,相当于辨别四和八的能力。

Miller 讨论的第二种认知限度是记忆广度。记忆广度指的是在呈现给被试项目后,被试在 50% 试次中能迅速按正确顺序回述的最长项目串(例如,数字、字母、单词)。Miller 观察到年轻成年人的记忆广度大约是 7 个项目。他注意到对于具有完全不同信息的刺激语料,记忆广度几乎是相同的。Miller 认为记忆广度单位不按比特,而是按语块受到限制。语块是一个人识别所呈现语料的最大的有意义单位,因此,语块主要依赖于被试的知识。例如,一个单词对本族语者是一个语块,但对完全不熟悉这种语言并且把一个单词视为语音片段的二语者来说就是诸多语块。

Miller 意识到一维绝对判断限度和短时记忆广度限度间的联系仅仅是一个巧合。仅仅是第一个限度而不是第二个限度就可以按信息理论表达方式来描述(大致上按持续不断的比特数量)。因此,对于数字 7 并没有什么"惊奇",Miller 仅在修辞上使用此表达方式。然而,"神奇数字 7"这个概念激发了人类对认知容量限度的严密和不严密的更多理论推理。数字 7 构成了一个有用的探索性论据,它提醒我们:同时记忆和加工比 7 更长的序列对人类来说更加艰难。

1.5.2 神奇数字 7 和工作记忆容量

研究者对短时记忆和工作记忆的实验表明,即使按一系列组块来测量记忆广度,也不是不变的。大脑的短时记忆使用组块作为保存一组组信息的方法,以便学习者更易于提取。

Shiffrin & Robert（1994）提出,组块可以很好地发挥作用的标志是:一个人综合新信息,然后充分练习,最后使之进入长时记忆,了如指掌。这些组块必须以一种信息可以被拆分成必要数据的方式便于学习者储存信息。储存容量依赖于被储存的信息,例如,学习者的长单词的广度比短单词的广度更低。Schweickert & Boruff（1986）因此提出对语料的短时记忆的有限容量并不是一个"神奇的数字",而是一个"神奇的魔法"。Baddeley（1992,2000）认为,工作记忆模式中的一个成分（语音回路）能保留大约两秒的声音,然而,短时记忆限度也不能轻易地描述为一个恒久不变的"神奇魔法",因为记忆广度还依赖于包括言语持续时间等其他的因素。

1.6 大脑中的定位(localization in the brain)

随着脑成像方法（ERP、PET 和 fMRI）的出现,人类大脑功能的定位已变得更加容易。研究证实了大脑前额叶皮层区域涉及工作记忆功能。20 世纪90 年代,更多的争论集中在大脑前额叶皮层的腹侧较低区域和背侧较高区域:一种观点认为背侧区域负责空间工作记忆,而腹侧区域负责非空间工作记忆;另一种观点提出了一种功能差别,即腹侧区域更多涉及纯粹的信息维护,而背侧区域更多涉及一些被记忆语料的任务加工。此争论并没有完全得到解决,但是大多数的证据支持了功能差别（Owen, 1997）。

脑成像研究也表明工作记忆功能不只限于大脑前额叶皮层。Smith & Jonides（1999）的研究表明,在工作记忆任务中的激活区域分散在大部分皮层:空间任务倾向于征用更多的右半球区域,而言语工作记忆（verbal working memory)和客体工作记忆(object working memory)往往征用更多的左半球区域。言语工作记忆任务中的激活可以分为一个在左后顶叶皮层中显示维持的成分和一个在左额叶皮层(布洛卡区,涉及言语产出)显示默读复述的成分(Smith et al.,1998)。

大多数研究认为,工作记忆任务使用前额叶皮层和顶叶区的网状系统。Honey et al.(2002)的研究表明,在工作记忆任务中,这些区域间的联系增加了。目前的讨论涉及这些大脑区域的功能。Kane & Engle(2002)认为,在执行功能的各项任务中,前额叶皮层很活跃。许多研究者纷纷提出前额叶皮层在工作记忆中的角色是控制注意、选择策略和操纵信息,而不是维持信息。Curtis & D'Esposito(2003)和Postle(2006)把维持功能归因于大脑的更后部区域,包括顶叶皮层;而Collette et al.(2006)则把顶叶皮层中的活动解释为反映了执行功能,因为相同的区域也在其他需要注意,而不是记忆的任务中被激活。

60个神经成像研究的元分析发现:左额叶皮层涉及低任务需求的言语工作记忆,而右额叶皮层涉及空间工作记忆。当工作记忆必须被不断更新、当按时间顺序的记忆不得不维持时,加工者需要征用上额叶皮层中的布洛德曼区6、8、9。在腹侧额叶皮层中的右布罗德曼10和47更经常涉及对操纵的需求,诸如双任务需求或心理操作。Wager & Smith(2003)认为后顶叶皮层的布罗德曼7也涉及所有类型的执行功能。

工作记忆包含两个加工过程,分别位于大脑额叶和顶叶两个不同的神经区域(Bledowski et al.,2009):首先,提取最相关项目的选择操作;其次,改变注意焦点的更新操作。更新注意焦点涉及尾部额上沟(caudal superior frontal sulcus)和后顶叶皮层的短暂激活。Coltheart(2006)认为涉及工作记忆脑区的不同功能主要依赖于能区别这些功能的任务。

对工作记忆的大多数脑成像研究使用了识别任务,诸如延迟识别一个或几个刺激语料或者n-back任务。识别任务的优点是它们要求被试执行最小的任务活动(仅仅按两个键中的一个键),可以使扫描器中头部的固定变得简单。然而,工作记忆中个体差异的实验研究广泛使用了回述任务(例如,阅读广度任务)。我们并不清楚什么程度的识别和回述任务反映了相同的加工过程和相同的容量局限。脑成像研究一直与阅读广度任务或相关的任务同时进行。在这些任务中发现了大脑前额叶皮层,同时在几项研究中也发现了前扣带回(anterior cingulate cortex)的增强激活。任务执行得更好的被试在这些脑区表现出更大的增强激活,这些激活随着时间更加相关,表明这两个区域的神经活动可能由于更密切的联系协调得更好(Kondo et al., 2004;Osaka et al., 2004)。

1.7 提高工作记忆

1.7.1 学习

Daneman & Carpenter(1980)提出,工作记忆与读写和计算这些必不可少的学习相关。由于测试的性质,测试被称为复杂广度任务,其结果正确评估了一个人的工作记忆,特别是他们的中央执行系统。并不奇怪的是,任务中被试的成功与他/她的阅读理解能力紧密相关。Swanson & Beebe-Frankenberger(2004)发现了相似的结果,小学生工作记忆的表现准确预测了解决数学问题的表现。此外,Alloway & Alloway(2010)的纵向研究证实了一个 5 岁孩子的工作记忆比 IQ 能更好地预测学业成绩。

在大规模筛选研究中,教室中 1/10 的孩子有工作记忆缺陷。Alloway et al.(2009)的研究表明,除了智商,大多数孩子在学业成绩上表现得相当差。同样地,在课程年龄低至 7 岁的低成绩学习者中发现了工作记忆的缺陷(Gathercole & Pickering, 2000)。如果没有适当的干预,这些孩子的成绩会落后于同龄人。Alloway(2009)一项对 37 个有严重学习残障的学龄孩子进行的研究表明:测量的工作记忆容量而不是智商预测了 2 年后的学习结果,这说明工作记忆受损与较差的学习结果相联系,将成为孩子学习成绩不达标的一个高危险因素。明显的相同模式出现在有学习缺陷的孩子中,这些缺陷诸如诵读困难(dyslexia)、注意力不集中和发展协调紊乱(developmental coordination disorder)(Pickering, 2006;Roodenrys, 2006)。

在课堂学习中,工作记忆受损的常见特征包括不能记忆指令和不能完成学习的各项活动。Gathercole & Alloway(2008)认为,如果没有早期的诊断,工作记忆受损会消极地影响孩子学习生涯中的表现。然而,Alloway(2010)提出,教育者可以针对学生工作记忆概况的特定优点和缺点总结出一些策略。

1.7.2 训练

工作记忆训练直接影响额叶皮层、顶皮层和基底核等大脑皮层活动以及中枢系统多巴胺受体浓度（dopamine receptor density）（McNab et al.,2009）。被试经过训练后，他们与工作记忆相关的大脑活动在前额皮层增加了，许多研究者认为前额皮层是与工作记忆功能相联系的区域。

一项有争议的研究表明，工作记忆任务（双 n-back 任务）的训练提高了健康年轻成年人特定的液态智力（fluid intelligence）测验的表现（Jaeggi et al.,2008），即提高或增强大脑的工作记忆能力增加了液态智力，研究者对这种结论褒贬不一。

Klingberg（2009）提出了加工者可以通过接受大量神经激活来提高工作记忆，他指出加工者的脑图可以通过这种激活来改变，从而通过特种的感觉体验创造出被激活的更大脑区。例如，学习弹吉他，一个吉他手通过对乐器的感觉印象被激活的脑区比非吉他手更大些。Zanto & Gazzaley（2009）的实验证据表明最佳的工作记忆表现与神经能力相关联。此能力把注意力集中于与任务相关的信息，并且忽视分散注意力的信息，与练习相关的工作记忆的提升是由于增加了这些能力（Berry et al.,2009）。同时，工作记忆表现也可通过高强度练习得到提高。Lo Bue-Estes et al.（2008）一项通过对久坐和活跃的 18～25 岁女性的实验来测量短时练习直到筋疲力尽对工作记忆的影响，被试的工作记忆在练习过程中和练习刚结束后降低了，同时被试的工作记忆在恢复后提高了。

第二章

短时记忆与外语学习

人们常把外语学习不好、单词记不牢，归咎于记忆力不好。学习一个新的单词，有的学习者需要反复练习才能记住，有的只需老师提一下便记住了，学习起来一点不费劲。开始学习外语时，孤立地记外语单词很不容易，把单词放在上下文背景中记忆就容易多了。这些现象无不与记忆有关。

一些心理学家认为记忆系统由三个阶段组成：感觉记忆、短时记忆和长时记忆。感觉记忆阶段是一个短暂的和直接感知的阶段。此阶段的言语信息一般在一两秒钟之内便会消失，只有当它受到注意时才会转移到另一个相对稳定的短时记忆阶段。在短时记忆阶段，信息处理的容量较小，但持续的时间稍长，约为17秒。短时记忆中的信息经编码处理后便会转移到记忆系统的第三个阶段——长时记忆。信息是否从短时记忆进入长时记忆，在很大程度上取决于大脑对停留在短时记忆中的信息进行处理的程度。在长时记忆阶段，学习者能长期储存信息，但这些信息不一定容易提取。

2.1 短时记忆的特点

短时记忆是指将所接受的信息暂时储存的那部分记忆，与此同时对信息进行分析理解，等到语句中的信息或内容被理解了，这些资料就成为永久性记忆（长时记忆），而语句本身则再无用处，可能会逐渐从短时记忆中消失（Richards et al., 2000: 283）。

短时记忆的容量很有限,大概是 7±2 个单位,信息停留的时间短。心理学家 Miller（1956）写过一篇重要论文《神秘数字 7±2》。他认为数字 7 在我们的生活中具有神秘的作用,短时记忆的广度大概在 7 个单位左右。Miller用"块"的概念表达他所说的单位,一个"块"是一条有联系的编码单位,其中一部分可帮助记忆另一部分。例如,电话号码 750326 被看成是孤立无联系的块,就不易被记住,如果联系为出生年月日就不会被忘记了,表示为 3 个有联系的"块"。Atkinson & Shiffrin（1968,1971）指出,我们不可能一次记住多达几十个的一系列单词,回忆出来的项目取决于它在系列中的排列位置。系列首尾两头的项目最容易记忆,中间的项目最容易忘记。心理学家把末尾项目容易回忆的现象称为近因效应,此效应可解释为:当人们开始回忆时,末尾项目的单词仍旧储存在短时记忆中。开头项目容易回忆的现象被称为首因效应:开头项目的单词仍旧储存在长时记忆中,就是说开头项目的单词比其他单词的排列次数多,因而更有可能从长时记忆中提取。学习者孤立识记外语单词时往往发生这种情况。

长时记忆是指将信息较长期地储存下来的那部分记忆系统,容量无限。长时记忆如同数据库,信息通过短时记忆存入长时记忆,然后从长时记忆中提取并被用于短时记忆;短时记忆扮演着通往长时记忆的通道的角色。存放在长时记忆中的信息一般都处于非活动状态,要提取这些信息必须有个激活的过程;当信息被激活,它就成为短时记忆的一部分。激活过程需要时间,因此再现在长时记忆里的信息比在短时记忆里的信息要慢得多。

信息在短时记忆中的保存,如不加以复习,就会被遗忘。短时记忆中的信息能否转移到长时记忆,取决于强度和频率。对短时记忆中信息的复习可使之转入长时记忆,一旦终止复习,旧信息会很快被新信息取代,并从短时记忆中消失。Atkinson & Shiffrin（1968,1971）提出信息从短时记忆向长时记忆转换理论。他们集中研究口头练习（verbal rehearsal）。Craik & Lockhart（1972）提出深层处理原理（depth of processing theory）:口头练习并不是行之有效的记忆方式,死记硬背对于只拨一次的电话号码是适合的,但是如果我们想记忆信息足够长的时间,它却有许多缺点;死记下来的东西未必能够被理解,只有理解了的东西才更容易被记住。

Baddeley et al.（2009）对短时记忆进行了详尽描述。工作记忆包括保存和操纵听觉信息的语音环、保存和操纵视觉和空间信息的短时储存器以及对有限数据进行加工和对整个系统进行控制的中央执行器。从功能上来说,语音环和视觉、空间储存器与短时记忆的概念相似,因为它们都分别保存视觉和听觉信息。Cowan（1995）和 Engle（1998）在区别工作记忆和短时记忆时指出:短时记忆是工作记忆的一个组成部分,短时记忆通常被看成是被动地储存信息的仓库,短时记忆的重要功能是通过使用语音环和视觉空间储存器来保持被激活的记忆编码;工作记忆则体现了对记忆过程的一种动态的观点,它同时具有储存和加工两种功能。

2.2　短时记忆与外语学习的关系

从外语学习的角度研究短时记忆的实验研究中,Cook（1977）和 Call（1985）的实验研究最为引人注目。Cook 实验研究证明了识记物体名称需要借助长时记忆中的深层信息,而包括背景知识在内的深层信息往往是外语学习者所欠缺的;短时记忆的容量有限,外语学习者与本族语学习者需借助长时记忆中的知识,都需尽快地对短时记忆中的信息进行释义处理。Call 通过实验证实了短时记忆是听力理解的一个重要组成部分,对句法的记忆能预测听力技能。

同时,陈吉棠（2002）也通过实验证明了收听内容的量、收听内容与听者的经验知识之间的关系对短时记忆的质与量都有直接的影响。

成功的外语学习应具备三种能力:能理解所学事物,能记住所学事物和能运用所学事物。外语学习模式如图 2-1 所示。

我们把将要学习的事物定义为输入。图 2-1 的右栏代表学习者,左栏代表他／她的环境。当倾听某人谈话时,输入是一种口头的过程。如果学习者想完全理解,首先要集中注意力于所听所学的知识,所注意的程度主要依赖于学习者的动机(箭头显示学习者集中注意力于外部输入,同时也要注意非语言的上下文或情景)。所有学习者在任务开始前就应集中注意力于手头的工作,以便有充分的思想准备。对听力训练做充分准备的学习者总是精力集中、安静并且专心致志;同时,不集中注意力也不会产生理解。

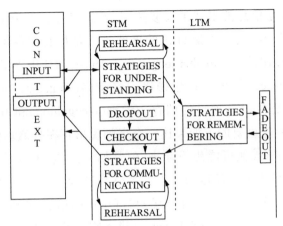

图 2-1 外语学习模式（Abbott et al., 1981:28）

当学习者接收了输入，一连串的语音经过他/她的耳朵进入一个把这些外在的声波转换成内在意思的系统（短时记忆）。由此，学习者的短时记忆总是不断地把连续的语音分割成语音单位，通过识别和使用语调作为界限。短时记忆中的理解策略（strategies for understanding）把连续的语音分割成有意义的词组，这些有意义的词组被依次转换储存在长时记忆中；同时，在存在的意义网络中给它们一个合适的位置，意思就这样被保存下来。尽管学习者会忘记他/她的朋友所确切地表达的内容，但在短时间内可以记住他/她的信息。如果信息按外语编码，至少有两个困难可能出现：第一，短时记忆可能会使学习者感觉到输入信息的速度太快，以至于没有足够的时间处理进入的信号；第二，即使信号速度不是太快，部分编码也可能不为学习者所熟知。当我们收听的时候，时间是一个致命的敌人，短时记忆容量有限，因此非常迅速的语音串不可能被完全解码，更不用说完全被理解了。进来的信号或者把以前还没有得到充分处理的信息排挤掉，或者当短时记忆还集中注意于以前的输入信息时，它们便会自动退出。任何输入在这个时期以任何方式消失，都会成为退出（dropout）。

如果学习者需要收听正常语速的英语，他们就需要提高听力水平，减少dropout。学习者训练的次数越少，时间对于他们来说就越紧迫。即使短时记忆对输入信息完好地储存和解码，如果学习者没有机会反复练习，有一些输入信息还是会迅速退出。反复练习是一种迅速的、私底下重复新信息的过程。

在语言学习中,是信息的形式被反复练习,意思将被提取出来。当学习者在反复练习时,用于学习一种新外语的理解策略是指我们参阅所有以前的经验,包括使用母语的经验(mother tongue experience)和使用外语的经验(foreign language experience),是短时记忆操纵记忆策略(strategies for remembering),长时记忆仅仅是对记忆项目的储存。识别(recognition)和再现(recall)的区别在语言学习上是重要的。如果让一个老师说出正在打篮球的、以前教过的一个学生的名字时,他可能想不起来;但是如果问他"你记得汤姆吗",他可能说"当然,他是那个打篮球的学生",那就是说,他可能认识他,却不能记得他。长时记忆包含可记忆(或可再现)和可认识的信息,但是如果不受注意,可认识的信息容易逐渐消失(fade out)并进入忘记的行列。消失包括忘记(也就是不认识)和几乎忘记(几乎不认识)。正如反复练习是一种使输入信息保留在短时记忆的手段,练习的目的之一是保证信息储存在长时记忆中。有效地识别新语音需要听力的训练,而有效地产出则需要发音的练习。最好的策略是使每个人能集中注意力练习听力,尝试口语模仿,努力发现规则。当信息储存在长时记忆时,让学习者掌握规则比记忆练习中所有的例子更好,因为规则占据的储存空间少,规则能运用于新的经历中。对语言来说,规则是规律,因此我们收听句子时,强调句法是重要的。对句法的短时记忆能减少听力的负担,一旦知识被成功地储存于记忆中,便已经学会了。因此,学习者是否掌握一门语言依赖于学习者运用外语交流的能力。最后,我们谈谈交际策略(strategies for communicating)及监控(monitor 或 check out)。运用外语交流的学习者可分为两组:那些把自己置身于任务中、并没意识到如何犯严重语言错误的学习者和那些一点不愿张口说话、唯恐犯语言错误或语言听起来可笑的学习者。一些学习者似乎有一个十分严重的监控以至于阻止了外语的表达,这种现象经常发生在青春期,孩子在这个发展阶段(通常 12、13 岁)会从精听练习而不是口语训练中受益。

2.3　提高外语学习效率的基本思路

　　首先,我们应根据短时记忆的特点,增加短时记忆的容量,从而扩大语块,减少短时记忆中的项目数量,因为组块可减少重复学习信息的时间。其次,由于短时记忆的容量有限,我们应依靠长时记忆中的信息,经验知识是长时记忆的体现,因此从长时记忆向短时记忆的信息转换是提高外语学习的重要方式,提高处理效率是提高短时记忆容量的有效方式。

Postovosky(1974)提出,对语言输入的解码需要认识知识(recognition knowledge),而对语言输入的编码则需要保留在长时记忆的提取知识(retrieval knowledge)。当学习者理解一个句子时,他/她会把语言知识在短时记忆中保留较短时间,直到被进一步处理并且与长时记忆中的知识相一致。如果他/她没有足够的认识知识的积累,很难提取并使用储存在长时记忆中的知识。英语教师不应低估认识知识积累的过程,应尽最大努力在学生能流利地表达目标语之前为他们创造尽可能多的大量吸收语言知识的机会;学生也应意识到这个过程的重要性,随时准备通过收听或阅读来吸收尽可能多的知识。因此,在听力和阅读过程中发展认识知识比发展提取知识更重要。

第三章

短时记忆在国内二语习得中的研究述评

3.1 引言

近年来,在二语习得方面涉及心理过程的研究日益广泛(Ellis,1994)。在二语课堂和二语日常使用中,短时记忆牵涉到每天的语言运用,学习者每天使用第二语言所做或所说的每一件事情在某种程度上都与短时记忆相关。

3.1.1 短时记忆和工作记忆的关系

在 20 世纪 60 年代,短时记忆——在短暂的时间段在大脑中存储少量信息——研究构成了认知心理学发展的要素。研究者在尝试构建短时记忆信息处理模式方面产生了一些争议。遗憾的是,借助当时适用的方法无法解决这些争议,而这也导致了 20 世纪 70 年代大家对短时记忆研究兴趣的减弱,甚至随后宣告了该项研究的终结(Crowder,1982)。正当短时记忆这一旧观念逐渐失宠时,它被并入到一个更为复杂的体系——工作记忆中了。工作记忆概念的提出主要源于对短时记忆系统特性的研究。工作记忆主张利用多成分系统取代单一储存体系,即通过大脑所储存的信息促进复杂的认知活动,诸如学习、理解和推理(Baddeley & Hitch,1974)。Baddeley 和 Hitch 的工作记忆模式不仅在认知心理学,而且在神经系统科学和发展心理学领域都极具影响力,由 Baddeley(1986)修改更新。到了 20 世纪 80 年代,人们对工作记忆的研究兴趣持续升温。20 世纪 90 年代,得益于功能成像技术的发展成果,整个大西洋地区对工作记忆的研究有了更进一步的飞速发展,正是认知心理学和工作记忆神经心理学二者之间的关系很好地助推了这一发展。

传统的短时记忆概念描述了一种几乎被动的短暂记忆储存,通过即时串行回忆信息来评定容量(Atkinson & Shiffrin, 1968)。从时间上说,工作记忆的概念更时新一些,它描述的是一种更动态的体系,在认知活动中涉及信息的短暂保留和转换(Baddeley & Hitch, 1974)。Baddeley 等人的工作记忆模型分为三部分:视觉空间模板、语音环和中央执行系统。工作记忆同时具有储存和加工两种功能,储存功能相当于短时记忆的功能,即在一定的时间内保存一定的信息;而加工的功能则和加工容量的概念有关(桂诗春,2000)。工作记忆对语言学习(主要是母语学习)的诸多方面(如词汇习得、语言理解与语言表达、阅读理解能力的发展)都具有深远影响(Gathercole & Baddeley, 1993; Baddeley et al., 1998; Baddeley, 2003)。从信息加工模式看,无论是 Broadbent (1953)提出的模型雏形,还是后来备受心理学家关注的 Atkinson & Shiffrin (1965, 1969)的三级加工模型,都强调短时记忆是信息加工中不可缺少的重要阶段,并且短时记忆在功能上起着工作记忆的作用。由于 Baddeley(1986)提出短时记忆是按照工作记忆的方式来活动的,所以认知心理学家认为工作记忆就是短时记忆概念的延伸,短时记忆和工作记忆起源相同。

3.1.2　短时记忆的特点

(1)练习效应

Atkinson & Shiffrin(1968, 1971)论述了从短时记忆向长时记忆转换信息的理论,强调了短时记忆和长时记忆的相互关系,提出了三项促进习得知识的控制处理策略:练习、编码(coding)和意象(imaging)(三种初始的学习方法)。Atkinson & Shiffrin(1968)集中研究一种口头练习:口头练习被认为是一种死记硬背的学习方式(form of rote learning)(通过重复而不是通过理解记忆),因为这意味着反复练习信息直到学会。因此,在学习抽象和无意义的材料时鼓励使用练习。

Craik & Lockhart(1972)提出深层处理原则,认为重要的不是信息被练习多长时间,而是在多深的层次得到处理,强调死记硬背并不是行之有效的记忆方式,忘记开始于背诵停止的那一时刻,因此只有通过深层的、有意义的记忆处理方式,才能更好地记忆。相对来说,短时记忆中的忘记比较迅速,这是因为被记忆的项目是在一个相对浅的听觉(视觉)层次被分析。同样,记忆项目在长时记忆中的保持归因于深层处理,尤其是分析记忆项目的意义。我们越是把当前经历与以前储存的信息相结合,越容易记住他们。深层处理原理推翻了 Atkinson 和 Shiffrin 的口头练习转换到长时记忆的原理。

(2)编码不同

Conrad(1962—1971)、Baddeley(1966, 1972, 1976)、Kintsch & Buschke (1969)、Shulman(1966, 1970—1972)、Conrad & Hull(1964)、Wickelgren(1965)和 Wickens(1970, 1972)从不同角度进行试验,归纳出两种编码形式:听觉代码形式和语义代码形式。

(3)保留功能(retention function)

短时记忆保存信息时间短暂,如未得到复述,将会被迅速遗忘;同时,只要记忆项目的数量不变,识记材料性质的改变对短时记忆的遗忘进程就没有多大影响(Peterson & Peterson, 1959; Brown, 1958)。因此应减少干扰(release from proactive interference),我们可以通过排列信息结构,即减少信息中的同类项来把干扰减小到最低程度(Wickens et al., 1963)。

3.1.3　短时记忆的信息提取

所谓信息提取(又称检索),指的是把储存在假定的记忆系统中的特定信息提取出来以便使用(朱智贤, 1989)。它涉及许多问题,并且引出不同的假说,迄今没有一致的看法。

最早开展短时记忆信息提取研究的是 Sternberg(1966, 1969)。他在研究中提出了相加因素法,认为加工者短时记忆信息提取过程中做了系列搜索(serial search),而不是同时对所有元素进行检查(平行加工, parallel processing)。因此 Sternberg 认为短时记忆信息提取是从头至尾的(exhaustive)系列扫描方式,而不是自我停止的(self-terminating)扫描。在这个过程中,加工者会对识记项目与记忆集中的每个项目进行比较、匹配,然后做出是或否的选择判断。Sternberg 的观点后来遭到 Carballis(1972)、Theios et al.(1973)、Townsend(1972)和 Morin(1976)等人的反对。

Wickelgren（1973）和 Eysenck（1977）提出直通模型（直接存取模型，Direct Access Model）：提取不是通过比较或搜索，而是直接通往所要提取的项目在短时记忆中的位置，即直接提取。

Atkinson & Juola（1973）将搜索模型和直通模型结合起来，提出了搜寻—直通混合模型。该模型认为，被试是基于探测词在主观熟悉量表上或高或低的值来做出反应的。

研究者们对作为信息加工最后阶段的信息提取的研究，无疑对揭示短时记忆的规律有重要作用。

3.2　国内短时记忆研究

根据从中国知网（CNKI）上搜索的相关学术期刊来看，语言输入比语言输出方面的研究多一些。研究者从心理语言学角度探讨二语学习者的认知与心理过程，开始关注短时记忆／工作记忆的认知功能对二语学习过程的影响。同时他们还围绕短时记忆／工作记忆和语言输入（听力和阅读）、语言输出（口语和写作）之间关系展开了丰富的理论探索与实证研究，见表3-1。

表3-1　工作记忆和语言输入和输出之间关系的理论探索与实证研究

语言学习		年限	篇数	研究内容	研究方法
语言输入	听力	1988—2004	21	通过短时记忆提高听力理解	以理论介绍、教学经验总结为主的非实证性研究
		2002	3	句法简化、短时记忆与听力	调查实验；统计分析；实证研究
		2005	4	抑制机制、可理解性输入、短时记忆和听力	问卷调查与实验调查相结合；实证研究
		2006	3	做笔记、听力和短时记忆	访谈和学生内省；实证研究
		2008	3	认知负荷理论、工作记忆、视听材料和听力教学	问卷调查和访谈；定量与定性相结合的实证研究
		2009	4	听写、收听笔头记录、听力焦虑、听力动机与工作记忆／短时记忆	理论分析；问卷调查与定量研究相结合实证研究
		2010	2	多种输入方式、工作记忆与听力	理论介绍；实证研究
		2011	4	图式、注意与工作记忆对听写的影响、信息结构与听力	理论介绍；实证研究
		2012	2	英汉互助记忆、语块、短时记忆与听力	理论介绍；实证研究

语言学习		年限	篇数	研究内容	研究方法
语言输入	阅读	1995—2005	5	阅读速度、推理模型、图式、控制性阅读、预测与短时记忆	以理论介绍和教学经验总结为主的非实证性研究
		1998	1	句法歧义与工作记忆	实证研究
		2006、2007	2	阅读技能迁移与工作记忆、词汇量与工作记忆	实证研究
		2008、2009	2	工作记忆障碍与阅读、课程资源开发与短时记忆	以理论介绍和教学经验总结为主的非实证性研究
		2010—2013	6	工作记忆、句子处理与阅读	实证研究
语言输出	口语	2007—2012	3	语调输入、语块教学、双语控制与工作记忆	以理论介绍和教学经验总结为主的非实证性研究
		2009	1	工作记忆与口语流利性	实证研究
		2012	2	口语输出、语音回路与工作记忆	实证研究
		2013	1	口译的源语理解与记忆负荷	实证研究
	写作	2010	3	策略构思、修改策略的个体差异、干预时机与工作记忆	实证研究
		2012	2	工作记忆超载、有效负荷与写作	实证研究

从表 3-1 中可以看出,语言输入方面的研究起步较早,1998 年在阅读方面有实证研究,2002 年在听力方面开始实证研究;语言输出方面起步较晚,2009 年在口语方面有实证研究,写作的实证研究开始于 2010 年。在这四个分水岭之前,绝大部分研究属于思辨性的理论探讨和经验介绍,研究内容主要集中在强调短时记忆/工作记忆在语言学习中的重要性方面。分水岭之后,研究逐渐从短时记忆/工作记忆的理论介绍和经验探讨走向理论与教学实践相结合的研究;研究方法也逐步从描述性的思辨研究走向定量与定性相结合的实证研究。然而,由于国内在这方面的研究起步比较晚,还有不少课题有待探讨:二语学习者如何更有效地利用短时记忆/工作记忆进行学习?短时记忆的信息是如何提取的?与大量调查成年人工作记忆与语言理解之间联系的研究相比,针对儿童的此方面研究相对较少。

国内短时记忆的研究起步较晚,研究者们纷纷从不同角度来进一步论证短时记忆对二语学习的影响。吴潜龙(2000)从认知心理学角度分析二语习得过程,提出一种以工作记忆为中心的模式。桂诗春(2003)认为记忆在语言学习中占有中心地位,应通过增加可理解性来优化输入。温植胜(2005,2007)认为工作记忆是外语学能的重要构成要素,并对外语/二语学习产生了重大影响。戴运财、蔡金亭(2008)提出工作记忆本身并不能等同于语言学能,因为学能综合体还包含其他的认知能力。因此,本书从以下两个方面进行讨论。

3.2.1　语言输入方面

通过阅读、听力或观看有标志的符号或图像来进行语言理解需要花费时间。为了理解说话者(或写作者)所表达的整体思想,听者(阅读者)首先要在一句话被表达完整之后记住句子开头的几个单词或词组,这就是短时记忆的目的,即在阅读和听力中提供持续性。McCarthy & Warrington(1990)提出短时记忆的三种功能:语言理解、问题解决和通往长时记忆的途径。

(1)听力

在国外,从外语学习的角度研究短时记忆的实验为数不多,值得一提的有两个实验。一个是 Call(1985)的听力实验,Call 认为短时记忆是听力理解的一个重要组成部分(王初明,1990:142)。徐方(2005)复制 Call 的实验并运用到以英语为外语的中国学生中,得出的结论是:短时记忆是听力理解的重要组成部分,对句法的短时记忆在提供可理解性输入方面起了重要作用。国内对短时记忆在听力方面的研究相对较多,陈吉棠可谓开国内短时记忆与听力研究的先河:从 1995 至 2005 年共发表关于短时记忆是听力理解影响因素之一的论文四篇,从 1997 至 2012 年共发表研究短时记忆与听力理解关系的论文六篇,著名的六次"论记忆与听力理解"在国内掀起了短时记忆与听力理解研究的热潮;通过理论介绍、问卷调查和统计分析探讨了如何通过提高短时记忆来提高听力理解。苏静(2002)认为句法简化能促进听力理解:长句和复杂句对短时记忆带来太大负担;长句变成简单句后,短时记忆便能每次承受一个简单句的信息,使听力理解变得简单。姜维焕(2006)通过访谈和学生内省探讨了工作记忆与听力的关系,认为应通过大量言语感知和实践扩大长时记忆中的各种资源的容量,从而将受控过程变成自动过程。卢敏(2006)认为处在感觉储存阶段的信息保留时间相当短暂,只有受到注意时才能进入短时记忆；同时，笔录是保障短时记忆中的信息转移到长时记忆的一种手段。王萌、谢小苑（2008）认为工作记忆由语言系统和图像系统两种认知系统组成；个体的记忆能力非常有限，但可以通过利用视觉和听觉相结合的方式输入信息，以便将工作记忆的能力最大化，从而提高听力理解。王艳（2008）论证了工作记忆被用于理解过程中的信息储存和加工：加工者遇到一个词就需要马上加工，而不是储存起来留作将来加工，因此工作记忆的有限容量和连接性推论方面的不足是产生解析阶段听力困难的主要原因。周罗梅（2009）综述了国内外工作记忆与听力理解的相关研究，并表明工作记忆与听力理解显著相关。梁文霞（2009）论证了工作记忆的直接影响：一方面与工作记忆组成部分中的语音回路和中央执行系统的功能相关，另一方面与听力过程本身的特点也有关联；同时，听力考试焦虑程度越高，可用的工作记忆资源越少。杨学云（2009）论证了学习者利用组块的特点可以克服短时记忆的局限性；短时记忆理论是听写式语言输入的理论依据，同时，听写式语言输入对听力能力的提高具有显著的促进作用。冯兰（2012）也通过实验，以语块为单位对被试进行记忆训练来提高听力理解。邱东林、李红叶（2010）运用工作记忆的心理模型，论证了应避免干扰工作记忆而造成的注意力分散和信息遗漏，因此建议与语言输入无关的画面越少越好；同时，在听力过程中，应以听为主，视为辅。王红阳（2011）论证了对于词汇量大的短文理解类听力来说，信息的解码和编码难度要比对话类听力高许多，这样会加重短时记忆的负荷；以信息结构为单位来区分新旧信息，并强调信息中心，可以减少短时记忆的负荷，对听力理解起着至关重要的教学指导作用。

（2）阅读

作为一种有限容量的加工资源，工作记忆往往使个体能够在加工信息的同时存储信息，而这种基本认知能力往往与阅读等高级认知活动密切相关（Graham，1997：223-234；Friedman & Miyake，2000：61-83）。吴诗玉、王顺同（2006）研究发现工作记忆与心理表征建构之间有着直接的联系，同时工作记忆还通过与抑制机制之间的关系间接地影响心理表征建构；工作记忆与抑制机制在受到语言水平的直接影响的同时还影响心理表征建构。闫嵘（2007）证明在语音信息加工过程中，听觉言语工作记忆、词汇量对篇章阅读理解有直接影响，需要以听觉言语工作记忆为中介。周明芳（2010）认为通过"组块识别"可以提高工作记忆的加工效率：工作记忆激活相应图式，原有图式得到证实或修正，从而生成理解。任虎林（2010）论证了高工作记忆比低工作记忆的中国学习者的阅读时间少，说明工作记忆在阅读时间方面起积极作用；但高工作记忆比低工作记忆的学习者理解时间长，说明工作记忆在理解方面起消极作用；同时，高工作记忆的中国学习者、本族英语学习者与低工作记忆的中国学习者在理解准确性方面几乎一致，说明工作记忆高低对理解准确度没有显著影响。马拯、王同顺（2011）证明外语学能和工作记忆显著相关，得出教学启示：教师应关注外语学能和工作记忆对不同阅读水平英语学习者的影响，以便提高阅读者的工作记忆容量。戴运财（2011）指出工作记忆容量大、中的学习者的关系从句习得效果明显比工作记忆容量小的学习者好；工作记忆容量和教学方式都对关系从句习得有明显影响，但两者却没有发生相互作用。孙聪颖（2012）认为，加工成分引起英语工作记忆的储存成分对英语阅读者阅读理解有影响；汉语工作记忆的加工成分以英语工作记忆的加工成分为中介，间接作用于英语阅读者的阅读理解。李晓媛（2013）运用实验和行动研究相结合的方法证明，教学辅助手段和不同的理解测试任务对二语阅读理解中的内部认知负荷产生不相同的作用，而这种作用受到学习者工作记忆容量的影响和制约。

3.2.2　语言输出方面

（1）口语

工作记忆理论认为发音（pronunciation）对语言处理和学习起重要作用。如果我们不能很快地说出话语，我们的短时记忆广度将会受到限制并因此面临语言处理和储存语言到长时记忆的严重困难。近年来，语言教学中不强调发音重要性，阻碍了学生发音能力以及处理和学习语言基本能力的发展。作为言语和理解的基础，发音应该受到重视。研究者证实了工作记忆的语音部分涉及言语处理（Adams & Willis, 2001）。尽管对成年人的研究显示工作记忆的语音部分不牵涉有技能的语言处理（Shallice, 1988），但近年来的研究表明，儿童工作记忆的语音部分和语言技能之间存在显著关联。事实上，很多证据已证明工作记忆的语音部分在学习语言过程中扮演了重要角色（Baddeley et al., 1998）。巫淑华（2009）论证了工作记忆容量大比容量小的学习者的口语流利程度明显高,因此应重视工作记忆的影响,培养学习者语块意识,减少工作记忆处理信息的负担,从而提高口语的流利性。宋美盈(2012)论述了语言回路构成了工作记忆中的一个重要部分,其主要功能是加工和存贮语音信息;证明了语言回路在二语词汇学习中对所有二语学习者和英语母语使用者都起作用,但其作用的大小依据学习者母语背景的差异而不同。金霞(2012)的研究显示了工作记忆容量与二语口语流利度和准确度显著相关,但与口语复杂度并不显著相关,说明工作记忆容量是约束二语口语产出的重要认知机制;同时,随着学习者二语水平、口语产出编码自动化程度的提高,工作记忆容量对二语口语流利度的制约作用会降低。赵晨(2013)的实验证明,词汇歧义和工作记忆负荷影响了读后口译的源语理解;通过对比高、低工作记忆容量学习者在加工句首、句末音译词时的异同,论证了只有高容量学习者在读后口译中阅读句末音译词的时间比控制词明显快得多。

(2)写作

Abu-Rabia(2003)证实了工作记忆与二语写作之间显著的相关性。张正厚(2010)认为,策略构思和充分构思都可以减少工作记忆的负荷,增加工作记忆可使用的空间,并提高限时写作质量;充分构思还可以增强学生对在线构思和监测的注意力。闫嵘(2010)证明了工作记忆对修改策略的显著影响:当时间限制修改任务并且提高对工作记忆负荷的要求时,工作记忆能力较低的个体往往强调对局部错误进行修正,而无法同时在表层和意义两个层面进行全面的更正;高工作记忆容量组修改得分和修改总分都比低工作记忆组明显高。王丹斌(2010)证明了多稿法比修改法有效:修改时,学习者可以节省出不少花费在写作内容和结构上的认知资源,减少短时记忆的认知负担,节约更多的资源空间去发现新错误,并有机会使错误成为短时记忆通往长时记忆的桥梁;成功的作者能同时运用短时记忆和长时记忆与读者进行双向的知识转换。蔡艳玲(2012)认为,学习者能否在二语写作中合理调配认知资源、有效地运用近似母语写作的认知策略尤其重要;学习者语言技能自动化程度越高,就越有可能在作文意义建构中投入大量的认知资源,增大工作记忆信息处理量。易保树、罗少茜(2012)的实验证明工作记忆容量对语言产出准确度有明显的影响,高容量组学习者语言产出准确度要比低容量组学习者高得多;工作记忆容量对书面语产出流利度和复杂度都没有显著影响。

3.3　国内短时记忆研究的发展趋势

通过对二语短时记忆教学研究的回顾及分析,可预想该领域的研究将会呈现以下几个发展趋势。

国内的研究都没有直接评估实时(在线)处理言语理解或言语产出过程中儿童工作记忆能力的个体差异的影响,因此评估儿童工作记忆技能与他们在线(实时)理解和产出语言之间的关系将会成为今后研究的主要课题。

在研究内容上,短时记忆的研究会呈现跨学科与多学科综合的趋势,短时记忆研究的多层次和多方位趋势将更加突出。短时记忆教学研究已与认知语言学、心理语言学交叉融合,今后将与其他学科如神经科学、脑科学、神经心理学等自然科学相融合,其研究视角和思路将会进一步拓展。

在研究方法上,多元化、规范化的趋势将更加突出。短时记忆的研究正逐步从以前的侧重理论性和经验性探讨的研究转向后来的注重教学实践的定量与定性相结合的实证研究。可以预测,借助于统计分析、认知科学等方面的知识和方法,短时记忆理论应用于英语教学实践的研究将更为明确化和具体化。

第四章

二语习得视域下句子理解中的工作记忆研究综述

4.1 引言

"工作记忆"这个术语是由 Miller et al.（1960）在他们的重要著作《行为结构与计划》中提出的。工作记忆不仅与言语、学习、运算、理解和推理等高级复杂认知活动有着密切联系，在其中扮演着重要角色，同时还在发展心理学、神经科学和认知心理学等领域中得到了普遍的研究和大量的推广应用。

4.2 工作记忆理论

4.2.1 工作记忆与短时记忆

工作记忆概念的提出源于对短时记忆系统特性的研究。从机能角度来说，工作记忆同时具有暂时存储和加工处理两种功能：存储功能相当于短时记忆的功能，即在短暂的时间内存储一定的信息；而加工处理的功能则和加工处理的容量这一概念相关联（桂诗春，2000）。从构成上看，短时记忆指的是一种单一成分的单元体系；而工作记忆则是由多个独立成分组成的多元体系。Engle et al.（1998）和 Engle & Oransky（1999）认为短时记忆是工作记忆的一个组成部分。由于受到 Cowan（1988，1995）研究的影响，Engle et al.（1998）提出了工作记忆组成部分相互关系模型，见图 4-1。该模型把中央执行系统从短时记忆中分离出来,并且单独罗列了各种控制策略,例如分组和编码策略。Engle 模型的一个重要特征是将控制性注意作为中央执行系统的首要功能的重要职责。Cowan 和 Engle 认为短时记忆和工作记忆的区别是短时记忆的首要功能是通过使用语音回路和视觉空间模板来维持被激活的记忆编码,而中央执行系统的首要功能是控制注意力。Engle & Oransky(1999)提出测量工作记忆容量的个体差异反应了控制性注意的差异,这些差异仅仅在鼓励或需求控制性注意的情景中反映出来。Unsworth & Engle(2008)和 Unsworth et al.(2009)在 Baddeley 的基础上指出:语音回路和视觉空间模板相当于言语信息和视觉空间信息的短时记忆系统,即工作记忆相当于由短时记忆和中央执行功能两部分构成。

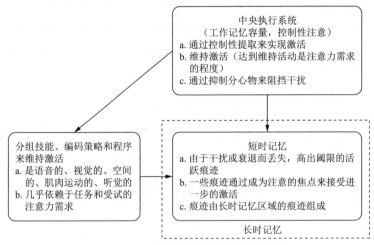

图 4-1　工作记忆组成部分相互关系模型

4.2.2 工作记忆的理论模型

Atkinson & Shiffrin(1968)提出了著名的记忆三级加工模型。Baddeley & Hitch(1974)推出了三成分工作记忆模型,此模型保留了三级加工模型的一些观点,即工作记忆由中央执行系统、语音回路和视觉空间模板三部分组成:中央执行功能是工作记忆模型最为重要的部分及核心;语音回路与短时记忆中的听觉编码相似,由语音储存和发音控制加工两部分组成,与之相对应的工作记忆是言语工作记忆;视觉空间模板与短时记忆中的视觉编码相似,由视觉元素(与颜色形状有关)和空间元素(与位置有关)两个元素组成,与之相对应的工作记忆是空间工作记忆(Baddeley,2003,2007;Smith,1998)。Baddeley(2000)补充完善了自己的理论模型,提出了工作记忆模型的第四个成分,即情景缓冲器。以下为工作记忆的四个成分及其功能(表4-1)。

表4-1 工作记忆的四个成分及其功能

工作记忆的成分	各成分的功能
中央执行功能	主管信息加工的计划协调、注意控制和策略选择,同时还负责协调各成分之间的活动以及与长时记忆保持联系
语音回路	主管存储和控制加工以声音为基础的信息,暂时存储言语材料
视觉空间模板	主管保持、控制和加工视觉、空间的信息
情景缓冲器	负责各成分之间的互动、信息存储和整合,并为各子系统和长时记忆的相互联系提供桥梁

Miyake & Shah(1999)总结编写了《工作记忆模型——主动维持和执行机制》一书,共罗列了十种工作记忆模型,见表4-2。

表4-2 工作记忆模型

序号	工作记忆的主要模型
1	Baddeley 的多成分模型
2	Cowan 的过程嵌套模型
3	Engle、Kane 和 Tuhoski 提出的控制性注意框
4	Lovett、Reder 和 Lebiere 的 ACT-R 模型
5	Kieras 等的执行—过程 / 交互控制模型
6	Young 和 Lewis 的 Soar 建构模型
7	Ericsson 和 Delaney 的长时工作记忆框架
8	Barnard 的交互认知子系统模型
9	Schneider 的控制和自动加工建构模型
10	O'Reilly、Braver 和 Cohen 的基于生物学的计算模型

4.2.3 工作记忆和句子理解的测量工具

4.2.3.1 工作记忆的测量工具

工作记忆的测量工具可以划分为:① 按任务复杂度划分——简单测

试(Ulf, 2010; Elvira & Susan, 2005)和复杂测试(Daneman & Carpenter, 1980; Unsworth, et al., 2005; 金霞, 2011, 2012);② 按所测子系统划分——中央执行系统和语音回路的工作机制与语言习得的关系最为紧密。常用的工作记忆测量方式都可以划分到这两个子系统的测量方式中。在语言习得领域,测量中央执行系统的普遍使用的工具包括阅读广度测试(也有研究者将其称为句子广度测试)、运算广度测试、口语广度测试,这几种工具都属于复杂测试,都是通过布置双重任务来确保受试对输入的信息进行储存与加工处理。测量语音回路的普遍使用的工具包括字母广度测试、数字广度测试、词语广度测试、非词回述测试,这几种测量工具都属于简单测试,只是测试储存功能并需要受试简单地表述所呈现的信息,如图4-2所示。

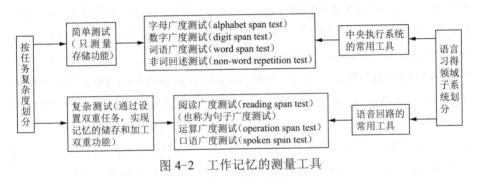

图4-2　工作记忆的测量工具

4.2.3.2　句子理解与工作记忆的测量工具

神经认知语言学所采用的一些关键技术主要有两类:① 第一类是功能性神经成像(functional neuroimaging)技术,此类技术包含正电子辐射断层摄影(PET)和功能磁共振成像(fMRI)等,这类技术主要用于考察在语言加工过程中脑区域是如何定位的;② 第二类技术更准确地描述了语言加工过程中的心理过程或时间历程,主要有脑磁描记法(MEG,可能是观测脑活动的空间特征和时间特征最好结合的无损伤测量技术,但是由于录制设施SQUID非常昂贵,MEG还没有被广泛使用)、经颅磁刺激法(transcranial magnetic stimulation,是暂时性、可逆性地损害人类大脑的特定区域来观察测量的技术)和红外线光学成像等,但是这些技术在当今语言研究领域中尚处于初级探索阶段,还没有被广泛应用于研究句子理解。近年来,随着认知神经科学的发展,脑成像技术如脑电图(EEG)、fMRI(以 fMRI 为核心的观测脑活动的空间特征的技术)、ERP(以 ERP 为核心的观测脑活动的时间特征的技术)等无损伤测量技术被引入工作记忆的研究领域。事件相关电位技术是相对成熟和可靠的高时间分辨率的实时研究技术,主要探究是否存在一个专门用于句法加工的工作记忆资源,可以对句子的加工非常灵敏(McKinnon & Osterhout, 1996)。无论是高速整合的,还是处于无意识状态下的句子加工过程,此技术都能够测试,并可以解决在数毫秒内发生事件的时间历程与初步的脑定位问题。随着事件相关脑电位技术的大量应用,研究者对工作记忆在语言中的加工和工作记忆在句子理解和加工中作用的了解都取得了丰硕的成果。与工作记忆过程相关的各种 ERP 成分包括 N400、ELAN、LAN、P600 和 SAN(sustained anterior negativity)。句子加工过程中存在着语义分析和句法分析这两个相对独立的成分:N400 效应和语义加工相关联(Kutas & Federmeier, 2011; Kutas & Hillyard, 1980a, 1984); P600 效应和句法加工、句子再分析相关联(Hagoort et al., 1993; Osterhout & Holcomb, 1992; Osterhout et al., 1994; Osterhout & Nicol, 1999; van Herten et al., 2006)。句法违反主要受到三个 ERP 成分的影响,分别是左前部负波(LAN, left anterior negativity)、早期左前部负波(ELAN 或 early LAN, early left anterior negativity)和中央顶部正波(P600)。ELAN/LAN 和 P600 分别反映了句子加工过程中的不同阶段:ELAN 是时间为 150～200 毫秒引起的词语种类错误(word category errors)句法违反;LAN 是在句子分析加工过程中时间为 300～500 毫秒表现出的形态句法违反(morphosyntactic violations); P600 是时间为 600 毫秒引发的后期高度控制性的句子重新分析和修改过程。ERP 中的持续前部负波(SAN)技术对于测量句子加工过程中的工作记忆负荷来说还不够敏感(Phillips, 2005)。

19 世纪末,法国学者 Lamare、Jaral 以及 Heuy 开始研究眼动技术。后来,人们尝试通过研究眼动中注视点的顺序和眼跳动来探究阅读背后的知觉过程。眼动技术能够更好地反应句子加工过程中,加工者何时、何地会出现加工的困难并且解决这些困难,所以眼动技术更适合了解和探讨歧义句的加工和处理过程(Kemper et al., 2004)。

4.3　二语习得中的工作记忆与句子理解

工作记忆在句子理解中发挥着重要的作用。工作记忆中的视觉空间模板在理解直观性和形象性的信息方面扮演着重要角色；语音回路对于理解复杂句起着至关重要的作用；而中央执行系统对理解言语有两个关键作用：一个是暂时存储与激活有用信息，另一个是抑制无用信息（陈平文，2007：9-12）。Ellis & Sinclair（1996：238）认为，工作记忆的语音回路部分不仅对二语的词汇学习产生重要作用，而且也会影响二语的句法学习。

4.3.1　国内二语习得中的工作记忆与句子理解

从中国知网进行检索的全文数据库和优秀硕士论文数据库来看，工作记忆与句子理解相关的文章共计 115 篇，其中期刊文章 58 篇、优秀硕士学位论文 52 篇、博士学位论文 5 篇。

4.3.1.1　国内二语习得中的工作记忆与二语语法

陈宝国、高怡文（2009）利用语法判断任务，探究了晚期二语学习者工作记忆容量的限制如何影响和制约第二语言（英语）语法的加工和处理。实验证明：在高工作记忆负荷条件下，被试的语法判断成绩明显比低工作记忆负荷条件下成绩低。研究证实：第二语言语法加工受到个体工作记忆容量差异这一关键因素的影响和制约。

4.3.1.2　国内二语习得中的工作记忆与二语复杂句

任虎林、金朋荪（2010）利用 3 组学习者，考察不同英语水平中国英语学习者的工作记忆在处理两种自嵌式英语复杂句时的差异：前 2 组是英语水平较高的中国英语学习者，分别是 25 名工作记忆力较高者和 25 名工作记忆力较低者；第 3 组是母语为英语的学习者，即 25 名工作记忆能力较高的、本族语为英语的硕士研究生。实验研究发现：英语本族语学习者处理英语复杂句时间最短，并且成绩也最好；而工作记忆能力较高的中国英语学习者比工作记忆能力较低的学习者处理句子所用时间短，同时，二者理解句子的准确率却几乎相等。实验证明：在处理英语复杂句的反应时间方面，中国英语学习者在一定程度上受到工作记忆的影响和制约，而复杂句的处理却几乎不受工作记忆的影响。任虎林（2013）对中国英语学习者的工作记忆容量大小在两种复杂、少见的英语形态结构复杂句加工中的作用进行了研究,研究结果表明:工作记忆容量大小是直接制约二语学习者复杂句阅读速度快慢的重要影响因素,这种影响和二语复杂句的形态结构没有直接联系;工作记忆容量大小不是直接影响二语学习者复杂句理解时间和理解准确性的关键原因。

4.3.1.3　国内二语习得中的工作记忆与二语关系从句

戴运财(2011)考察了工作记忆和教学方式在英语关系从句习得中的作用,分别使用显性和隐性教学方式进行四种关系从句知识的教学,并在教学后进行即时测试。实验发现:当学习者的工作记忆容量是大和中等时,习得关系从句效果明显比工作记忆容量小的学习者要好;尽管工作记忆容量与教学方式两者并没有相关性,但是工作记忆容量与教学方式是影响学习者关系从句习得时的关键因素。

4.3.1.4　国内二语习得中的工作记忆与二语句子加工和理解

赵婧、王金铨(2012)根据内隐与外显加工相分离的任务,研究了工作记忆对中国二语学习者内隐与外显句子加工的影响。实验证明:工作记忆与句法启动没有高度相关,但对即时句子回忆任务有明显影响;在后继词组序列与诱导词视觉呈现的双重干扰条件下,低工作组的诱导词替换率明显高于高工作组。药盼盼、王瑞乐、陈宝国(2013)利用自定步速的两个阅读实验来操纵动词偏好等信息,探讨了第二语言(英语)句子加工中动词偏好信息利用是如何受到工作记忆容量差异的影响。研究证明:只有当句子加工对工作记忆要求相对较低时,第二语言学习者动词偏好信息的利用才会在一定程度上受到工作记忆容量差异的影响。唐瑜婷、陈宝国(2014)探讨了在句子阅读过程中,语境限制强度、句子长度和工作记忆容量如何影响第二语言的词汇学习。实验表明:在句子阅读条件下,工作记忆容量是影响第二语言词汇学习的显著制约因素,高工作记忆容量对第二语言词汇学习起了促进作用。研究结果证明:个体工作记忆的容量和阅读材料等变量都是影响自然阅读条件下第二语言词汇学习的显著因素。陆辉、谢贵华(2015)考察了中国英语学习者工作记忆广度和语言水平差异对隐喻句这一特定句型理解的影响,实验表明:中国英语学习者的英语语言水平、英语工作记忆广度与其隐喻理解能力有很高的相关性,工作记忆和语言水平高低两组 t 检验结果均呈显著性差异,说明工作记忆广度及语言水平是影响中国英语学习者隐喻理解的两大重要因素，因此英语学习者应该通过拓宽知识面及培训工作记忆来增强自己的隐喻理解能力。

4.3.2　国外二语习得中的工作记忆与句子理解

4.3.2.1　国外二语习得中的工作记忆与二语语法

Miyake & Friedman（1998）通过实验发现，由于二语学习者受到工作记忆容量的限制，因此通过解释晚期二语学习者语法加工的困难能够更好地解释关键期假设不能解释的现象，但关于个体工作记忆容量的差异是否影响第二语言语法的加工还没有得出统一的答案。实验得出结论：工作记忆容量高的阅读者比容量低的阅读者语法加工的成绩更好。William（1999）和 Williams & Lovatt（2005）通过实验，研究了成年人英语学习者工作记忆中的语音回路因素如何影响其二语习得过程中对语法规则的归纳学习能力。实验结果证实：语音短时记忆（语音环）与非记忆因素都对学习者语言规则的归纳学习产生显著作用和影响；对语法规则的归纳学习很大程度上依赖于各音系形式（phonological forms）之间建立起来的关联（主要是语音环的作用），而不是通过对形式—意义之间的关联进行归纳分析所能完成的。Juffs（2006）和 Felser & Roberts（2007）等探讨了工作记忆容量的差异如何影响和制约二语语法加工。实验表明：工作记忆容量的大小在二语语法加工中没有发挥显著的作用；工作记忆容量大小的影响在二语者句子加工中没有体现，而只在母语句子处理中才能体现出来。McDonald（2006）研究发现，工作记忆容量与二语语法判断的成绩有着显著的相关性，由此说明：第二语言语法加工在很大程度上受到工作记忆容量大小的影响。Leeser（2007）实验证明，工作记忆容量的差异在学习者理解和处理语法形式中扮演着一些角色，工作记忆还依赖受试者对文本话题的先前知识。

4.3.2.2　国外二语习得中的工作记忆与二语复杂句

Ellis & Sinclair（1996）认为处理句子的效率受到句法复杂性的影响和制约，而工作记忆能力强弱又与句子处理相关联。Kuno（1974）曾指出工作记忆能力与关系句的处理难度高度相关。基于 Kuno 的结论，Izumi（2003）对一些英语学习者理解中心嵌入和右嵌入式的句子进行实验，这些英语学习者是英语为第二语言的不同母语(例如意大利语、汉语、德语、朝鲜语)学习者,实验证实了 Kuno 理论的准确性,即这些学习者理解右嵌入句子要比理解中心嵌入句容易得多。Baddeley & Hitch (1974)和 Caplan & Waters (1990)都承认语音回路对于理解冗长而复杂的句子的作用,但 Baddeley 等人的"后分析"理论强调促进句法结构的分析是语音编码的主要功能,所以语音回路主要在语言理解的初始阶段才起作用;而 Caplan 等人的"前分析"理论则强调意义、句法的加工和处理是即时的,语音编码主要出现在句子加工的后期,也就是说只有将句法、意义加工的结果、经验和现实进行对比时才会产生影响,因此语音回路只有在理解的高级阶段才会产生影响和发挥作用。Just & Carpenter (1992,1996)的容量限制理论认为,只存在一个一般性的言语工作记忆系统,语言加工的各个方面直接受到该系统的有限容量的影响和制约,例如,语义提取、句法角色的指派、词汇通达和其他以语言为媒介的认知活动。Ardila (2003)详述了工作记忆是处理复杂句的重要因素,因此二语学习者和本族语者相比,需要有更强的工作记忆能力和更长的理解时间来理解和处理复杂的句子,而在句子理解准确率方面却比本族语者低。Dussias & Piar (2010)的实验研究证实:采用通达性信息研究从最初错误到正确的长距问题时,只有工作记忆容量大的、母语为汉语的英语学习者才能具备和本族英者一样利用通达信息处理复杂句的水平。

4.3.2.3 国外二语习得中的工作记忆与二语句子理解及加工

Miyake & Friedman (1998)指出,工作记忆容量的差异制约实时二语加工的质量和效率,所以工作记忆是二语能力的关键。Friedman & Miyake (2004)的实验证明句子的加工时间在阅读广度任务中很大程度依赖于句子的位置:随着加工者句子加工越来越靠后,句子的加工时间成线形增长势态。这说明随着被试记忆负担的增大,加工的效率受到了很大的影响,致使加工和储存之间难以区分。Sagarra (2005)利用 RST 方法,考察了工作记忆如何影响和制约二语西班牙语学习者的句子处理,实验发现工作记忆能力只有短期效应而没有长期效应。Fiebach et al. (2005)通过实验证明在线理解句子时,布罗卡区在句法工作记忆中起着重要作用。Dan & Penny (2007)通过实验证明工作记忆容量是隐喻加工的一个关键因素:实验 1 证实高度工作记忆个体比低跨度个体能更迅速、准确地产生隐喻理解;实验 2 证实高度工作记忆个体比低跨度个体能产生更合适的隐喻;实验 3 证实数字广度反面比数字广度正面能生成更优质的预测隐喻。实验结果证明言语常识和工作记忆功能对于隐喻加工起着同等重要的作用。Felser & Roberts（2007）探究了英语学习者（母语为希腊语）加工处理填充语－空位(filler-gap)依存句的模式。实验结果证实:二语句法加工并不受到工作记忆容量高低的影响和制约。Yuan et al.（2010）通过实验证实二语句子理解时被试对工作记忆的独特需求。

4.3.2.4　国外二语习得中的工作记忆与二语句子回忆

Potter（1993）提出了"瞬时概念记忆系统"假设,强调瞬时概念记忆系统的作用是主管与长时记忆中的概念系统发生相互影响,同时准确而详实地表征句子意义。Potter（1993）没有从工作记忆角度加以详述,但是从功能角度来看,Baddeley（2000）所提出的情景缓冲器功能与瞬时概念记忆系统相吻合,即二者在短时记忆和长时记忆之间架起了桥梁。Rummer & Engelkamp（2001）的实验证明语音编码促进了即时句子回忆,并且该影响是迅速的、短暂的。Alloway & Gathercole（2005）采用语音启动进行实验研究,研究证明:在即时句子回忆中,儿童易受长时记忆中同义词的影响,而且高工作记忆组使用的语义替换比低工作记忆组少。Baddeley et al.（2009）采用系列句子回忆进行实验研究,又一次证实了情景缓冲器的功能。

4.4　总结与展望

在过去的二十年间,二语习得视域下句子理解和加工中的工作记忆研究取得了巨大的进步,但仍存在一些问题和不足。

工作记忆基本理论研究者和脑成像研究者之间还存在脱节,前者不擅长脑成像技术,后者缺乏文献理论知识。

研究者还需进一步了解与工作记忆过程相关的各种 ERP 成分(如 N400、LAN、SAN 和 P600)的精确性质。将 ERP 技术与 fMRI 技术紧密结合起来,才可以更为翔实和严密地研究和论证工作记忆能力强弱的差异对句法歧义消解的影响。

句法意识研究面临的一个问题是如何测量加工者的精确句法意识,当前急需解决的一个问题是:如何在句法意识任务中抑制语义加工的干扰和工作记忆的负荷。

研究者应该从认知心理学的角度出发来探究工作记忆容量的差异和与二语句子加工之间的联系，从而进一步论证认知能力如何与二语加工能力相关联。

国内外研究表明工作记忆和句子理解之间存在显著相关，但是在实验数据的控制、测试工具的选取等方面仍有待进一步优化。未来研究可以采取更为精确的实验数据控制和评分测量标准，以便对工作记忆容量的高低进行测试和计量，从而研究工作记忆个体差异如何影响和制约二语句子的理解。

从言语工作记忆（语音回路）的角度研究歧义句加工和语法等句子理解的实验相对较多，但从空间工作记忆（视觉空间模板）的角度研究句子理解和加工的实验相对较少。这将是今后研究二语习得中工作记忆和句子加工值得进一步探讨的问题。

第五章

神经机制下工作记忆和二语句子理解研究述评

　　二语句子理解涉及的是输入信息和个体变量相互作用的过程。在个体变量中，除了二语习得者的年龄、先前知识（包括第一语言、第二语言的语言学知识和世界知识）外，Skehan（1998）提出，一些学习者处理输入信息更有效可能是因为他们拥有更大的工作记忆容量或是他们能以更快速度执行工作记忆中的分析过程。心理语言学通过行为测量来研究二语习得者如何在线处理和理解句子，引起了许多争议。本章从神经认知科学角度回顾工作记忆和二语句子理解实验研究，运用神经认知科学的测量技术（ERP、fMRI、PET）测试脑活动来探讨习得年龄、一语向二语迁移与内容熟悉度是如何与工作记忆相联系来制约和促进二语句子理解，从而更好地解决心理语言学行为测量的一些矛盾问题。

5.1　工作记忆概述

5.1.1　神经成像研究中的工作记忆

　　工作记忆容量通常由广度任务来测量。早期的神经成像研究集中于辨别工作记忆中的维持和处理过程：维持信息通常没有外在刺激（例如，练习），而处理和重组被维持的信息通常由中央执行功能来完成。神经成像研究主要集中于大脑的三个额区：① Ventrolateral（VLPFC）= BA 44, 45, 47，即大脑腹侧前额叶皮层是布罗德曼区 44、45、47 号，负责维持信息；② Dorsolateral （DLPFC）= BA 9, 46，即大脑背侧前额叶皮层是布罗德曼区 9、46 号，负责处理信息；③ Anterior（APFC）= BA10，即大脑前额皮层前部是布罗德曼区 10 号，负责更高层次的控制过程；同时，神经成像研究还集中于 BA7、40 号，即大脑顶叶区是布罗德曼区 7、40 号，此区域可能存在包含大脑前额叶皮层和顶叶皮层的注意神经回路。

额叶内的前额叶皮层被普遍认为在工作记忆中扮演着重要角色。大多数模型认为储存信息的主要场所不在额叶内，而是在后皮层。前额叶皮层的功能是根据当前目标保持信息活跃或者处理这些活跃信息。

Smith & Jonides（1997）通过 PET 研究工作记忆得出结论：不同的神经回路影响言语、空间和物体工作记忆，空间记忆是右侧向（right lateralized），而言语和物体记忆是左侧向；同时，涉及每一种工作记忆的一些皮层区存在差异：空间工作记忆激活枕叶区和下额区，物体记忆是下颞区（inferotemporal area）活跃，而言语记忆激活布罗卡区。

Müller & Basho（2004）通过 fMRI 发现听—视—运动处理流的输入汇集激活场所位于左侧大脑下额叶：下额叶皮层是语言习得的重要场所之一；下额叶皮层的功能由于工作记忆容量的增大而进一步增强，使之在句法解码时必不可少。

5.1.2　前额叶皮层的两个结构原则

前额叶皮层的两个结构原则是认知分层（cognitive hierarchy）与自动化程度（degree of automaticity）。

语言一直以来被认为具有分层结构的特点：音节由音素组成，单词由音节组成，词组由单词组成，然后词组组合构建成句子。前额叶皮层一直沿着前部到后部轴心有系统地组织，并依赖于认知分层变化的层次，即前部区域涉及更高层次而后部区域涉及更低层次；同时，分层加工的神经基础涉及大脑的背侧前额叶皮层。Jeon & Friederici（2015）提出自动化程度是前额叶皮层组织的要素，后部至前部梯度体系表明二语（低自动化程度）脑前部控制的过程，而以后部为主的体系表明本族语（高自动化程度）主要涉及脑后部自动化过程。

5.1.3 工作记忆各成分在二语学习中的角色

研究者们纷纷通过实验证明工作记忆在二语习得中扮演的角色。二语研究者提出个体在工作记忆中的差异会限制注意,因此影响二语习得。语音记忆(phonological memory)和中央执行功能在二语和本族语的学习中尤其重要。

首先,处理语音信息对语言学习和使用至关重要。Baddeley 工作记忆模式中的语音环操纵着语音短时记忆,此成分在本族语发展中扮演着重要角色。语音环支持语言学习,包括词汇发展、流利性和一些对理解的测量。语音环的功能不是记忆熟悉单词,而是帮助学习新单词。语音记忆在儿童和成年二语发展中扮演着重要角色。学习新声音模式中的语音记忆功能对二语词汇学习、涉及诸如性别一致性依存关系的形态规则和二语语法学习都至关重要。许多研究者把语音短时记忆和语言学习间的联系归因于语音环对新语音材料形成稳定、长时心理表征的重要性,这些表征对语音知识尤为重要,例如,单个的单词和语块。短时记忆容量可以预测语块能力,"组块"是记忆和恰当使用二语固定词组的能力,组块能力又反过来与以后创造性地运用语言相关联。其次,中央执行功能与阅读理解和全面言语能力相关。控制注意是中央执行器的主要功能,已适用于二语研究。注意控制与工作记忆是同义词。基于工作记忆的中央执行成分的控制注意功能,工作记忆与二语词汇和语法学习有着直接联系。研究者们对视觉和空间记忆的研究并没有引起语言研究学家的重视。迄今为止,二语学习中还没有对新增加到 Baddeley 模式的情景缓冲器的研究。

5.2 影响二语句子理解中工作记忆的因素

5.2.1 一语向二语迁移与工作记忆

已有大量证据证明,一语的语音、拼写、语素词汇、词汇—语义和句法特性会影响二语句子理解(Frenck-Mestren & Pynte, 1997; Hernandez et al., 2005; Marian & Spivey, 2003; Scheutz & Eberhard, 2004; Tan et al., 2003; Weber & Cutler, 2004; Jeong et al., 2007)。

充分迁移观点(full transfer view)认为,二语者持续习得二语不仅会在二语加工时使用这些语言特征和加工路线,还会习得一语中没有的二语特点。"建构理论"模式指出熟练的阅读者会抑制不恰当的意思来建构庞大、连贯的分层结构,其中每一个新成分都被组合并激活前面相关成分,反复受到激活的成分更易于回忆。一语阅读向二语转换时,熟练的本族语阅读者能在阅读后回忆一语语境文本成分,并构建一个连贯结构以便以后回忆这些成分;如果二语水平与文本相符合,他们会很好地处理二语语境中的每一个句子,也可以回忆这些成分。

5.2.2　内容熟悉度与工作记忆

由于加工者有限的工作记忆容量,加工一系列句子时,语境能提供加工益处。储存的语境可以提前激活与理解相关的概念、关系和图式以便于加工随后的句子。背景知识在阅读中有利于词汇学习或单词意思的推断。Hambrick & Engle(2002)提出领域知识和工作记忆对理解的相互作用:相关背景知识或领域知识能在理解时弥补加工者的低工作记忆能力,而高层面领域知识可以削弱甚至抵消工作记忆的促进性影响;高工作记忆能力提高了相关领域知识,代表了"丰富—更丰富"假设,即如果加工者拥有足够的背景知识,更大的工作记忆容量可以促进理解。有三个模式涉及工作记忆容量和领域知识对认知表现的影响:补偿模式、丰富—更丰富模式、独立影响模式。

5.2.3　习得年龄与工作记忆

自从 Lenneberg(1967)和 Penfield & Roberts(1959)首次提出二语习得生物限制期假设,研究者对于关键期假设(critical period hypothesis)(Lenneberg,1967)又提出许多新观点。大多数理论认为习得二语的能力像本族语一样受到成熟期限制(maturational constraints),在儿童期开始下降并在青春期消失。反对关键期假设的一个观点是二语习得不仅是语言学习年龄跨度的总下降,还反映与年龄相关的其他认知资源(例如,工作记忆)的下降。

Newport et al.(2001)认为语法习得受到关键期的影响。儿童期和青春期的发展变化引起本族语和二语中语法加工的差异。陈述—程序模式提出由于成熟因素,程序记忆体系涉及的二语加工比本族语更少些。此提议基于与语言加工相关的两个大脑记忆体系的差别:陈述性体系促进被记忆单词和词组的储存,位于包含内侧颞叶(medial temporal)和额前皮层区的特定脑结构网络;程序性记忆体系涉及加工语言的组合规则,依赖于包含额—基底神经节巡回和额下回(BA44 或布罗卡区)的网络。晚期二语学习者过度依赖陈述性体系(如语法加工),主要由于儿童期和青春期发生的成熟变化,而本族语者依赖于程序性体系。

5.3 神经机制下二语句子理解

二语习得的研究使用了许多测量技术。心理语言学家一直使用一系列行为测试来研究二语习得者在理解过程中是如何进行在线语言加工的。神经科学家一直使用脑活动测试,来研究二语理解过程中推断不同种类信息牵涉到大脑的什么组织,从而调查一个大脑存放两种或更多语言的认知和神经结果。

5.3.1 二语句子理解中的 ERP 成分和工作记忆

N400 被用来间接测试工作记忆容量对更严格分析句法各方面的影响。Garnsey et al.(1989)通过 N400 探测加工来选择暂时句法歧义句引起的语义花园路径。花园路径是由于工作记忆容量的限制,N400 可以帮助以一种更抽象方式在句法层面反映工作记忆需求。与更小的工作记忆负荷相比,适中的工作记忆负荷与介于 250 和 600 毫秒间更大的负波相关,尤其出现在左半球中央电极区。

LAN 是工作记忆负荷(与暂时储存在工作记忆中的填充词相关)更综合的指标。LAN 的神经区域是(左)前额叶皮层,特别是布罗卡区。Kluender & Kutas(1993)研究了长距离依存关系的 wh- 句和关系从句:加工者必须在工作记忆中保存填充词一段时间,直到完成填充词—空位委派;至少两类词引发 LAN,即保存在工作记忆中正在被加工的填充词和在随后位置正进行题元角色委派的词,因此工作记忆负荷能融入正在构建的句子表征中。Neville et al.(1992)观察到由功能词引发的位于脑后部、偏左侧 N400—700 成分:大多数英语功能词的重要特征是支持最初句法分析、介绍新句法成分、决定句子中词组结构,功能词在语法中扮演重要角色。因此,一个功能词本身就反映了更大的工作记忆负荷,从而引发了 N400—700。

5.3.2 fMRI / PET 和二语句子理解

Friederici（2002）提出本族语的神经加工阶段：神经基础的第一个加工阶段是左颞上回前部（anterior portion of the left superior temporal gyrus，STG）和深额岛盖（deep frontal operculum）；第二个阶段的词汇—语义／题元信息以及形态句法信息的综合主要依赖于颞上回后部（posterior STG）、颞中回（middle temporal gyrus，MTG）和额下回（inferior frontal gyrus，IFG）（通常被认为是布罗卡区）；最后再分析加工主要激活包含颞上回后部和基底神经节的皮质—皮质下体系。

布罗卡区位于左额下回，按功能分为三个区域：语音、语义和句法，但也对非语言功能（如，认知）控制起重要作用。一部分布罗卡区（BA 44，岛盖部（pars opercularis））主要加工句法信息，而左额下回更低部分（BA 47，眶部（pars orbitalis））有选择性地加工语义信息。布罗卡区对本族语仅是语言器官，而左额下回其余部分对二语起作用（Scoresby-Jackson，1867）。

5.4 神经机制下工作记忆和二语句子理解实验研究

到目前为止，学者们从脑神经机制的角度研究工作记忆和二语句子理解的论文不多，这是有待于进一步发展和探索的领域。表 5-1、表 5-2、表 5-3 分别从工作记忆以及与工作记忆相关的习得年龄、一语向二语的迁移、内容熟悉度四个方面研究回顾了二语句子理解 ERP（7 个）、fMRI（10 个）、ERP 和 fMRI（1 个）、PET（2 个）实验结果。

5.4.1 ERP 实验

ERP 实验分为语音和语义相结合、语义、句法、语义和句法相结合四个方面，见表 5-1。

表 5-1 与习得年龄、语言迁移、内容熟悉度和工作记忆相关的二语句子理解 ERP 研究回顾

作者	习得年龄	语言迁移	内容熟悉度	工作记忆	二语句子理解 ERP 结果
语音和语义相结合					
Sinai et al.（2003）	晚期二语为英语，本族语为西伯来语	没报道	受到语境影响	低级识别信号脑电波表明更高的认知加工，至少包含部分语义加工	二语单词 P3 振幅增强；二语比一语引发振幅更小的 P2

续表

作者	习得年龄	语言迁移	内容熟悉度	工作记忆	二语句子理解 ERP 结果
语义					
Martin et al. （2013）	晚期二语为英语，本族语为西班牙语	没报道	句子语境使预期的名词比不预期的名词更易于组合	关键单词基于工作记忆中的语境信息组合	二语者对于不预期冠词没能引发 N400 的振幅增加
句法					
Hahne et al. （2006）	晚期二语为德语，本族语为俄语	没报道	没报道	复数违反没引发 LAN，说明工作记忆负荷	分词：LAN 和 P600；规则复数引发 P600，而不规则复数引发 N400
Gillon Dowens et al. （2008, 2010）	晚期汉语—西班牙语 L2（2008）；晚期英语—西班牙语 L2（2010）	受到一语向二语迁移的影响	没报道	第二个句子位置没引发 LAN，说明需要更长时间在工作记忆中保存一致性特征，工作记忆负荷增大	第一个句子位置（句首）引发 LAN 和 P600；第二个句子位置（句中）仅引发 P600 以及两个句子位置的数和性别违反的重要振幅和潜伏期差异
Gillon Dowens et al. （2011）	晚期二语为西班牙语，本族语为汉语	二语句法加工受到一语向二语迁移的影响	没报道	缺少 LAN 说明工作记忆负荷；仅引发 P600 是更不自动反映	违反性别和数一致都包括 P600 效应
Reichle et al. （2013）	晚期二语为法语，本族语为英语	没报道	没报道	随着本族语工作记忆容量增加，二语 N400 振幅增加	二语学习者主语—动词一致性违反只引发 N400。主语与动词不相邻，二语者 N400 振幅减小
语义和句法相结合					
Weber-Fox et al. （2001）	早期汉语—英语（L2），习得年龄：1～3、4～6、7～10；晚期汉语～英语（L2），习得年龄：11～13、大于 15 年	没报道	没报道	二语学习者言语工作记忆能力相似	7 岁后浸入二语者封闭类词峰潜伏期更晚些；语义违反引发 N400，只对晚期二语者显示出渐增的峰潜伏期

续表

作者	习得年龄	语言迁移	内容 熟悉度	工作记忆	二语句子 理解 ERP 结果
Sugiura et al. （2018） （fNIRS- ERP）	晚期二语为英语，本族语为日语的初中生	没报道	没报道	性别差异：随着水平的提高，男孩呈现降低的负荷，而女孩理解语法不正确的句子时能充分利用语言知识和工作记忆	收听二语句子时，男孩依赖于涉及基于规则的句法加工的前额区，女孩依赖于涉及语音、语义和句子加工的后部语言区域

5.4.2　fMRI 实验

fMRI 实验分为语音、句法、语义和句法相结合、自动化程度四个方面，见表 5-2。

表 5-2　与习得年龄、语言迁移、内容熟悉度和工作记忆相关的
二语句子理解 fMRI 研究回顾

作者	习得年龄	语言迁移	内容 熟悉度	工作记忆	二语句子 理解 fMRI 结果
语音					
Tan et al. （2003）	晚期二语为英语，本族语为汉语	执行英语单词语音任务，应用一语体系到二语阅读	没报道	语音加工汉字使用对空间工作记忆和作为中央执行系统协调认知资源起作用的皮层区	语音加工英语单词神经系统最活跃
句法					
Hasegawa et al. （2002）	晚期二语为英语，本族语为日语	没报道	句子中的否定结构是二语语境中出现的难点	言语工作记忆从属区域左缘上回、左中央前沟、辅助运动区表现出强烈和一致影响；后古典语言区与认知控制相联系	二语在左颞区、后古典语言区引发更大激活；二语否定句比肯定句引发更大激活

续表

作者	习得年龄	语言迁移	内容熟悉度	工作记忆	二语句子理解 fMRI 结果
Yokoyama et al.（2006）	晚期二语为英语，本族语为日语；习得二语的年龄影响二语理解时的皮层表征	一语和二语时使用相似皮层区；句子中不同的语法结构影响皮层表征	没报道	控制工作记忆的影响	日语被动句比主动句在左三角部、运动前区和顶上小叶引发更大的激活，二语没有
Hernandez et al.（2007）	早期二语为英语，本族语为西班牙语；晚期二语为西班牙语，本族语为英语	没报道	没报道	晚期二语者显示广泛分布在前额叶皮层前部并延伸到 BA44/45 的激活群	一语和二语激活基本重叠，但早期和晚期二语学习者存在提取差异
Suh et al.（2007）	晚期二语为英语，本族语为韩国语	一语和二语句法加工的皮层区是共同的，但是潜在的神经机制不同	没报道	不同的左额中回激活表明不同的工作记忆负荷	一语和二语激活区重叠，但一语和二语句法复杂性存在不同
Jeong et al.（2007）	晚期二语为日语，本族语为韩国语；晚期二语为英语，本族语为韩国语	一语和二语句法相似性影响二语皮层加工	没报道	右小脑、左额下回在言语工作记忆中合作来识别形态句法错误	句法结果一语和二语相似，但二语额外激活是由于跨语言不同的作用
语义和句法相结合					
Rüschemeyer et al.（2005）	晚期二语为德语，本族语为俄语	没报道；但俄语一语者对词组结构违反与德语一语者显示相似的激活	没报道	受到句法复杂性和句子中工作记忆需求的影响，部分下额叶皮层逐渐被激活	一语和二语者对于语义违反比句法违反表现出更相似的激活增加模式；二语者使用额颞语言网络特定部分
Rüschemeyer et al.（2006）	晚期二语为德语，本族语为俄语	没报道	没报道	句法复杂性与更高的工作记忆需求相关；左额下回激活增加使用了短时记忆体系	句法结果一语和二语相似，但在一些脑区二语激活程度增加

续表

作者	习得年龄	语言迁移	内容熟悉度	工作记忆	二语句子理解 fMRI 结果
自动化程度					
Wang et al.（2007）	晚期二语为英语，本族语为汉语	没报道	没报道	语言转换涉及工作记忆中的前额叶皮层	当转换到二语时，二语加工表明了左前额叶皮层 fMRI 反映增加
Jeon et al.（2013）	晚期二语为韩国语，本族语为德语	没报道	没报道	二语学习者必须使用额外认知资源工作记忆来弥补低效率	二语显示明显渐倾激活模式，最高层面使用前额叶皮层最前部区域

5.4.3 ERP 和 fMRI 实验相结合

ERP 和 fMRI 实验反映了自动化程度，见表 5-3。

5.4.4 PET 实验

根据语音和语义相结合来考察言语记忆，共有两个实验研究，见表 5-3。

表 5-3 与习得年龄、语言迁移、内容熟悉度和工作记忆相关的二语句子理解 ERP 和 fMRI、PET 研究回顾

作者	习得年龄	语言迁移	内容熟悉度	工作记忆	二语句子理解 ERP 和 fMRI、PET 结果
自动化程度					
Rodriguez-Fornells et al.（2002）	早期西班牙语—加泰罗尼亚语（L2）双语	没报道	没报道	抑制加工一种不相关语言时，二语左前额叶皮层 fMRI 反映增加	（ERP）双语者对非目标语词频不敏感。（fMRI）双语者颞平面对三个重要条件引发更大激活
语音和语义相结合					
Kim et al.（2002）	晚期二语为英语，本族语为韩国语	没报道	没报道	低水平二语视觉更高层控制在工作记忆加工时起重要作用	（PET）二语工作记忆激活了大脑右背侧前额叶皮层和左颞下回后部
Halsband et al.（2002）	晚期二语为英语，本族语为芬兰语	两种语言的脑机制使用相同成分	没报道	编码与前额和海马激活相联系；记忆提取任务	（PET）二语具体单词引发角形脑回和缘上回更大激活

5.5　启示

表 5-1 工作记忆与二语句子理解 ERP 研究数据表明，高水平二语学习者句法的加工接近于本族语，往往引发 P600，可是涉及二语句法加工的、与工作记忆负荷相关的左前额负波经常缺失；而低水平的二语学习者通常引发语义加工的 N400。实验证明工作记忆是影响语言理解的关键因素。工作记忆和短时记忆是学能模式中更高层次语言水平技能的重要组成部分。

大多数二语研究 LAN 的缺失表明二语句子加工时自动化程度显著降低，尽管涉及加工局部语法依赖的自动化程度会随着二语水平的提高而提高。然而，涉及复杂分层结构的二语句子加工是否能完全自动化还有待于进一步研究。神经影像研究已表明：二语结构复杂句的脑皮层激活增加，说明二语理解比本族语理解需要更多的加工。如果加工非局部依存对工作记忆有更大需要，此领域学习者的困难可能源于加工二语时缺少工作记忆资源，而不是语法知识。

表 5-2、表 5-3 工作记忆与二语句子理解 fMRI、PET 研究数据表明，首先，与二语相关的递增大脑活动出现在斡旋一语的脑区或这些脑区附近（例如，左额下回或颞上回）；其次，与认知控制相关的特定的、额外的脑区活动出现在左前额叶皮层、前扣带回和基底神经节。

对控制的需求与前额叶皮层活动增加相联系。一项任务越得到越多的练习，对控制（和前额叶皮层）的依赖便会减小，因为练习加强了大脑其他结构与任务相关的神经通路的联系。这些巡回可以随时间独立于前额叶皮层而运行，执行任务变得更自动化。神经成像研究表明学习初始阶段前额叶皮层表现出更大激活，随着学习经历和练习的增加，前额叶皮层内的神经活动变弱。高效率处理句子常常来自练习或是一些指导性干预。阅读中强化训练同样可以对一些理解成分加工产生更大效率。为了增加总工作记忆容量，练习可以征集更多激活或额外的加工，复述依赖于恢复（refreshing）的过程，此过程涉及对选项的持续注意。记忆依赖于学习者对材料的熟悉度并随着练习而增强。因此在二语教学中，教师应根据学生水平在考试前给予学生适当指导，并辅以练习题来巩固和强化所学知识。

大脑前额叶皮层执行工作记忆。来自亚利桑那大学的教授 Yuan（2014）

表明前额叶皮层体积越大和 PFC 皮层越厚,学习者会有越好的执行表现,因此学习者应参加各种认知活动来锻炼前额叶皮层使之增强。因此,在二语教学中,教师可以通过记录笔记、遵循指示和忽视干扰来锻炼学生的加工能力,从而提高工作记忆容量。

如果工作记忆与注意容量或者控制中央执行功能相联系(可以抑制来自一语的竞争压力),那么二语学习者可以集中于二语形式并努力抑制一语的影响。许多学者认为一语迁移是不可避免的,控制注意资源并抑制影响是成功二语学习的关键。二语学习者前额叶皮层被逐渐激活,说明在加工低水平二语时,前额叶皮层阻挡来自更强本族语的更优势的、不相关的反应,从而有利于加工与任务相关的弱势二语表征。背侧前额叶皮层与抑制和注意相联系说明工作记忆不是一个与其他执行功能完全分开的加工。因此在二语教学中,教师应帮助学生激活图式(schema),即优先与任务相联系的反应,并抑制不恰当的反应。对任务图式更有效率的管理是让具备更大工作记忆容量的二语学习者能更迅速地排除竞争信息中的干扰。因此,如何成功抑制将是今后二语研究的课题。

Hernandez et al.(2007)、Suh et al.(2007)、Jeong et al.(2007) 和 Rüschemeyer et al.(2006)(表 5-2)的实验表明,不同的模式(听力或阅读)证实了一语和二语者句法加工使用相似的脑区,也就是说,一语和二语激活区重叠。然而,二语句法习得应存在激活脑额区和颞区的交替使用,特别是左前额皮层与句法规则学习相联系。因此,未来研究应该更详细地调查二语者句法语言加工时脑额区和颞区(Rueschemeyer et al.,2005,2006)(表 5-2)间交替使用的特性。成年二语学习者习得二语语法不依赖用于加工本族语的相同脑结构(额纹状体网络,fronto-striatal network)。随着语言水平的提高,介于本族语和二语学习者之间的最后神经差异会消失。句法复杂性与二语者更高的工作记忆需求相关。语言理解个体差异已表明高容量者更大的可塑性;同时,最大、最一致的可塑效应易于在前额区域和纹状体(striatum)观察到,并且调查工作记忆的神经成像研究经常激活这些区域。随着句法复杂性的增加,高容量阅读者更大程度地运用前额区域和终脑皮层表明了高容量阅读者比低容量阅读者有更有效的句子理解措施。个体可塑性差异与相关信息积极、轻松地转换到皮层加工中心相联系,这种能力对于语言理解以及需要维持和处理信息的其他任务(如,工作记忆容量)都至关重要。为了更好地了解二语句法分析体系与工作记忆的关系,从语言学、神经生理学层面以及构成二语句法习得的脑基础来考虑和调查多重结构微妙之处是十分必要的。

Jeong et al.(2007)(表5-2)和Kim et al.(2002)(表5-3)的实验表明,二语低水平学习者使用右半球更多区域来弥补语言的低水平。语言理解中右半球的功能是什么? 此问题一直争论不休,更别说二语研究。因此,对于语言任务,大多数人一致地激活左半球语言区域,而右半球的作用在个体和任务间变化,研究者难以概述。通过使用脑神经设备,涉及二语加工的右半球个体差异将得到系统研究,此类困难和问题会被逐步攻克。

Weber-Fox et al.(2001)(表5-1)、Hernandez et al.(2007)(表5-2)和Rodriguez-Fornells et al.(2002)(表5-3)的实验表明:二语者习得年龄都是早期,可是实验并没有表明前额叶的大量活动是由于习得年龄,还是与二语水平相关的其他因素。研究者对二语儿童的神经认知学测量实验很少。Perani & Abutalebi(2005)对涉及语法加工的本族语者和二语者大脑活动进行对比:早期双语者(刚出生者)大脑活动没有差异;晚期二语学习者(六岁后)大脑语言相关区域牵涉更多活动。一语是在关键期的隐性(implicit)习得,而二语通常只能通过正式指导来显性(explicit)习得,因此,二语者加工二语语法知识并不是通过与隐性加工一语语法相关的神经结构(如布罗卡区和基底神经节)。Newport(1990)提出儿童时期的小工作记忆容量的优势,因此,儿童有限的工作记忆容量为语言学习时涉及的成分分析提供了优势。二语儿童学好外语涉及大脑的可塑性和关键期。通过神经认知科学的测量技术,研究者可以观测和解决如何在临界期通过提高工作记忆来提高二语儿童的语言水平。

第六章

工作记忆容量与歧义句
加工关系的研究述评

从试图理解句子的阅读者的角度来看,句法歧义是一种挑战,因为理解者经常会产生理解错误和句法再分析;同时,句子加工的认知机制受到工作记忆资源的限制,因为认知机制的工作记忆资源在存储和计算操作方面容量有限。本书试图通过相关研究来探讨工作记忆容量差异与句法歧义加工之间的关系,从而更好地解决工作记忆容量差异对二语句法歧义句加工的影响,以便提高二语句法歧义句的加工效率。

6.1. 文献综述

6.1.1 工作记忆与歧义句加工

工作记忆系统支持句子理解的程度和其在句子理解中的角色一直是持续不断讨论的话题(Just & Carpenter, 1992; Carpenter et al., 1994; Caplan & Waters, 1999, 2013; Just & Varma, 2002, 2007; MacDonald & Christiansen, 2002)。

6.1.1.1 涉及句法加工的工作记忆理论

工作记忆资源理论涉及句子加工过程,一直在一语心理语言学文献中存在争议。此争议集中于以下问题:是否存在一个单一工作记忆资源用于所有认知/语言加工过程(Caspari et al., 1998; King & Just, 1991; MacDonald et al.,1992;Miyake et al.,1994;Pearlmutter & MacDonald,1995;Just & Carpenter,1992,1996,1999);是否存在不同种类的工作记忆资源用于句子加工(Caplan & Waters,1990,1999,2002;Waters & Caplan,1996a,1996b,1996c,2001,2002;Hanten & Martin,2000,2001;Martin,1995;Martin & Feher,1990;Martin & He,2004;Martin & Lesch,1995;Martin & Romani,1994;Martin et al.,1994;Saffran,1990;Waters et al.,1991;Withaar & Stowe,1999)。Just & Carpenter(1992)认为单一的、统一体系用于整个加工过程,包括句法、语义以及语用方面。而Caplan & Waters(1999)持不同观点,提出了言语工作记忆的分开的句子解释资源模型(separate-sentence-interpretation-resource,SSIR),此模型在言语工作记忆内进行了更精细的区分,挑战了单一资源模型(主张句子加工行为中存在个体差异)所阐述的观点,即存在两种用于不同语言任务的子系统:解释性加工体系(interpretive processing system)和后解释性加工体系(post-interpretative processing system)。

Waters & Caplan(1996a)提出了两种分开的语言资源,一个是更自动的言语加工,一个是更加具有控制性的言语加工。同时,Caplan & Waters(1999)和 Caplan et al.(1998)对中央和模块语言加工过程进行了区分:解释性加工是模块化的、自动的语言加工过程,后解释性加工是中央的、控制性的加工过程(Caplan & Waters,1999)。第一种资源指的是"心理语言学资源库",利用此资源库的加工过程是强制性地(自动地)遵循句子输入(例如,声学—语音转换、词汇通达、句法分析、题元角色指派和信息结构)的所有工作,句法加工由单词识别、句法构建、韵律和语义表征、题元角色指派组成,这种解释性加工从当前正被加工的句子中提取意思。句法复杂句比句法简单句对此资源需求更高,但对控制言语加工的资源库的需求是相同的。失语症患者此"自动"资源减少。控制言语任务,例如,言语推理或在语义记忆中刻意搜寻一条信息,使用第二种资源库。此资源(控制性言语加工任务)中的词汇受到认知资源有限的影响。在此加工过程中,通过解释性加工提取的意思来完成其他的言语任务,例如,把信息储存在长时语义记忆中,基于句子意思推理、基于句子意思计划行动等。低广度阅读者和阿尔兹海默病患者比高广度阅读者具有更少的容量,但两者"自动的"资源类型并不存在差异。并且,额外负荷仅对"控制性的"资源库需求更高。模块的/解释性的加工过程包括结构建构以及题元角色指派,句法和角色指派在解释性工作记忆中执行加工过程,而利用世界知识发生在后解释性工作记忆中。区分这两种工作记忆的一个重要方式与复杂性相关,特别是 Caplan & Waters 认为句法复杂性影响解释性工作记忆的加工,而后解释性工作记忆会受到非句法复杂性的影响。Caplan & Waters 进一步指出解释性加工(大约相当于在线句法加工)中并不存在个体差异,而他们从在线句法加工中提取意思的后解释性离线加工中观察到了差异。因此,先前研究通过在线方法探讨了关系从句挂靠,集中于加工的解释阶段;而使用离线强迫选择范式(offline forced-choice paradigm)的研究,集中于后解释性阶段(post-interpretive stage)。同时,先前研究探讨关系从句挂靠的混合结果可能是由于调查了加工的不同阶段(解释性加工相对于后解释性加工)。Waters & Caplan 总结了阅读者的阅读广度、额外的负荷和加工时的句法结构,认为阅读者句子加工时并没有利用相同的资源库。并且,他们从实证和理论方面质疑了单一资源假说,并由此产生了大量辩论来探讨涉及构成语言理解基础的言语工作记忆资源的特性(Caplan & Waters,1995;Waters & Caplan,1996a,1996b,1996c;Just et al.,1996;Miyake et al.,1995)。

Waters & Caplan(1996a)认为 Just & Carpenter(1992)的单一言语资源理论通过在相同实验中操纵三项变量(句法复杂性、额外的负荷和广度)可以与他们的分开的资源理论(SSIR)区别开来,即两种理论对额外负荷和广度差异对句法加工的影响作出了不同的预测:单一言语资源理论预测阅读者的句法加工在额外的高工作记忆负荷下变得更难,尤其是对于低广度阅读者来说;而分开的资源理论预测阅读者的句法加工应该不受负荷和广度差异的影响。两种理论都预测了句法复杂性对加工有消极的影响。

综上所述,基于工作记忆容量对歧义句加工的影响,存在以下三种不同的预测理论。

(1)单一言语资源理论

单一言语资源理论(single verbal resource theory)(Just & Carpenter,1992,1996,1999)认为只存在一种单一的言语工作记忆资源,工作记忆中的两种成分涉及再分析、存储和加工,同时两成分共享相同的资源库。分析者最初把歧义词的多种解释储存在工作记忆中,这样会消耗额外的工作记忆资源。随着句法分析的持续,如果剩余的工作记忆资源不足以加工随后的信息,加工者可能不得不放弃更不优先的解释。当额外的工作记忆负荷较高时,句法加工会变得困难,特别是对于工作记忆广度低的加工者来说。低广度阅读者不同于高广度阅读者,他们具有更少的言语容量来激活两种句法表征以便持续更长的时间。因此,低广度阅读者相比于高广度阅读者,更易被带入花园路径。

（2）独立言语资源理论

独立言语资源理论（separate verbal resource theory）（Caplan & Waters,1999,2002; Waters & Caplan,1996a,1996b,1996c,2001,2002）认为存在两个独立的、更加专门化的语言资源。此理论提出句法加工与阅读广度任务中的表现无关。低广度和高广度阅读者同等程度地受到句子结构中的句法复杂性影响。句法加工不受额外的工作记忆负荷和言语工作记忆广度这两个因素的影响。在调查工作记忆容量和暂时歧义句加工之间关系时,Caplan & Waters 发现不同工作记忆广度的被试在离线句子接受任务中加工花园小径句时不存在差异。

（3）句法分析策略理论

句法分析策略理论（Mecklinger et al.,1995; Friederici et al.,1998; Vos et al.,2001）提出高广度和低广度阅读者在句法分析策略方面存在差异。一些阅读者运用更有效的加工策略,即他们可能需要更少的资源来完成相同的任务。高广度阅读者托付单一优先结构（single preferred structure）更有效率,因为他们可以建构仅仅一种句法结构（早期托付模型）（early commitment model）（Mecklinger et al.,1995; Friederici et al.,1998; Vos et al.,2001）,即与输入信息相符合的、最简单的句法结构。低广度阅读者保持多重句法表征活跃更没有效率,所以没有显示出解歧效应（没有再分析）。例如,组块加工可能是对输入信息更有效的加工（Daneman & Carpenter,1980）。

6.1.1.2　涉及工作记忆的歧义句加工模型

为了解释句法分析者最初的句法优先解释和随后的修改,研究者们提出了几个工作记忆限制影响歧义句加工的理论模型。

（1）容量限制句法分析模型

Just & Carpenter（1992）介绍了容量限制句法分析模型（capacity

constrained parsing model)(MacDonald et al.,1992)。此模型认为句法分析策略依赖于个体工作记忆容量的差异。个体的工作记忆容量总体上制约句法加工过程,尤其是句法歧义的加工。当阅读者碰到句法歧义时,他们最初总是构建多重表征,也仅仅是在构建这种初始多重表征后,具备高或低工作记忆容量的阅读者的加工出现了差异。

在容量限制句法分析模型理论中,下面句子(a)中的动词 warned 是主动词,soldiers 是施事;而句子(b)中 warned 引导的是关系从句,soldiers 是 warned 的受事,而不是施事。

(a) The soldiers warned about the dangers....

(b) The soldiers warned about the dangers conducted the midnight raid.

MacDonald et al. (1992)采用自控速阅读范式,通过实验证明了工作记忆容量对句法歧义加工的影响,高广度理解者(再分析)比低广度理解者(没有再分析)在解歧点阅读时间更长,判断句子准确率更高,是因为高广度理解者构建了多重表征。

① 单一表征模型

单一表征模型(single representation model)(Frazier, 1979;Marcus, 1980),即系列模型(serial models)(Frazier & Rayner, 1982)认为低广度阅读者更没有效率,只激活暂时句法歧义的一种可能的句法表征,即最简单的结构或优先的解释(preferred interpretation)。因此,低广度阅读者可能放弃最初接受的更低激活层面的表征,即低频率、语用上不合理和句法上更复杂。

② 多重表征模型

多重表征模型(multiple representation model)(Kurtzman, 1985;Gorrell, 1987,即并行模型(parallel model)(Altmann & Steedman, 1988)认为高广度阅读者激活暂时句法歧义的两种理解(readings)。高广度阅读者保存优先的解释和不优先的解释(unpreferred interpretation)。实验结果表明,高广度阅读者(再分析)比低广度阅读者(没有再分析)在解歧点阅读时间更长,判断句子准确率更高,是因为使用了多重表征模型。这种情况在加工短句(10～12 个单词)的时候特别明显,但对更长的句子(13～15 个单词)来说,情况并非如此。这说明高广度阅读者可能并不是同时保存对句子的多重解释。

（2）花园路径效应

花园路径效应（Bever, 1970）（经典例句：The horse raced past the barn fell.）指的是加工花园路径句时显示出了（至少）两种结构之间的暂时歧义，其中一种比另一种结构更不符合预期；在更不符合预期结构的解歧点，花园路径句的加工速度变慢，并因此产生了花园路径效应（garden path effect）或歧义效应（Rayner et al., 1983）。

① 约束满意理论

约束满意理论（constraint satisfaction models）（MacDonald et al., 1994；Trueswell & Tanenhaus, 1994；Trueswell, 1996）认为基于词汇、语义、语境、句法等多种语言信息，加工者形成句法结构，并在句法歧义结构中同时建构多种句法分析。句法分析器会组合词汇亚范畴、语义合理性、语境等多种语言信息来选择最合理的句法结构，从而完成句法消歧。因此，该理论认为如果在句法歧义位置的所有可能的句法分析都具备同等激活强度的话，那么，该位置的加工将会需要更多的认知资源来解决句法分析间的竞争，因而工作记忆容量的差异会影响歧义句加工。

MacDonald et al.（1994）、Trueswell & Tanenhaus（1994）等把句法歧义归因于词汇这个层面。他们认为，词语的许多特性影响甚至决定歧义结构的理解。例如，动词作为分词使用的频率是不同的，动词"raced"更经常被用于主动的、不及物形式，因而这会抑制所需要的被动的、及物动词的解释。然而，当句子中的动词经常以过去分词形式出现或者语义合理性支持减缩关系构式时，花园路径效应会减小或消失，这就产生了约束满意理论。此理论认为最初产生和建构两种句法解释是根据可能性信息，例如，动词频率和语义合理性（MacDonald et al., 1994；McRae et al., 1998；Spivey-Knowlton & Sedivy, 1995；Spivey & Tanenhaus, 1998；Trueswell et al., 1994；Trueswell & Tanenhaus, 1994）。同时，MacDonald et al.（1994）的实验证明高广度被试迅速、高效地运用词汇语义合理性信息成功消解句法歧义，而没有显示出花园路径理论阐述的园径效应。

② 花园路径理论

花园路径理论（garden-path model, fixed-choice two-stage models）（Ferreira & Clifton, 1986, 1996；Ferreira & Henderson, 1990；Frazier, 1979, 1987a, 1987,

1989，1995；Frazier & Fodor 1978；Frazier & Rayner，1982；Rayner et al.，1983；Traxler et al.，1998）和类似的序列句法加工理论（serial syntax-first model）（Frazier，1996；Gorrell，1995）认为特定的句法分析器仅产生对输入信息"最简单的"句法结构分析，"简单性"的定义可能在序列模型中变化，但总是出自句法理论。该理论认为句法分析按照最少节点挂靠原则（minimal attachment）（Frazier，1978）。当遇到歧义结构时，句法分析器将建构尽可能简单的结构，更简单结构会部分受到更易于被保存在工作记忆中观点的激活（Frazier & Fodor，1978）。另一个加工原则被称作迟关闭原则（late closure）（Frazier，1978）、近现（recency）（Gibson et al.，1996）或右联（right association）（Kimball，1973，1975），该原则提出当存在一个结构挂靠歧义时，根据最终句法分析的结构复杂性，消歧模式并不存在差异，那么句法分析器会支持局部整合，即把输入语料挂靠到当前正加工的词组上，因为非局部整合（把输入语料挂靠到更早已被加工的成分）需要再激活这个早期成分。因此，非局部整合根据记忆资源比局部整合（不需要再激活）更费力。这样，如果最初的句法分析遵循最少节点挂靠原则和迟关闭原则，那么语言系统只进行一种单一分析，因为一次计算超过一种句法结构是超负荷的，并且不立即计算一种结构会迫使单词未被分析就被保存在记忆中，从而造成工作记忆的负荷。语言系统倾向于采用最小语法分析（minimal grammatical analysis），是由于系统的工作记忆容量有限。

（3）句法谓语位置理论

基于工作记忆的理论由 Gibson（1998，2000）在句法谓语位置理论（syntactic prediction locality theory，SPLT）中提出。该理论认为，加工者句法分析歧义句中某一个成分时，会预测即将出现的其他句子成分，随着加工者所需预测的成分增加，工作记忆的负荷增大。

句法谓语位置理论合并了工作记忆需求与计算负荷来解释复杂句（例如，关系从句、被动语态、花园路径句）的加工困难。此理论区分了整合负荷成分（integration cost component）和记忆负荷成分（memory cost component）：整合负荷成分决定了认知资源的量，而认知资源负责把新的语言输入信息整合进对句子的心理表征；在句子加工过程中，记忆负荷源于对词汇范畴的句法预测，即最小地要求词汇范畴把当前的输入信息转换成不得不在工作记忆中保存的语法句。另一方面,当新输入的信息被整合进对句子的当前结构表征时,加工者产生了整合负荷,并且整合负荷会随着被整合成分之间的距离而增加。

6.1.1.3　歧义句加工和执行功能

另一个试图把工作记忆与歧义句加工相联系的问题是工作记忆的个体差异是否与容量本身相关,或与储存在记忆中的项目的干扰相关(Gordon et al.,2002,2006;McElree et al.,2003;van Dyke & McElree,2006)。

研究者们更多地研究了与句子加工相联系的执行功能——工作记忆。工作记忆通常运用阅读广度任务的一些版本来测量(Baddeley,1986,1996;Baddeley & Logie,1999;Caplan & Waters,2002;Daneman & Carpenter,1980;Kane et al.,2004;MacDonald & Christiansen,2002;MacDonald et al.,1992;Waters & Caplan,2001)。大量研究集中于探究支持句子加工的记忆资源是类别特异性(domain-specific)(Just & Carpenter,1992;Caplan & Waters,1999),还是类别一般性(domain-general)(Kane & Engle,2002;Fedorenko et al.,2006)。一些研究者更支持句子加工的类别一般性学说,即句子加工可以与包含其他认知功能(例如,执行控制)的更大系统共享(Fedorenko & Thompson-Schill,2015;Hsu et al.,2017)。

Baddeley(1986,2000,2007)工作记忆模型在调查二语习得和加工中的工作记忆研究时具有影响力。此类理论可以被看作由三部分组成的模型(tripartite models):狭窄的注意焦点、工作记忆成分和独立的长时记忆存储。个体差异归因于信息的容量限制,即个体可以一次把信息活跃地保存在工作记忆中的信息量。对于句子理解,研究者们提出了工作记忆容量的个体差异影响加工者可以活跃地保存多少单词或句子,或者一次可以征用的不同类型的句法和非句法信息源(Daneman & Carpenter,1980;Just & Carpenter,1992;Just et al.,1996)。因此,根据一语和二语者在特定时间点可以保持信息活跃的量,基于容量的方法描述了一语和二语的差异(McDonald,2006;Hopp,2006,2010)。相反,由两部分组成的模型(bipartite models)认为没有分开的工作记忆成分(McElree,2006)。此类模型认为加工者一次可以在注意焦点激活的信息量严重受限,并且比在广度任务中测量得更少(Cowan,2001;McElree,2006);同时,此类模型强调涉及记忆编码、储存和提取的加工过程,以及涉被带进和带出焦点注意的项目间转换注意的加工过程。

句子理解部分地受到认知加工过程（例如，执行功能和工作记忆）的支持。事实上，神经心理学家把工作记忆看作执行功能的子过程。尽管工作记忆可能是分离的（Lehto，1996）或重叠的资源（Baddeley，1986，2010），工作记忆和执行功能存在着复杂的关系。Baddeley（1986，1996，2003，2010）发展了工作记忆概念，以便联系各种概念来描述不同的记忆能力，包括对刺激语料的通道特异性（modality-specific）短时存储、在短时存储中加工刺激语料、对刺激语料加工的控制和长时存储。在 Baddeley 工作记忆模型中，通道特异性短时存储体系、语音环和视觉空间模板以活跃的状态保存信息，但是当加工者需要操纵信息时，中央执行系统执行操纵加工。中央执行系统也会负责有意识地引导注意或引导短时存储系统到外部事件或内部思想和观点。短时存储体系和中央执行系统的关键特点是它们具有有限的容量，即有限的信息可以在任何时间被保存在语音环或视觉空间模板，或者受到中央执行系统的操纵。

大量研究表明，阅读者在歧义句中修改不正确预测的能力受到执行功能的支持（Fedorenko，2014；Mazuka et al.，2009；Novick et al.，2005，2010；Ye & Zhou，2009）。中央执行系统是工作记忆中的控制成分。工作记忆的执行加工过程可以再细分为不同的成分功能：转换（shifting，在工作记忆内转换注意）、抑制或干扰消解（inhibition，阻止不相关信息在工作记忆中变得活跃）和更新（updating，更新工作记忆的内容）（Engle et al.，1999；Zacks & Hasher，1994；McCabe et al.，2010；Smith & Jonides，1999；Miyake et al.，2000；Miyake & Friedman，2012；Friedman & Miyake，2004；Nee et al.，2007，2013；Bledowski et al.，2010）。尤其与花园路径复原（recovery）相关的执行功能的一个方面，是成功操纵"表征冲突"的情境的能力，即在对刺激语料惯常的解释和当前任务需求之间引发的冲突中的情境。当句子加工体系需要放弃一种分析句子时的偏爱方式来支持最初不偏爱的方式时，加工者的执行功能的抑制控制和冲突监察/消解成分会被征用。花园路径复原中的个体差异与和执行功能以及认知控制相关的总认知能力的差异相联系。Engle 等人（Broadway & Engle，2010；Conway et al.，2003；Engle，2002；Engle et al.，1999；Heitz et al.，2006；Kane & Engle，2002）大量调查了工作记忆容量和执行注意之间的关系，他们把执行注意定义为工作记忆(控制当前在记忆中活跃的信息)的一部分。Engle 等人认为工作记忆和执行功能是分离但高度相关的资源。

一种可能性是,当句子理解更具挑战性时(例如,当句子理解在更不理想的条件下发生,或当句子本身不寻常地复杂时),加工者征用执行功能来帮助进行自上而下的加工。执行功能总体上可以使理解更容易或更有效率(Fedorenko,2014)。涉及句子加工和执行功能的大量证据尤其依赖于歧义句加工,是因为歧义句引发了可能必须被抑制,然后被修改的曲解。这种抑制和修改与执行功能加工过程并行。加工者执行功能的个体差异与他们理解句法歧义句的能力相联系,同时,提高加工者执行功能的干预也提高了他们加工这些句子时修改不正确预测的能力(Novick et al.,2014;Vuong & Martin,2014)。执行功能帮助阅读者和听者减少不正确解释的激活并增加正确解释的激活。歧义句为调查执行功能和句子加工之间的关系提供了一种好的测试例证。

(1)歧义句加工中涉及工作记忆潜在机制的两种主要假说

句中歧义通常会被后面的信息(阅读者用来修改不正确的预测)很快消解。歧义句中或者包含具有多种意思的单词(词汇歧义,lexical ambiguity),或者包含具有不同语法角色的词组(句法歧义,syntactic ambiguity)。对歧义消解的研究表明,工作记忆资源对保存在工作记忆中的句子歧义区的两种解释至关重要,是一种有利于后期消解歧义的策略(Mitchell,1994;MacDonald et al.,1992)。歧义句加工中,还同时存在着涉及工作记忆潜在机制的两种主要假说。

① 激活假说/基于容量的学说

激活假说(activation hypothesis)(句法歧义)(Just & Carpenter,1992;King & Just,1991;Miyake et al.,1994)或者基于容量的学说(MacDonald et al.,1992)认为工作记忆可以帮助激活所有支持句子加工的相关信息:高广度阅读者有更好的激活资源,在工作记忆中可以维持解歧点的两种意思;而低广度阅读者只能保存占主导地位的意思。

② 抑制假说

抑制假说(inhibition hypothesis)(词汇歧义)(Gernsbacher & Faust,1991;Gernsbacher,1990,1991;Faust & Gernsbacher,1996;Gernsbacher & St. John,

2001；Friederici et. al.，1998；Gunter et al.，1999，2003；Engle，1996）认为高广度比低广度被试更容易抑制不相关信息或从属意思，更不可能执行多重分析。

Kidd et al.（2018）认为这两种相反的假说产生了对工作记忆和歧义句加工之间潜在心理机制的完全不同解释。

6.1.2 与歧义句加工相关的 ERP 成分

电生理研究对于词汇—语义和句法加工过程的差异提供了大量证据。涉及与歧义句加工相关的 ERP 成分主要是 N400 和 P600。

6.1.2.1 N400

N400 反映了语境上不恰当的单词在刺激语料后大约 400 毫秒产生最大振幅的负波，通常出现在句子末或嵌套在句子内（Kutas & Hillyard，1980a，1980b，1980c，1983，1984；Kutas & van Petten，1994）。

N400 是出现于关键词后 300～500 毫秒之间的负波，一般位于大脑的中后部。N400 通常与语义整合的难度有关，即加工者的语义整合越难，N400 的波幅越大。然而，在一些研究中，句子加工中的重分析过程也会诱发 N400 效应。重分析过程诱发的 N400 效应通常出现在歧义句的加工中。此类句中动词所提供的信息（如动词的格、数、所提供的世界知识、动物性）具有解除歧义的作用，当动词把句子解歧为非优势结构时就会诱发 N400 效应（Schlesewsky & Bornkessel，2006；Haupt et al，2008；Wang et al.，2009）。

6.1.2.2 P600

研究者们纷纷报道了各种各样的句法违反引发的 P600 振幅增加：最常见的违反是主语—动词一致违反（Vos et al.，2001）；Muente et al.（1998）在正字法违反中发现了 P600 效应；P600 效应还在对歧义句中更不偏爱的句法结构中发现（Osterhout & Holcomb，1992，1993；Osterhout et al.，1994；Kaan et al.，2000）；对于不可能事件也观察到了 P600 效应（Coulson et al.，1998）。

P600 的功能意义值得我们进行大量探讨。P600 振幅的调整反映了句法加工（Hagoort et al.，1993）、句法整合困难（Kaan et al.，2000）、句法再分析（Friederici，1995；Osterhout et al.，1994；Roesler et al.，1998）、更全面的句子再分析（reanalysis）（Muente et al.，1998）或者甚至是类别一般性认知加工过程（Coulson et al.，1998）。

在句子加工的 ERP 文献中,再分析现象主要是与特定的 ERP 成分相关,即所谓的 P600 或句法正漂移成分(Friederici, 2002; Hagoort et al., 1993; Osterhout & Holcomb, 1992, 1993; Osterhout et al., 1994)。此效应一般发生在关键词出现之后的 500～1 000 毫秒,与许多句法歧义中的不优先消歧(dispreferred disambiguation)相关:关系从句挂靠歧义(relative clause attachment ambiguities)(Carreiras et al., 2004; Kaan & Swaab, 2003);主动词—缩约关系从句歧义(main verb-reduced relative clause ambiguities)(Osterhout & Holcomb, 1992, 1993; Kotz et al., 2008);直接宾语—嵌入主语歧义(direct object-embedded subject ambiguities)(Osterhout et al., 1994);相似的成分也与主语—宾语歧义的再分析相关(Bornkessel et al., 2004)。P600 反映了从花园路径句中复原的两个必要指标:更高加工负荷(Osterhout & Holcomb, 1992, 1993; Osterhout et al., 1994)和修改加工过程(Mecklinger et al., 1995; Friederici, 1997)。

在加工句法信息时,研究者已发现两种不同的 ERP 模式:P600 和 LAN。花园路径句和复杂句中的解歧单词和(歧义)关键单词分别在 300～900 之间引发正走向电波,此正极称作 P600:介于 300～600 毫秒之间的正波出现在不同的句法加工过程中,例如,再加工(reprocessing,因修改最初句法结构而变得必要时)和修复加工过程(repair processes,因面对句法上不正确的输入信息而变得必要时)。同时,晚期正波也在被试加工句法复杂的句子时发现。

(1)与再分析相关的正波

Osterhout & Holcomb(1992, 1993)实验发现花园小径句中关键的解歧单词引发了 600 毫秒左右的晚期正波,被称为 P600。对于必要修改(revisions)的 P600 反应,研究者已在英语不同类型的句法构式中观察到(Osterhout & Holcomb, 1992; Osterhout et al., 1994)。Mecklinger et al.(1995)调查了德语主语和宾语关系从句,也发现了被试由于必要的再分析引发的正波(P345),然而潜期更短。短暂的潜伏期是由于被试经历了从德语主语关系从句到宾语关系从句的修改过程。Friederici et al.(2002)在关系从句中又一次发现 P345,然而伴随着大约 600 毫秒更晚和更小的正波。这些实验数据表明两种修改加工过程可能存在差异,即判断需要再分析和实际的再分析的加工过程;前者反映在早期正波,后者反映在更晚期的正波。

（2）与修复相关的正波

然而,涉及句法违反时,语言加工中的晚期正波不仅在与结构再分析相关的加工过程相关中观察到,而且在与修复的加工过程相关的过程中观察到(Coulson et al.,1998;Münte et al.,1998)。与句法违反相关的正波在大约在600毫秒达到最大值。在对词组结构违反、动词论元和形态句法违反的反应中都观察到了晚期正波。因此,就结构歧义来说,晚期正波不仅反映了再分析的加工过程,而且反映了修复的加工过程(Friederici,1998)。Brown et al.(1999)评论了相关的 P600 研究,指出可能存在着歧义消解引发的 P600（与再分析相关的 P600）和由句法违反引发的 P600（与修复相关的 P600）之间的分布差异:前者更加以前额分布为特征(Osterhout & Holcomb,1992),而后者更以中央顶头皮分布为特征(Coulson et al.,1998)。总之,根据被试对晚期正成分的不同反应,晚期正成分中可能存在三种不同的子成分。第一种子成分是 P345,反映了加工者判断和从不偏爱的结构中即时复原,这些加工过程迅速、自动,因为一些实验已证明 P345 不受语义(Mecklinger et al.,1995)、概率变体和额外的记忆负荷(Vos et al.,2001)影响。第二种子成分是额中央分布的、与再分析相联系的 P600,反映了结构再分析的加工过程;此子成分对概率变体和额外的记忆负荷(Vos et al.,2001)敏感,反映了不自动的加工过程。第三种子成分是与修复相关的 P600,此成分中央顶分布,受到语义(Gunter et al.,2000)、概率变体(Hahne & Friederici,1999)的影响,再次反映了不自动的加工过程。

6.2　英语歧义句分类

依据动词、关系从句挂靠和直接宾语／主语歧义,可以把歧义句分为三类,见表 6-1。

表 6-1　英语歧义句分类

英语歧义句分类		
汉语名称	英语简称	例句
1.动词 （1）主动词/减缩关系从句歧义	MV/RR	The horse *raced* past the barn fell.

续表

英语歧义句分类		
汉语名称	英语简称	例句
（2）直接宾语／句子补语歧义	DO/SC	Jane convinced her *parents* are interested in their children.
2. 关系从句挂靠歧义 （1）局部性歧义		
关系从句高挂靠歧义	RC/HA	The *writer* of the letter that had blonde hair arrived this morning.
关系从句低挂靠歧义	RC/LA	The letter of the *writer* that had blonde hair arrived this morning.
（2）全局性歧义		
关系从句任意挂靠歧义	RC/EA	The sister of the *writer* that had blonde hair arrived this morning.
3. 直接宾语／主语歧义	DO/S	While the man hunted the *deer* ran into the woods.

6.3　对英语歧义句的本族语和二语的研究

母语中许多的研究发现，工作记忆的容量影响句法歧义句的加工（Swets et al.，2007；Kim & Christianson，2017；Just & Carpenter，1992）。但是，对于工作记忆是否影响第二语言（L2）歧义句的加工目前分歧较大：有研究者认为工作记忆不影响 L2 歧义句的加工，例如，Juffs（2004）；而另外一些研究者则发现了此影响，例如，陈宝国和徐慧卉（2010）、Kotz et al.（2008）。

6.3.1　动词引发的歧义

6.3.1.1　工作记忆容量差异对主动词／减缩关系从句歧义句加工的影响

MacDonald et al.（1992）探讨了一种包含暂时句法歧义的花园路径句（"The experienced soldiers warned about the dangers conducted the midnight raid."）。通常，当阅读者把第一个动词"warned"最初（并且不正确地）解释为句子的主动词（而不是缩约关系从句的动词），再遇到第二个动词"conducted"时，便会产生困难；因此消解需要修改最初的分析（Bever，1970；Clifton, et al.，2003），涉及句子加工过程中保存句子备选的分析。以下为国内和国外学者纷纷选用 MacDonald et al.（1992）的实验语料进行实验，得出的不一致结果。

（1）工作记忆容量差异对本族语主动词/减缩关系歧义句加工的影响

Kemper et al.（2004）的实验选用以英语为母语的老年阅读者（相当于低容量的被试）和青年阅读者（相当于高容量的被试）作为被试，通过眼动技术发现被试在名词短语区和歧义区加工的首次注视时间不存在差异，尽管在解歧区的注视时间增加，但是被试的主效应不显著。实验的结果支持独立加工资源的理论。

Kemtes & Kemper（1997）运用在线自控速句子阅读任务，发现了工作记忆广度、句法歧义类型（歧义相对于非歧义）和句法歧义消解类型（主动词相对于关系从句）之间的相互作用，影响了年轻被试和老年被试在线的阅读时间和离线的句子理解。

Osterhout & Holcomb（1992）（阅读）和 Osterhout & Holcomb（1993）（听力）测试了本族语被试主动词/减缩关系从句的歧义加工。实验结果证明了工作记忆容量差异对主动词/减缩关系从句歧义句加工的影响，即具备高广度记忆的被试对于不定式标记"to"引发了 P600，而对于句子最后的单词"door"引发了 N400。

Clifton Jr. et al.（2003）的实验运用眼动技术，通过操纵句子主语的生命性、结构歧义和副中央凹预视句法上解歧材料，探讨了加工包含减缩关系的歧义句，两个实验都显示出无论主语是有生命性还是无生命性，被试在减缩关系从句的 by- 词组部分加工的中断，而有生命的主语使歧义加工更难。高和低广度阅读者显示出非常相似的加工模式。实验结果支持序列、句法第一解析模型，同时支持独立加工资源理论。

Kurthen et al.（2020）的实验选用 29 名健康老年人（年龄 61～76 岁）听力理解包含缩约关系从句和宾语关系从句的英语歧义句，并记录他们的脑电图。实验发现被试在早期缩约关系从句加工时，听力阈值和工作记忆预测了 P600 振幅，而个体的 alpha 频率（alpha frequency）在更晚期的时间点预测了 P600 振幅。具备更好的听力和更大的工作记忆容量的被试同时激活对缩约关系从句的优先和不优先两种解释，而具备更差听力和更小工作记忆容量的被试仅激活了一种优先的解释。实验结果支持老年被试在句子加工过程中运用不同的策略，即依赖于他们的听力和认知能力，并且并不存在单一的能力统一地预测句子的加工。

Yoo & Dickey（2017）的实验证明年轻被试和老年被试在加工缩约关系从句过程中存在差异，但是工作记忆和抑制都没有预测到反应时的延长。

（2）工作记忆容量差异对二语主动词／减缩关系歧义句加工的影响

国内学者陈鸿标（1998）利用 MacDonald et al.（1992）的实验语料来探讨句子歧义是由动词引起的。实验结果表明工作记忆容量的大小对中国英语学习者理解句法歧义句的过程并无明显的影响。

陈宝国、徐慧卉（2010）实验的被试为 31 名大学本科一年级非英语专业学生，其中高、低工作记忆容量被试分别 16 人和 15 人，采用眼动技术，以句子阅读过程中句子不同区段的首次注视时间作为句子即时性加工的指标，回扫次数和总的注视时间作为句子非即时加工的指标，考察非熟练的汉—英双语者的工作记忆容量差异对第二语言（英语）暂时句法歧义句加工的影响。实验结果表明：对于非熟练的汉—英双语者，工作记忆容量的差异既影响英语句法歧义句即时性的加工，也影响非即时性的加工；工作记忆容量的差异既影响英语句法歧义句初始的句法加工过程，也影响句法的重新分析过程；研究结果在一定程度上支持工作记忆容量限制的理论。

Kotz et al.（2008）探讨了本族语与二语被试加工主动词／减缩关系从句歧义句。ERP 实验结果表明：与暂时句法歧义引发的 P600 相比，词组结构违反的两组被试振幅更大、头皮分布更后部；暂时句法歧义引发的 P600 比词组结构违反引发的 P600 小并且广泛分布，在起始 650～800 毫秒延迟且有更低的振幅；两组被试的歧义句句末发现负波，然而句法分析词组结构信息时，非本族语比本族语阅读者振幅更小；此实验是第一例在线二语暂时句法歧义 ERP 加工的研究，但是并没有考察工作记忆容量的个体差异对二语歧义句加工的影响。

6.3.1.2　工作记忆容量差异对直接宾语／句子补语歧义句加工的影响

（1）工作记忆容量差异对本族语直接宾语／句子补语歧义句加工的影响

Osterhout et al.（1994）运用 ERP 成分（P600 或 SPS）研究句子加工中的再分析现象。实验结果表明，当句子包含一个及物偏好的动词时，句法分析器会错误地指派直接宾语角色给句子中没有显性补语标志的名词词组；

尽管包含纯粹的及物动词或及物偏好动词句子的助动词引发了 P600 效应，但及物动词的 P600 振幅最大；及物动词句中的助动词引发了双向反应：介于 300～500 毫秒的负向成分和大约 500 毫秒开始的正向成分（P600）；及物动词偏好句中的助动词引发了 P600，而不是 N400。但实验没有考虑被试的工作记忆容量差异对本族语直接宾语／句子补语歧义句加工的影响。

（2）工作记忆容量差异对二语直接宾语／句子补语歧义句加工的影响

药盼盼、王瑞乐、陈宝国（2013）采用自控速句子阅读的实验范式，通过操纵动词偏好等信息，考察工作记忆容量的差异对二语学习者（英语）句子加工中动词偏好信息利用的影响。实验结果表明：工作记忆容量在一定程度上影响二语学习者动词偏好信息的利用，但是这种影响是有条件的，即影响只出现在句子加工对工作记忆要求相对较低时。

6.3.2　关系从句挂靠歧义

Gilboy et al.（1995）提出加工者关系从句的挂靠偏好不仅受到结构原则的影响，而且受到语义因素或语义关系的影响，其他因素包括韵律也影响关系从句挂靠歧义。Gibson et al.（1996）认为语言在原则的相对层级中存在差异：首先，就近原则支持把语料与最近的、可获得的名词整合；其次，一种竞争原则，即谓词接近原则（predicate proximity），支持通过定语从句尽可能地就近挂靠到谓语词组的中心词（head）来修饰主要成分；如果就近原则胜过谓词接近原则就是低挂靠，反之谓词接近原则胜过就近原则，就是高挂靠。总之，加工者对低挂靠的结构就近偏好（structural recency preference）不仅受到非结构词汇—题元、语用因素的影响，而且受到韵律因素的影响。

研究者大量涉及挂靠偏好个体差异根本原因的研究一直集中于工作记忆容量，但是产生了不同的结果（Swets et al.，2007；Kim & Christianson，2012，2017；Traxler，2007，2009；Caplan & Waters，2013）。

6.3.2.1　工作记忆与本族语关系从句挂靠

一些实验研究发现本族语关系从句挂靠受到工作记忆的影响：在线实验的结果表明本族语关系从句挂靠与工作记忆正相关，即低广度被试倾向于低挂靠，而高广度被试倾向于高挂靠（Online, Felser et al.，2003；Traxler，2007）；一些离线、在线实验结果表明本族语关系从句挂靠与工作记忆负相关，即高广度被试倾向于低挂靠,而低广度被试倾向于高挂靠(Swets et al.,2007;Traxler,2009;Kim & Christianson,2012)。

(1)本族语关系从句挂靠与工作记忆正相关

一些在线研究发现了本族语关系从句挂靠受到工作记忆的影响,实验结果表明本族语关系从句挂靠与工作记忆正相关。

Felser et al.(2003a)通过自控速实验,调查了本族语英语儿童和成年人听力理解关系从句"The doctor recognized the nurse of the pupils who was/were feeling very tired.(高/低挂靠)"的挂靠偏好,发现本族语儿童的挂靠偏好依据听力广度存在差异,即儿童的歧义消解过程是以结构为主的,其他的信息(比如语义信息)在儿童歧义加工的早期阶段并不起作用:(a)具备低工作记忆容量的儿童低挂靠了第二个名词词组(NP2 attachment),采用就近原则,即把语料与最近的、可获得的名词整合;(b)高广度儿童高挂靠第一个名词词组(NP1 attachment),依赖于谓词接近原则,即通过定语从句尽可能地就近挂靠到谓语词组的中心词来修饰主要成分。

Traxler(2007)改编了 Traxler et al.(1998)的实验语料,采用眼动实验考察 96 名本族语为英语的被试阅读主语—修饰关系从句(subject-modifying RCs)(例如,"The writer of the letter that had blond hair arrived this morning."),发现工作记忆容量和关系从句挂靠显著相关,即低广度被试倾向于低挂靠,而高广度被试倾向于高挂靠。实验在线研究了儿童和成年人关系从句挂靠,发现了被试记忆广度和挂靠偏好之间的关系受到以记忆为基础的近现策略的制约。

(2)本族语关系从句挂靠与工作记忆负相关

一些离线、在线实验结果表明了本族语关系从句挂靠与工作记忆之间的负相关,这些实验结果指出工作记忆容量和关系从句挂靠偏好之间的相反关系,即高广度被试倾向于低挂靠,而低广度被试倾向于高挂靠(Mendelsohn & Pearlmutter,1999;Kim,2010;Swets et al.,2007)。

Mendelsohn & Pearlmutter(1999)的实验发现低广度被试显示出对高挂靠的偏好,而高广度被试并没有显示出挂靠的偏好。

Swets et al.(2004)报道了对本族语离线句子加工的研究,关系从句挂靠偏好受到被试工作记忆容量的影响,即具备更大容量的被试与更小容量的被试往往具有不同的挂靠偏好。

Swets et al.（2007）研究了 150 名本族语为英语的被试的离线挂靠偏好，对"The maid of the princess who scratched herself in public was terribly embarrassed."句子执行强制选择判断任务（forced-choice judgment task），实验结果发现：（a）被试的工作记忆容量和关系从句挂靠偏好（RC attachment preference）之间呈负相关，即具备更高工作记忆广度的被试显示出更高比例的低挂靠偏好，反之亦然（与 Kim & Christianson（2012）结果相似）；（b）在离线判断任务中，被试的阅读广度与高挂靠偏好之间显示出负相关，因为低广度阅读者容量有限，会运用组块策略把关系从句分割成单独的韵律短语（与 Kim（2010）结果相似）。

Traxler（2009）采用的实验语料与 Traxler（2007）相同，在线眼动实验支持任务中工作记忆对挂靠偏好的不同影响：（a）被试的阅读广度与高挂靠偏好之间存在负相关，即高广度被试偏爱低挂靠；（b）韵律因素解释了低广度阅读者对高挂靠的偏爱，低广度阅读者会插入隐性韵律来间断复杂名词词组和关系从句，因为分割从句降低了对句法分析的需求；同时，高广度被试根据韵律来整合关系从句和名词短语，而低广度阅读者把句子分成两大组块（复杂的名词短语和关系从句），因此更愿意把关系从句挂靠到以篇章为主的第一个名词上（Fodor，2002）。

6.3.2.1　工作记忆与二语关系从句挂靠歧义加工

在二语关系从句挂靠的歧义研究中，工作记忆是否影响第二语言关系从句挂靠的歧义加工目前分歧较大：一些研究者认为工作记忆不影响二语关系从句挂靠的歧义加工（Nakano & Wang，2011；Omaki，2005）；而另外一些研究者则发现了这种影响（Hopp，2014；Kim & Christianson，2017）。

（1）二语关系从句挂靠歧义加工不受到工作记忆的影响

一些研究者探讨了二语关系从句挂靠与阅读广度之间的关系（Nakano & Wang，2011；Omaki，2005），并没有发现工作记忆容量的差异对二语歧义加工的影响。

Omaki（2005）研究了本族语是日语的晚期高水平英语被试执行嵌入关系从句（a）和补语关系从句（complement relative clauses（b））阅读任务。

（a）The babysitter that［the sister of the schoolgirl who burned herself the other day adored] was very nice.

（b）The babysitter said that [the sister of the schoolgirl who burned herself the other day was very nice].

不考虑关系从句的类型,二语被试组无论是离线判断还是在线阅读任务,都没有显示出任何挂靠偏好。并且,被试的挂靠模式并没有受到阅读广度差异的影响。

Nakano & Wang（2011）通过眼动实验,由本族语是日语、二语是中—高水平英语的被试执行阅度广度任务、判断歧义句（例如,"The doctor recognized the nurse of the pupils who was/were feeling very tired."）（高 / 低挂靠）发现:（a）离线任务中,高广度组微弱地支持高挂靠,而低广度组并没有显示出任何偏爱;（b）在线阅读任务中,高广度被试组显示出不一致的模式,即在首通测试（first-pass measures）中显示出高挂靠偏爱,而回归和总阅读时间显示出微弱的低挂靠偏爱;同时,低广度组并没有在高和低挂靠中表现出差异。实验结果表明二语歧义句加工中的挂靠偏爱不受记忆广度的影响。

（2）二语关系从句挂靠歧义加工受到工作记忆的影响

另一种二语关系从句歧义消解集中于工作记忆以及个体阅读广度的差异可能影响挂靠偏好的程度。

Hopp（2014）调查了本族语是德语（高挂靠）的英语（低挂靠）学习者在线（眼动）和离线（判断）任务,测试他们的关系从句挂靠偏好以及阅读广度。二语水平和阅读广度成绩显著相关。离线任务中,二语被试显示出与本族语相同的高挂靠偏好,二语被试的阅读广度与高挂靠反应呈负相关。换句话说,具备更低阅读广度的被试更愿意选择高挂靠（与近现原则期待的相反）。此结果与更早的 Swets et al.（2007）对本族语被试所报告的相似,即不考虑语言,具备更小工作记忆广度的被试偏爱高挂靠,而具备更大广度的被试选择优先低挂靠;与 Fodor（2002）隐性韵律假设（implicit prosody hypothesis）一致,即低广度阅读者在第二个名词词组（NP2）和关系从句之间插入间断（break）,产生了高挂靠偏爱。同时,这些结果与 Felser et al.（2003a）结果相反:Felser 和同事们用自控速听力任务和听力广度任务来测试本族语为英语的儿童（平均年龄 6 岁;平均年龄 8 岁）,低听力广度组儿童对涉及低挂靠的语料显示出更快的反应时,而高广度组对高挂靠语料反应更快。

Kim & Christianson（2017）通过两个自控速阅读实验调查了本族语是韩语的高水平英语学习者工作记忆容量对加工整体歧义关系从句（globally ambiguous relative clauses）的影响。高水平二语学习者加工歧义结构时，相同被试的一语和二语之间并不存在加工策略的差异，而阅读者的不同工作记忆容量存在差异。实验数据支持具备更大工作记忆容量的被试对于释义判断任务反应时更长。此结果与容量限制句法分析模型（MacDonald et al.，1992）的预测相一致，说明足够大的工作记忆容量可以使被试具备对整体歧义敏感和把两种解释保存在工作记忆中的能力。Kim & Christianson（2012）研究韩国二语学习者对于复杂句的低挂靠偏爱。Swets et al.（2007）报道了英语中受到工作记忆容量调节的挂靠偏爱大于先前观察到的介于（低挂靠语言）英语和其他高挂靠语言之间的挂靠偏爱差异。当前实验结果显示了韩语被试显著低挂靠偏爱和英语被试的缺少显著挂靠偏爱，支持 Kim & Christianson（2012）和 Swets et al.（2007）的实验结果，说明尽管关系从句挂靠中存在跨语言差异，句子复杂性和工作记忆容量会比跨语言差异更重要。

Goad et al.（2021）调查了本族语为西班牙语的英语被试韵律线索对听力理解包含关系从句歧义句语料的影响。由于英语和西班牙语对于关系从句挂靠的默认偏爱（default preference）存在差异，即英语是偏爱弱的低挂靠（关系从句修饰 NP2），而西班牙语偏爱更强的高挂靠（关系从句修饰 NP1），实验推断出与 Felser et al.（2003a）本族语被试结果相一致的结论：具备低工作记忆广度的被试求助于近现原则来决定他们的偏爱反应，因为他们不能控制语料的分割。

尽管一语挂靠可以被解释为受到诸如谓语临近（谓语临近支持最近的名词短语）句法因素的引导（Gibson et al.，1996），二语者没有显示出挂靠偏爱，证明了二语者不详细的、浅层句法分析（Clahsen & Felser，2006a，2006b）。然而，二语者没有显示出明确的挂靠偏爱，说明对 NP1 和 NP2 的可变挂靠不一定涉及浅层句法分析。一语者对 Np1 和 NP2 可变的挂靠可以在一语歧义句加工中观察到（Traxler et al.，1998）。这些情况下的挂靠偏爱也受到一系列因素的影响，包括记忆广度测试的表现（Swets et al.，2007）和任务需求（Swets et al.，2008）。同时，相关研究也在二语者中显示出明确的挂靠偏爱。

二语学习者可以构建充分详细的句法分析，但他们在记忆提取过程中比一语者更易受到干扰。一语和二语在歧义消解过程中所存在的差异始终持续,尤其是当加工者成功的解释需要提取和修改先前在加工过程中建构的信息时。现存证据表明,一语和二语者关系从句歧义的不同挂靠偏爱受到诸多因素的影响,重要的是,不同句法挂靠表明了分析者选择了歧义消解,而不是浅层句法分析。二语学习者可能对歧义消解中语境的作用显示出递增的敏感(Pan & Felser,2011;Pan et al.,2015),这些发现表明二语学习者可能对采用语用上恰当的句法分析更敏感,而不涉及浅层的句法分析。这些结果也提供初步证据支持假设,即一语/二语差异可以根据句子加工过程中加工者如何执行记忆提取提示的差异来描述。二语学习者对加工关系从句时文本语境的作用显示出递增的敏感(Pan et al.,2015),说明二语学习者比一语者可能更主要依赖对记忆提取的、基于文本的提示。

6.3.3　工作记忆与直接宾语/主语歧义

6.3.3.1　工作记忆与歧义句中的非句法信息

早期研究考察非句法信息在句法歧义加工初期的作用,发现词汇频率、亚范畴(subcategorization)信息和语义合理性信息不同程度地影响句法歧义的最初加工过程。

Traxler(2002)通过自控速阅读实验调查儿童加工暂时歧义句(object-subject ambiguities)(结果与 Felser et al.(2003a)相似),实验结果表明 8 到 12 岁儿童倾向于把三个条件中动词后的名词错误分析为直接宾语,表明偏向结构上更简单的分析,而不考虑合理性或动词的题元特性。此效应在不及物动词条件中不显著,说明亚范畴信息可能部分被利用。实验结果表明成年人似乎更倾向于放弃不合理的错误分析来支持更复杂的构式,而儿童在实验中似乎倾向于结构上更简单的分析,不管语义是否合理。先前的研究表明儿童,尤其是更小的儿童(小于10岁)由于工作记忆限制,采取与成年人不同的加工策略(Tyler & Marslen-Wilson,1981;Traxler & Joye,2000)。Traxler(2002)的实验结果与这些研究相一致:儿童可能存在拆分先前加工的信息并因此增加了记忆负荷的现象;或者,句法再分析得益于表层信息的复原;由于儿童和成年人复原表层信息的能力差异,他们句法再分析的进程也存在差异。儿童比成年人保存表层信息有更多的困难(Tyler & Marslen-Wilson,1978),因此当他们最初的分析证明有缺陷时,他们更不可能复原必要的信息来执行另一种句法分析。

Juffs（2004）选用汉语、日语和西班牙母语者为被试,采用自控速句子阅读任务,考察了个体工作记忆容量的差异对 L2 句法暂时歧义句加工的影响。实验结果发现,工作记忆容量不同的个体不仅在回答问题的正确率上没有差异,而且在阅读花园路径句歧义词的时间上也不存在差异,即工作记忆容量对 L2 句法歧义句的加工未产生影响。

Hopp（2015）通过眼动实验调查了个体差异是否和如何影响二语学习者句法歧义加工（object-subject ambiguities）,实验结果表明工作记忆容量与阅读时间不显著相关。

6.3.3.2　工作记忆与歧义句的曲解残留

近年来,句法歧义研究更多地关注歧义句的初期错误分析后的重新分析过程,对最初的曲解残留存在一致的观点,但对于造成这种现象的原因还没有一致的观点。研究者把曲解残留（lingering misinterpretation）归因为浅层句法加工（Shallow Syntactic Processing）（Clahsen & Felser, 2006a, 2006b; Frisson, 2009）,即由句法分析者构建的不详细句法结构（Underspecified Syntactic Structure built by the parser）（Ferreira et al., 2002; Sanford & Sturt, 2002; Swets et al., 2008; Logacev & Vasishth, 2016）和足够好加工（把曲解残留归因为不完全的再分析）（Christianson, 2016; Christianson et al., 2001; Ferreira et al., 2001; Karimi & Ferreira, 2016; Qian et al., 2018）。花园路径中的曲解是加工者由于基于最初句法和语义的分析而进行的解释并残留在他们的长时记忆中,随后与他们对句子的解释相互干扰（Slattery et al., 2013; Sturt, 2007）。

文献对足够好加工提出两种机制来解释曲解残留:第一种机制被称作不完全再分析（incomplete reanalysis）,是加工者最初的曲解语义取消了充分再分析的句法结构,产生了不完全的再分析和残留的曲解;第二种机制被称作曲解残留（lingering misinterpretation）,是加工者完成了再分析后,但来自最初分析的解释和再分析的解释共同存在。换句话说,根据足够好加工学说,如果加工者对句法结构的再分析不完整,或者成功进行了句法再分析,但两种分析同时存在,那么最初的曲解会残留。

阅读者经常把花园路径曲解保存在来自许多暂时歧义句中获得的最后表征里(Christianson et al., 2001; Engelhardt et al., 2010; Ferreira et al., 2001; Patson et al., 2009; Van Gompel et al., 2006)。阅读者仅仅部分地再分析花园路径句,形成了一种理解观点,被称为足够好理解(good-enough comprehension),即阅读者形成了浅层和表层表征(Ferreira et al., 2002, 2009; Ferreira & Patson, 2007; Sanford & Sturt, 2002; Sturt, 2007)。句子理解的"足够好"观点是基于资源有限的主要假设,反映了阅读者面对困难时采取的一种省力策略,即减少加工的努力和时间(Czerlinski et al., 1999; Gigerenzer, 2008; Gigerenzer & Goldstein, 1996; Gigerenzer & Selten, 2001; Tversky & Kahneman, 1974)。然而,对于资源限制观点(resource-limitation perspective),我们并不完全清楚个体差异如何影响"足够好"表征的形成。先前研究通常认为具备更低能力的个体更易于犯花园路径的错误(Christianson et al., 2001, 2006, 2018; Ferreira, 2003)。

工作记忆容量在花园路径消解中扮演着重要角色。当加工者由于额外的信息需要更新结构分析和解释时,已被加工的语料需要被带回到注意焦点,被再提取和再分析。事实上,成年人工作记忆容量的个体差异与他们加工复杂句(Just & Carpenter, 1992; Miyake et al., 1994)、暂时歧义句(Christianson et al., 2006; MacDonald et al., 1992; Caplan & Waters, 1999)的能力相关。

记忆提取也涉及歧义消解中的再分析加工过程。大量研究报道了花园路径句中最初委派的句子解释不总是被成功地再分析(Christianson et al., 2001)。尽管"足够好"句法分析更早的研究描述了曲解(Ferreira et al., 2002; Ferreira & Patson, 2007),这些类型的曲解不需牵涉不详细的句法分析,而是由于来自记忆中没被充分删除的、最初被委派的句子解释的干扰(Slattery et al., 2013)。

由此,研究者们进行了工作记忆与曲解残留相联系的一系列研究。

(1)本族语的工作记忆与歧义句的曲解残留关系研究

在母语研究中,加工者原先的曲解与消歧后的正确理解并存的最终表征在一系列研究中得到证实。

Christianson(2001)报道了成年英语学习者有时不正确地把句子"While Anna dressed the baby that was small and cute spit up in the bed."中的"Anna dressed the baby"分析为直接宾语。尽管在递进的歧义句加工过程中,加工者最初的优先分析,最后却是不符合语法的。这种结果可能表明,阅读者并不总是构建充分详细的句法分析。

（a）While Anna dressed the baby played in the crib.

（b）Did the baby play in the crib?

（c）Did Anna dress the baby?

在传统研究中,如果被试可以准确回答句子(b)这种针对主句的理解问题,表明他们能准确理解该句。Christianson et al.（2001）在这种惯常的考察之外,又增加了针对从句的理解问题(c)句,他们发现被试回答(b)的正确率几乎达到了100％,但同时很多被试不能准确回答问题(c),这表明整个句子消歧后,"Anna给婴儿穿了衣服"这样的曲解依旧存在。一些研究者将曲解与消歧并存归因于认知加工资源的限制,花园路径句的局部歧义造成了较强的加工负荷,产生了曲解残留（Christianson,2005；Ferreira & Patson,2007）。

工作记忆容量在更年轻的成年人（Just & Carpenter,1992；MacDonald et al.,1992；Just & Varma,2002）、更年长的成年人（Kemtes & Kemper,1997；Kemper et al.,2004；Christianson et al.,2006）的花园小径歧义消解中都扮演着重要角色。Christianson et al.（2006）的实验证实了工作记忆容量影响句法理解的最终表征。他们发现工作记忆容量低的年长者在读完(a)这样的句子后,回答(c)问题的准确率很大程度上低于工作记忆容量大的年长者和年轻人。Christianson et al.（2006）的实验结果与 Just & Carpenter（1992）工作记忆容量理论提出的假设相符合:工作记忆容量会影响句子理解;工作记忆容量因人而异,这种个体差异可以解释语言理解多方面的差异。

Payne & Stine-Morrow（2017）通过眼动实验,证实了工作记忆训练可以影响句子理解,说明居家（home-based）训练工作记忆可以是探究老年人认知可塑性的范围和限度的一种切实可行的选择。

（2）二语的工作记忆与歧义句的曲解残留关系研究

目前就第二语言花园路径句理解中曲解和消歧并存现象所作的研究甚少,工作记忆容量及语言水平与最终不完整表征建构的关系尚不清晰,这正是我们的关注点。

就语言水平在句子理解中的作用而言,陈鸿标（1998）的实验研究发现,学习者处理歧义句比非歧义句的时间长，但是理解正确率并没有显著差异；语言水平高的学习者在处理较为简单的歧义句时与初级学习者无显著差异；但处理花园路径句时，其理解正确率明显高于初学者。

顾琦一、程秀苹（2010）测试材料改编自 Christianson et al.（2001）的实验语料。被试为某大学英语专业一、二年级的 106 名学生。实验结果表明：通过对花园路径句主句和从句理解测试、工作记忆测试和语言能力测试，在中国英语学习者花园路径句理解上发现了不完整的最终理解表征，即消歧与曲解残留并存的现象；同时，尽管工作记忆容量和语言水平影响花园路径句歧义的消解，但与这种不完整表征的建构都未发现显著相关。

王佩杰（2007）借用 Christianson et al. 的研究成果，对中国英语学习者进行了即时阅读实验来探究工作记忆的作用，初步证实第二语言理解中也有消歧和曲解的并存，并强调这与工作记忆的有限资源概念相一致。

侯建东（2014）实验证明：高水平被试因在初始分析时就已经能够成功消歧而未触发花园路径效应；中级水平受试则未能在早期成功解歧，因此触发了该效应且在成功消歧后仍出现了曲解残留问题。

陈士法、王邵馨、彭玉乐、崔馨元、杨连瑞（2022）通过眼动实验，利用 60 个花园路径句选自 Christianson et al.（2001）和 van Gompel et al.（2006）的实验句，探究了中国学习者加工英语二语"直接宾话／主语"类花园路径句的时间进程。线性混合模型分析发现：受试加工花园路径句的时间在从句动词和歧义名词区、消歧动词区和剩余成分区的不同眼动指标上都与加工非花园路径句的时间存在显著差异，实验表明中国学习者在此类花园路径句加工中存在着花园路径效应；只有高水平组在消歧动词区阅读花园路径句的回视路径时间显著多于非花园路径句的时间，二语水平影响了花园路径效应。这项研究并没有关注工作记忆与歧义句的曲解残留和消歧。

Brothers et al.（2021）采用眼动实验，调查了中—英双语被试和本族语英语被试阅读宾语—主语歧义句时对句法范畴和次范畴信息的反应。阅读过程中，单语者和双语者显示出与句法再分析相关的相似的花园路径效应，但是本族语者对于动词次范畴信息更敏感。具备更多语言经历和更大执行功能的阅读者对于动词次范畴信息显示出递进的敏感，但他们的句法分析却不受工作记忆容量的影响。

高水平者持续存在的一语／二语差异，可以依据二语者句子加工时记忆提取操作过程中递增地受到干扰来描述。二语者比所观察到的一语者加工时更多地依赖于语义和语用信息来帮助理解，此理论的主要依据来源于一些研究，即二语者对句法分析过程中的语义和语用信息敏感，但是在消解句法歧义（Felser et al.，2003b；Papadopoulou & Clahsen，2003）时建构表面上不详细的句法表征。

6.4 结语

研究者们对一语和二语者暂时歧义花园路径句加工的大量研究，显示了他们最初采用对歧义句句法上简单的分析。尽管这些研究结果表明一语和二语者跟随花园路径后试图再分析，然而很少有研究调查二语学习者句子加工时是如何成功再分析的。

与母语理解相比，二语学习者由于受到语言能力的限制，加工负荷会有所增加，很可能产生了非完整的理解表征，但是迄今为止相关的研究不多。语言学习者的语言水平很可能对花园路径句理解造成影响，其语言能力上的局限性也会造成学习者在歧义句加工过程中对工作记忆容量的要求与母语加工有所不同。

未来进一步的研究需要系统地调查：① 个体差异是如何在二语句子理解中影响加工者不同的记忆操纵；② 如果充分考虑加工者个体差异这样的问题，二语加工是否可以完全如同本族语的加工。对非本族语语境以外的双语句子加工的研究表明，记忆提取操作过程中一种语言所采用的提取提示可能影响双语者知晓的另一种语言的提取提示。

进一步研究需要调查的是二语学习者是否可以克服歧义句加工中一语／二语的差异。当前所研究的记忆编码、存储和提取中的个体差异在双语群体，而不是二语学习者歧义句加工中扮演的可能角色并不十分清楚，需要研究者们进一步调查研究。通过更好地了解这些加工过程，我们有希望理解不同的双语群体歧义句加工时的相似性和差异。

工作记忆和冲突消解能力一直是与歧义句加工密切相联系的两种加工过程。工作记忆是否对句子理解至关重要？冲突消解是否是构成工作记忆的基础？是否需要冲突消解来解决不同句子解释之间的干扰？研究者们对于这些问题一直争论不休。许多研究开始调查执行功能是否可能通过它在工作记忆中的角色或更直接地帮助消解不同句子解释之间的冲突来影响歧义句理解。当不同的词汇、语义和句法提示对句子产生不同的解释时，执行功能可能对句子理解至关重要。大量研究支持冲突消解在从多种选项中选择正确解释时的角色。执行功能支持对句子解释的修改，因此，二语学习者的执行功能在句法修改和语言学习中所扮演的角色值得研究者更进一步探讨。

竞争效应作为抑制干扰的证据，自然遵循着二语学习者歧义句加工更易受到提取干扰影响的这种假设。然而，研究者很难得出容量限制在一语/二语差异中不起作用的结论，歧义句加工中涉及的记忆编码、存储和提取操作的精确描述可以为描述一语/二语学习者歧义句加工的差异提供有希望的框架。

未来研究还应包括对工作记忆的测量，以便更全面地了解执行功能在花园路径再分析中的作用。

在许多日常语言交流中，我们会运用抑制来消解歧义（例如，花园路径句），而且，双语者经常会抑制一种语言（与当前语境不合适的语言）以便有效地交流。调查二语学习者在认知负荷下的歧义消解可以帮助研究者更进一步了解此加工过程。

第七章

短时记忆、外语听力理解与输入假设

7.1 引言

听力理解在外语教学中长期受到忽视,原因可能是听力理解被视为一种被动的技巧,而且教师认为使学生置身于听力环境中听材料便是听力教学的万全之策。这样便出现了一些不良现象:首先,听力教师只是习惯于通过操纵磁带和核对学生的答案来主宰听力课堂。其次,低年级学生总是收听远远超过他们听力水平的非常难的听力材料,使他们逐渐厌倦,失去兴趣。没有可理解性输入,任何学习都不会开始;在产出之前的理解性学习能使初级阶段的语言习得更加便利(Krashen, 1982)。最后,高年级学生认为:学习一段时间以后,听力水平仍停留在原来的水平;收听长篇资料很难取得理想的效果。低水平和高水平之间似乎存在着难以跨越的沟壑,其中一个重要原因是短时记忆的容量局限造成短时记忆信息提取受阻(陈吉棠, 1999)。

近年来,记忆与语言学习之间的关系问题已受到越来越多的关注,以往的实验研究中的被试都是来自其他的语言学习背景,而不是以汉语为母语的英语学习者。因此,根据短时记忆的特点,探讨英语作为第二外语的中国学生的听力学习,从而提高听力水平具有必要性和现实意义。

7.2 理论框架

7.2.1 短时记忆

记忆一直是心理学,尤其是认知心理学研究的重要课题。记忆按其持续时间的长短可分为 3 种不同的类型:感觉记忆、短时记忆和长时记忆。20 世纪 50 年代至 70 年代是对短时记忆研究的兴旺时期。短时记忆是指将所接受的信息暂时储存的那部分记忆,同时对信息进行分析、理解,等到语句中的信息或内容被理解了,这些资料就成为永久性记忆(长时记忆),而语句本身则再无用处,可能会逐渐从短时记忆中消失(Richards et al.,2000)。

短时记忆是短暂的记忆,容量有限。美国心理学家 Miller(1956)指出,在短时记忆中,一个人不能保持超过 7±2 个组块的信息量。长时记忆是将信息长期地储存下来的那部分记忆,容量无限,但要费力才可将信息转入长时记忆。接受信息的过程是:信息从外部环境通过感觉储存系统进入,对于此阶段的言语信息一般在一两秒钟之内便会消失,只有当它受到注意时才会转移到另一个相对稳定的短时记忆阶段;在短时记忆阶段,信息处理的容量较小,但持续的时间稍长,约为 17 秒,短时记忆中的信息经编码处理之后便会转移到长时记忆。如果在短时记忆中的信息得不到重复练习,将在 20~30 秒内被丢失。学习者不能在短时记忆中永久保留信息,因为总会有新信息进入,并随时把旧信息从短时记忆中排除掉。

Atkinson & Shiffrin(1968,1971)的实验研究一种口头练习,即死记硬背的学习方式。对于抽象无意义的材料,鼓励通过反复练习记住信息,这样可使信息转换到长时记忆中。Atkinson & Shiffrin 还指出近因效应和首因效应。

从 1963 到 1976 年,Conrad(1972)、Wickelgren(1973)、Winkens(1976)实验论证了二种编码形式:听觉代码形式和语义代码形式。基于声音的听觉代码是短时记忆的主要记忆代码,基于意义的语义代码是长时记忆的主要代码。

Waugh & Norman(1965)测试信息从短时记忆的消失是源于丢失还是干扰,实验证明干扰是重要原因。我们可通过排列信息结构,即减少信息中的同类项,来把干扰减小到最低程度。

（1）短时记忆与外语学习

迄今为止,从外语学习的角度研究短时记忆的为数不多,仅有的两个值得一提的实验研究都是国外学者做的:Cook（1977）和 Call（1985）(王初明,1990)。

Cook（1977）区分两种记忆:主要记忆,它不依赖语言,易于从本族语转移到外语;言语处理记忆（speech-processing memory）,它取决于语言的性质,外语学习者的言语处理记忆受句法使用能力的制约。比起物体名称来,表示数字的单词有限,外语学习者容易辨认。识记物体名称需借助长时记忆中的深层信息,而包括背景知识在内的深层信息往往是外语学习者所欠缺的。短时记忆的储存有限,外语学习者与本族语说话者需依靠长时记忆中的知识,尽快地对短时记忆中的信息进行释义处理。外语学习者与本族语学习者的重要区别在于:一是前者在长时记忆中的语言知识不如后者充足;二是前者因熟悉程度不够而造成处理语言速度减慢。

Call（1985）的听力实验的目的是研究短时记忆与外语听力之间的关系。结果表明,短时记忆是听力理解的一个重要组成部分,对句法的记忆能够预测听力技能。学习者必须学会利用句法帮助识别词与词之间的联系,使句子在短时记忆中保持较长的时间,以便弄懂意思。

（2）短时记忆与听力理解

如果我们想弄明白短时记忆在听力理解中所起的作用,首先我们应清楚在收听和理解话语时,声音被转换成意义所经历的一系列过程。当听者听到声音时,一个短暂的感觉储存(又称回声记忆)储存信息大约一秒钟。这时听者运用以前学过的规则把这一系列语音分割成有意义的单位。一旦语音组成的规则被识别出,它们便以单词形式进入短时记忆。在语言处理过程中,一般从句法结构的角度给记忆单位下定义。记忆单位通常表现为单词、短语或子句。一旦语音进入短时记忆,并按一定的结构合成适当的句法单位,它只保持一定的时间以供释义,接着便被清除,让位于新的输入。语音负载的信息不一定转入长时记忆。表达信息的确切单词在短时记忆中停留的时间一般不长,意思被提取之后,很快便会被忘掉。

尽管听力和阅读都被视为接收技能,但听力理解远比阅读理解难得多。在阅读时,读者可以回顾一下前面读到过的,也可以继续阅读以便了解下文的内容,然而对于听者来说,却不能这样做。稍不留神便会漏听重要的甚至全部的信息,因此记忆变得相当重要。尽可能多地记忆所听内容成为许多外语学习者追求的目标,特别是以英语为外语的学习者,他们语言能力欠缺,词汇量贫乏。运用好的听力技巧,可使听力材料在短时记忆中保持较长的时间,并能有技巧地激活长时记忆中的知识,使之转入短时记忆。总之,改善听力技巧能提高学习者的听力水平。

7.2.2　Krashen 的输入假设与听力理解

输入假设被简单解释为:人类习得语言仅仅通过一种方式——通过理解信息或通过接收“可理解性输入”(Krashen, 1985)引自 Cook(2000:51),即语言习得依赖于试图理解其他人所说的话。如果学习者听到有意义的言语并试图理解它,习得便会产生。语言习得通过理解性信息而产生。可理解性输入是 Krashen 输入假设的重要观点。如果语言材料中仅仅包含学习者已掌握的语言知识,它对语言习得不具有意义。同样,如果语言材料太难,大大超过了学习者目前的语言知识,它对语言习得也不具有意义。Krashen 定义为 $i+1$。i 代表学习者目前的水平,1 指材料的难度应稍高于其目前已掌握的语言知识。学习者当前的语言知识状态 i 与下一个发展阶段 $i+1$ 之间的“缺口”或者说“距离”是靠语言环境所提供的相关信息以及学习者以往的经验来弥补的。

对于听力,$i+1$ 可解释为学生熟悉的材料(i)和一些不熟悉的材料,其意思可从上下文中推导出来(1)。根据 Krashen 的观点,学习者的口语能力不是教会的,只有通过接受可理解性输入来提高语言能力,他们才能自然而然地获得口语能力;如果学习者接触到的语言输入是可理解的,并且有足够的输入量,学习者就能自动地获得必要的语法。

7.3　研究设计

7.3.1　研究问题

Call(1985)的实验研究对象为说西班牙语和阿拉伯语的英语学习者,因此以往的实验研究的被试都是来自其他的语言背景,而不是以汉语为母语的英语学习者。那么,对于中国英语学习者来说,对各种听力输入的短时记忆广度是否也同样影响听力成绩？下面的试验试图回答这几个研究问题：

（a）对有情节的一段短文中句子的短时记忆是否对听力成绩的变化影响最大？

（b）对孤立句子的短时记忆是否对听力成绩的影响居第二位？

（c）对随机安排的单词的短时记忆是否对听力成绩的影响居第三位？

（d）对随机安排的数字的短时记忆是否对听力成绩的影响最弱？

7.3.2 研究对象

参加实验的被试是 40 名青岛大学二年级非英语专业学生，年龄为 19～22 岁。被试者在中学已学过至少 6 年英语，其中 10 人已在大学二年级通过大学英语四级考试。

7.3.3 测试手段

首先，实验对学生进行前测验，测试学生听力水平，并将学生的听力水平分类。接着，实验对 Call（1985）所采用的方法略做改动，来测量被试的短时记忆。短时记忆测试分为 4 个小测试：对有情节的一段短文的记忆测试（probe subtest）、对一系列孤立的句子的记忆测试（sentence subtest）、对随机安排的单词的记忆测试（random word subtest）、对随机安排的数字的记忆测试（random digit subtest）。最后，实验设计了听力测试题来测量被试的听力理解能力。

7.3.4 实验步骤

测试 1：测试一段有情节的短文（包含 10 个句子）的短时记忆。要求受试听 1 个被中断 10 次的英文短故事，在每次中断后，受试会听到一个实义词提示铃（这个实义词是刚刚听到的句子的第一个实义词），要求受试写下提示铃后的单词。因此，像正常的听力一样，受试集中于所听的内容而不是语言形式。测试中，受试知道他们被要求回忆并写下所听的内容，但不知写下的材料有多长并且何时开始写，是测试一种连续记忆。

测试 2：测试 40 个孤立的句子的短时记忆。此测试排除掉上下文的因素，每一个句子与测试 1 中的句子在长度、句法复杂性和词频方面相似。在这种情况下，受试知道他们被要求写下所听到的每一个句子。因此，他们便能集中注意力于句法和词法结构，而不会受到语义内容的干扰。

测试3：测试随机安排的单词的短时记忆。此测试排除掉句法的因素，要求受试收听25串随机安排的实义词，每串实义词包括4～8个单词，并且这些实义词已出现在测试1、测试2中，此测试排除了句法提供的词的外在顺序。

测试4：对随机安排数字的短时记忆。此测试排除掉前面测试中的词汇意义的因素，听25串随机安排的数字，每串数字包括4～8个数字，数字是孤立的，意思清晰明确，不会产生语义干扰。然而一个孤立的实义词有几个意思，当听者听到一个单词时，会从长时记忆中提取几个意思，因此影响短时回忆的效率。由任意联想对一个单词造成的干扰也会影响提取，任意联想通常不影响数字，因此不影响短时回忆。

对短时记忆广度的四个小测试中，测试者在每个小测试前都要求被试不许动笔，直到外教读完每个测试项目，才可以写下所听到的单词或句子，以期达到短时记忆测试的准确性。在听力测试中，为确保测试的效度和信度，我们没有告诉被试参加实验测试，而只是通知他们参加摸底考试。

7.3.5　测验材料

测试1 probe subtest 中的 probe 指的是基本句型是 NP1+BE+V-ing+NP2 的句子中的第一个实义词（并且在它之前可有任何限定词）。这些句子在 NP1 或 NP2 的位置、名词短语的修饰类型（形容词、介词短语或关系从句）方面有所不同。测试1 probe subtest 与测试2 sentence subtest 在相对长度、句法复杂性和词频方面相似，用于测试1和测试2的实义词是从测试3 random word subtest 的实义词中选出的。相对长度由通过计算句子中单词数目、音节数目及（大约的）词素的数目，然后把三者相加除以3而得出，即相对长度

$$= \frac{单词数目＋音节数目＋（大约的）词素的数目}{3}$$

。测试2中1）中4个句子要与测试1中第1个句子在相对长度、词频和句法复杂性上相似，依此类推，测试2中2）中的4个句子应与测试1中第2个句子相似，3）中4个句子应与第3个句子相似，等等。

7.4 结果与讨论

运用 SPSS11.0 对所得各类数据进行统计分析,结果如下。

7.4.1 皮尔逊积矩相关系数

首先,为了证实听力测试的有效性,笔者比较了被试在此次的听力测试成绩与被试的两次期末成绩的平均分。结果显示:相关系数 r=0.842,显著意义水平 p<0.01,被试的听力测试成绩与被试的两次期末成绩平均分呈显著相关(统计表格从略)。

其次,皮尔逊积矩相关统计分析了短时记忆的每一个小测试与其余三个小测试的相关性,以及每个短时记忆小测试与听力测试的相关情况(如表 7-1)。成绩被分成两组,与 Call(1985)的 speech processing memory 和 primary memory 的分类相符。第一组:由 probe subtest 和 sentence subtest 组成,与听力成绩呈显著相关。第二组:由 random word subtest 和 random digit subtest 组成,与听力成绩呈弱相关。这些结果证实了 Call(1985)的发现,primary memory 并不比 speech processing memory 对听力成绩影响大。句子成绩(sentence subtest)被假设与听力成绩呈第二显著相关,却显示比 probe subtest 与听力成绩相关系数(r=0.53)(曾假设为最显著相关)高(r=0.699)。句子成绩与 probe subtest 显著相关(r=0.854),说明这两个测试发掘同一属性的处理语言输入的能力。其余两个变量显示出与听力成绩所假设的关系:句子成绩(r=0.699)比随机安排的单词成绩(r=0.336)显示稍高的相关系数;随机安排的单词比随机安排的数字成绩(r=0.214)显示稍高的相关系数,然而两个成绩之间的相关不是很显著(r=0.448),说明这两个小测试开发短时记忆的不同成份,证实了 Call(1985)的发现:对数字的记忆不同于对单词的记忆。

表 7-1 短时记忆四个小测试之间的相关系数以及分别与听力成绩的相关系数

	测试 1 有情节的短文	测试 2 孤立的句子	测试 3 随机安排的单词	测试 4 随机安排的数字	听力 理解
测试 1 有情节的短文	1	0.854**	0.492**	0.424**	0.530**
测试 2 孤立的句子		1	0.541**	0.399*	0.699**

	测试 1 有情节的短文	测试 2 孤立的句子	测试 3 随机安排的单词	测试 4 随机安排的数字	听力 理解
测试 3 随机安排的单词			1	0.448**	0.336*
测试 4 随机安排的数字				1	0.214
听力理解					1
** 显著性在 0.01 水平上（双尾）					
* 显著性在 0.05 水平上（双尾）					

7.4.2　多元回归分析

多元回归分析是说明听力成绩的变化是如何由四个小测试测得的四个自变量来解释的。如表 7-2 所示，各变量与自变量（听力成绩）的相关顺序从最高相关依次递减到最低相关。在 50.9% 的总数中，句子测试占 48.9%，probe 测试仅加了 1.7%，占 50.6%，说明这两个自变量是最强有力的。只要其他变量得到控制，单词测试和数字测试对听力成绩的变化没有影响。

表 7-2　自变量对听力成绩影响的多元回归分析

自变量	r	R	R 变化
测试 1 孤立的句子	0.699	0.489	0.489
测试 2 有情节的短文	0.530	0.506	0.017
测试 3 随机安排的单词	0.336	0.507	0.002
测试 4 随机安排的数字	0.214	0.509	0.001

如果自变量按相反顺序排列，以最弱变量排列在首位依次递增，其结果没有多大变化。对变量起最大作用的还是来自 Group 1：probe 和 sentence subtest。数据显示，由 sentence 和 probe subtest 测得的自变量对听力成绩影响最大，其余两项测试并不起多大作用（统计表格从略）。

实验证明，对孤立句子和有情节短文中句子的记忆是对听力的最好预测，因为这两项都包含对句法的记忆。同时，在对孤立句子的测试中，被试知道他们被要求写下 40 个句子，便能集中注意力于句法和词法结构，而不会受到语义内容的干扰，因此写下的每一个句子就比较完整和规范；在对由 10 个句子组成的有情节短文的测试中,要求被试写下提示铃后的单词,即每个句子的第一个实义词之后的单词,被试知道他们被要求回忆并写下所听内容,但不知写下的材料有多长并且何时开始写,因此写下的短句或短语很零乱并且不规范,这就是句子测试比有情节短文测试对听力成绩变化影响大的原因。

7.5　结论

根据实验结果,我们得出如下结论:首先,对听力输入的短时记忆是听力理解的重要组成部分;其次,通过对句子和有情节短文的测试,证明对句法的记忆是对听力技能的最好预测;同时,对单词和数字的记忆只能解释听力成绩的一小部分变化,这个不同点更清楚地解释了可理解性输入。可理解性输入解释为 i+1,即学生熟悉的材料(i)和一些不熟悉的材料,其意思能从上下文中推导出(1)。当学生被提供输入 i+1,他们运用他们熟悉的"关键单词"(名、动、形、副)(Krashen et al., 1984:266)以便理解输入信息中所表达的整体意思。上下文(语言和非语言)帮助学生理解不熟悉的单词,使之随后变成学生熟悉单词的一部分。结果显示,对句法安排的单词的记忆是听力理解的重要组成部分。由此,可推出句法在提供可理解性输入方法方面起重要作用,不熟悉句法规则而试图听懂外语材料无异于试图回忆那些随机安排的外语单词。实验结果表明:学生从句法中受益,能使他们把单词组成句法单位。

7.6　对教学的启示

(1)听力与口语的关系

外语学习者常常抱怨听力和口语是他们学习的薄弱环节,口语尤其是弱中之弱。这似乎表明,语言教学应以提高学生的口语能力为目的。实则不然,因为语言输入比语言输出更为重要。

一个学习者能以轻松自如的速度来调整相对狭小的词汇量表达观点;而当听答话时,便不再能控制词汇量的选择。一个人必须随时准备吸收那些是说话者积极词汇的一部分单词,并且必须适应说话者的语速。为了能操纵一个简单的对话,一个人在听力上必须拥有比在口语上大的能力和词汇量,尤其是在与说英语的本族人交谈时。

口语和听力相互补充。一个学生没有先学"+1",即没有吸收"i+1"输入,便不能产生"i+1"输出。另一方面,可理解性输入不能导致语言发展。因为在输出中积极利用新资料"1"的压力,将迫使学生有意识地分析信息所包含的语言形式。我们应意识到输入与输出的内在相关性,特别是一个学生的可理解性输出,经常会成为其他学生的可理解性输入。

(2)如何弥补短时记忆容量有限

如上所述,克服短时记忆的有限容量是提高听力的一个必要条件。首先组块可帮助减少短时记忆中的项目数量,增加短时记忆的容量。同时组块是建立不同项目之间联系的第一步,这种联系会便利对长时记忆中信息的回忆,组块可减少重复学习信息的时间。由于短时记忆容量有限,我们应依赖长时记忆中的信息。长时记忆中的信息必须被激活才能用于理解中。经验知识是长时记忆的体现,它对短时记忆具有熟悉效应和激活扩散的作用,使短时记忆在这些"效应"的基础上得到良好的保持,以便于信息联结和记忆扩展(陈吉棠,2002)。因此从长时记忆向短时记忆的信息转换是提高听力理解的最重要方式,提高处理效率是提高短时记忆容量的又一方式。

近年来,图式理论引起广泛关注,是长时记忆的一个分支。新信息应与人的先前学习知识与经验相联系,以便与长时记忆相结合。充分利用记忆中的图式能帮助弥补短时记忆的有限容量。

(3)对听力教学的启示

首先我们不应忽视上下文的因素,上下文可通过提供更多线索来减少信息的模糊性。标题在处理篇章中也起了重要作用。听者能利用有情节的上下文的线索增强理解。同时,教师应把重点放在听前准备阶段。听前充分的准备可提供语境和动机,它能帮助学生意识到听力输入的动机和目标。教师能帮助学生减少对听力材料的多余期望,并对相关材料集中注意力,以便减少听力负担。

许多学习材料强调听懂意思而未注意让学习者收听语言结构,形成意思的是这些结构,光有词汇知识不足以使一个学习者改善听力。学习者必须学会运用句法帮助识别词与词之间的联系,使句子在短时记忆中保持较长的时间,以便弄懂意思。识别句法结构的专门练习对提高听力是必不可少的。

在教授高年级听力课时,听力重点应从表层记忆向深层理解转换。着眼点是提高学生听力理解能力和概括能力,题型应从多项选择题(客观题)为主向主观题为主转换,指导学生改变思维,扩展短时记忆的角度,增加记忆范围,让学生善于根据自己的实际情况发现有助于脑记的笔记形式,学会把短时记忆与长时记忆科学地结合起来,从而提高听力理解。

第八章

工作记忆容量对二语句子加工中的生命性和世界知识影响的 ERP 实证研究

8.1　引言

大多数语言学家观点一致,认为句法和语义组成不同种类的信息(Chomsky, 1965)。对于心理语言学家来说,一个关键的问题是,我们在线加工句子时如何把这些不同种类的信息组合起来形成意义的最后表征。

在二语习得句子理解过程中,句子理解除了与习得者的早期环境浸入、更高学习动机和日常生活中经常使用的二语相关外,主要还与二语习得者的工作记忆容量、单词识别技巧、句法知识、语义知识、语用知识和文本输入的特点等相关联。在二语研究领域,关于个体基本认知容量是如何影响和制约二语阅读理解的研究很少。本章试图探究工作记忆如何与二语阅读理解中个体实时加工题元的(thematic)差异相关联。

8.2　理论文献

8.2.1　句子理解

8.2.1.1　模块论(modular approach)

Frazier(1987b)所提出的语法分析策略和语言理解中的模块论是相符合

的。总的来说,理解是由很多不同的模块相互作用的结果;每一个模块都对理解的一个特定方面起了作用(Fodor,1983)。句法分析首先由一个句法模块来执行,它不受更高一级的句子意义的语境因素或世界知识的影响。因此,Frazier(1987b)认为句法分析由句法模块来执行,而语境变量在后来的理解中才起作用。Forster(1979)的模型认为语言处理包括三个不同的独立系统,每一个系统都不受上一级系统的影响。第一个是词汇处理器,它在语音输入的基础上激活一些词项;第二个是句法处理器,接着处理器从词汇输出中提取信息,对句子进行分析理解,产生表层结构表征;第三个是消息处理器,它把语言表征转成代表语义意图的概念或意义结构。

8.2.1.2　互动模型(interactive model)

语言处理的互动模型认为句法和语义在理解过程中交互起作用(Britt et al.,1992;Crain & Steedman,1985;Taraban & McCleelland,1988;Tyler & Marslen-Wilson,1977)。这种模型是自上而下和自下而上的互动。句子的处理首先以自下而上的处理开始,听者的感觉器官首先感受和分解语音信号,然后向上面的音素、词语、句子结构进一步发展,直到辨解句法的语义关系,从而产生句子的意义。另一个过程则是从上而下处理,即使用各种语言和非语言信息来加速、辨析自下而上出现的信息的处理。这种模型认为句子处理过程中世界知识(world knowledge)和词汇—语义信息(lexical-semantic information)共同迅速作用影响。这种语言理解过程表明当听到话语时,需要同时进行句法处理和语义处理。

8.2.2　题元加工

语言理解理论在解释阅读者何时组合正展开的句子中不同的句法、语义和世界知识信息时存在着预测的差异。模块模型预测句法信息会首先被用来组成一个句子的结构,伴随着词汇—语义特征的整合。这些特征与对这些单词的表征储存在心理词典中(Frazier,1987a)。这种对言语输入信息更高层级的表征会进一步映现到我们对世界的认识中(Fischler et al.,1983)。互动模型预测阅读者在阅读理解过程中运用不同信息的时间进程不需要延迟(MacDonald et al.,1992)。许多研究结果表明了句子加工过程中世界知识和词汇—语义信息的极其迅速的影响。Hagoort et al.(2004)表明相对于词汇—语义信息，句子加工时并不存在对世界知识的在线整合的延迟。而来自许多其他的行为和电生理学研究结果表明了论元（argument）的生命性对阅读者理解句子时的极其早期的影响（Ferreira，2003；MacDonald et al.，1994；Marslen-Wilson & Tyler，1980；Markus et al.，2008；Kuperberg et al.，2007，Kim & Osterhout，2005；Nakano & Swaab，2005；van Herten et al.，2005；Hoeks et al.，2004；Kolk et al.，2003；Kuperberg et al.，2003；Ferreira & Clifton，1986）。

　　电生理测量（事件相关电位）能提供加工者实时句子加工时质的信息，而不需要他们即时的行为反应。两种 ERP 成分尤其与题元加工的研究相关：N400 和 P600。N400 对输入信息的语义方面敏感，并一直与词汇—语义信息的提取和整合相联系；当单词的意思与语境匹配时，N400 的振幅减小（Kutas & Hillyard，1980a；Swaab et al.，in press；Kutas & Federmeier，2000）。P600 传统上被解释为对语言输入信息的句法方面敏感；对于构成前面句子的句法上异常、复杂或歧义的接续词，P600 振幅增强（Kaan et al.，2000；Hagoort et al.，1993；Osterhout & Holcomb，1992）。然而，基于研究结果，研究者们又增加了一些与 P600 效应相关的语言加工的新观点，即 P600 效应在句法非歧义句中的关键动词的题元角色违反时发现（例如，"The eggs would eat toast with jam at breakfast."）（Kim & Osterhout，2005；van Herten et al.，2005；Hoeks et al.，2004；Kolk et al.，2003；Kuperberg et al.，2003）。尤其是当对句子结构（例如，S-V-O）的基于句法的分析受到句中单词的强语义关系的挑战时（Kuperberg，2007）和/或受到句中论元和动词的最合理组合的挑战时（Kim & Osterhout，2005；Bornkessel-Schlesewsky & Schlesewsky，2008），加工者会引发 P600 效应。Kuperberg et al.（2007）表明句子中个体单词间的语义关系，不会引发 P600 效应，因为置于语义上不相关的无生命论元名词词组前面的、题元上违反的动词也显示出了 P600 效应（例如，"For breakfast the eggs would plant..."）。这些发现说明，在英语主动句中，动词前面的论元生命性信息即时被计算，并且会影响动词的加工；当动词是前面语境的异常持续时，会产生动词引发的 P600 效应。

　　基于语义—题元违反的 P600 的发现，Kuperberg（2007）提出了两种加工语流平行运行的语言理解模式：基于语义记忆的语流（semantic memory-based stream），在句子成分中计算语义特征和关系，并且对语言输入信息逐渐发展的语义方面的违反主要反映在 N400 成分中；另一个组合语流（combinatorial stream）对语言限制敏感，包括对形态句法和题元角色关系的限制。当两种语流提供自相矛盾的输出时（例如，当第一种语流的语义解释输出与句子中的形态句法或题元信息相矛盾时），必须持续分析来解决这种不一致，并且是这种延伸的分析被反映在了 P600 成分中。van Herten et al.（2005）提出了对 P600 的一种不同的描述。这些研究者也强调了多种表征间的冲突。此外，他们还建议这种冲突会受到执行控制下监察过程的探测。

当前研究的目标是评估二语学习者理解简单、主动句时题元信息的个体差异。我们并不打算解决 P600 加工特性中的争论。然而，基于上面讨论的 P600 的发现，我们假设二语者在线句子理解时被考虑的信息会随着个体工作记忆广度的差异而变化，并且这会在题元加工时产生不同困难的电生理学特征（N400 或 P600）。

8.3　研究设计

8.3.1　研究问题

题元角色指派（谁对谁做了什么）要求对句法、语义和世界知识信息进行迅速组合。例如，下面三个句子：

（a）The dog is biting the milkman. —（control condition）控制条件

（b）The cook is biting the milkman. —（world-knowledge violation condition）世界知识违反条件

（c）The cup is biting the milkman. —（animacy violation condition）生命性违反条件

三个句子都有一个简单、主动、无歧义结构，并且是按英语语言中规范的主语—动词—宾语（SVO）顺序排列，但是介于动词和前置主语论元之间概念关系的合理性发生了变化。在例句（a）中，主语名词"dog"是动词"bite"的完全合法施事者，狗咬牛奶工的行为是一个合理事件。例句（b）违反了世界知识，尽管厨师可以咬牛奶工，但这样的事件与我们对世界的共识不符。例句（c）违反了生命性，这是因为句法加工产生了基于单词种类信息（名词—动词—名词）的主语—动词—宾语（SVO）结构，但是语义加工与这个结构不一致,这就产生了题元加工问题,因为句子的主语不能充当动词行为的施事者,见表 8-1。

表 8-1　本研究三种条件下使用的语料例示

条件	解释	例子
控制句	无违反	The **dog** is **biting** the **milkman**.
世界知识违反	根据我们的世界知识,动词不大可能是第一个名词短语中的名词的行为	The **cook** is **biting** the **milkman**.
生命性违反	动词不可能是第一个名词短语中的名词的行为	The **cup** is **biting** the **milkman**.

ERP 是以例句中的黑体字来测量的。

本实验依据 Nakano et al.（2010）的实验,略做改动。在实验中考察了低工作记忆容量和高工作记忆容量的被试是否和何时会利用生命性信息和世界知识理解简单、无歧义的句子时委派题元角色。本实验预测:相对于控制句（control）,不同的工作记忆广度的受试对于生命性违反条件和世界知识违反条件中的第一个名词短语（NP1）中的名词、动词（V）和第二个名词短语（NP2）中的名词所引发的 N400 效应和 P600 效应,预测问题为:

（a）相对于控制句,世界知识违反条件中的高广度和低广度被试都对宾语名词产生了语义加工困难,即 N400 效应。

（b）相对于控制句,生命性违反条件中的高广度被试对于主语名词产生了语义加工困难,即 N400 效应。

（c）相对于控制句,生命性违反条件中的高广度被试对于动词产生了句法加工困难,即 P600 效应。

（d）相对于控制句,生命性违反的条件中的低广度被试对于动词产生了语义加工困难,即 N400 效应。

8.3.2　被试

Nakano et al.（2010）的实验研究对象为英语本族语的学习者,而不是二语学习者。本实验的被试为二语学习者。

参加实验的被试是来自中国高校的 60 名大学生:他们均已参加过中国大学英语四级考试,成绩为 450～500 分。他们年龄为 19～29 岁（40 名女生、20 名男生）:10 名被试由于属于中工作记忆容量,被排除;10 名被试由于脑电信号中的过度眼动和肌肉活动对脑电数据造成的影响而被排除;剩余的40名学生中,20名被试被归为高工作记忆容量(13女、7男),20名被试被归为低工作记忆容量(15女、5男),均为右利手,视力或矫正视力及听力正常,没有脑外伤和神经系统疾病史。实验结束后,每人获得一定报酬。

8.3.3　实验材料

8.3.3.1　工作记忆容量测试

基于Daneman & Carpenter(1980)的实验,本实验分为2部分来测量被试的工作记忆容量:阅读广度测试(reading span test)和听力广度测试(listening span test)。鉴于Waters & Caplan(1996c)对于早期阅读广度测试只测试储存而忽略了加工的批评,本阅读广度测试中加入了语法判断任务(grammaticality judgement task)。阅读广度测试包含60个无关联的主动语态、简单句,其中30个句子语法正确,30个句子语法不正确,每个句子的长度是11～13个单词,每个句子由不同的单词结尾,被试判断正误并写下每句的最后一个词。听力广度测试也是60个句子,由30个正确句子和30个错误句子组成,所有句子均选自常识测试书,涉及生物、物理、地理、文学、历史、实事等各领域的知识,每个句子的长度是9～16个单词,每个句子由不同的单词结尾,被试听后判断正误并写下每句的最后一个词(见附录1)。

阅读和听力实验中的60个句子分别为3套(set),每套题中的句子数量分别为2、3、4、5、6,每个句子只呈现一次,被试需要在计算机房按两个键中的一个键判断每个句子是否正确。每个句子的间隔都是7秒,在每套的所有句子题(分别为3套的每套的2个句子、3套的每套的3个句子、3套的每套的4个句子、3套的每套的5个句、3套的每套的6个句子)被呈现后,一个文本框会出现在屏幕上,要求被试输入所记忆的每个句子最后的一个单词。

8.3.3.2　语料

根据3种条件,简单、进行时、主动语态的270个句子分别为90个控制句、90个世界知识违反句和90个生命性违反句。

我们把3个条件句分为3套题元关系:施事和行为(the agent and the action)(例如,"狗/厨师/杯子正在咬");行为与题元(the action and the theme)(例如,"正在咬牛奶工");施事、行为和题元(例如,"狗/厨师/杯子正在咬牛奶工")。为了保证 3 套题元关系的呈现顺序在被试之间抵消平衡（counterbalance），我们创建了 3 个区组（block），这样动词和第二个名词短语（例如，"is the milkman"）就不会在 1 个 block 中重复出现，但是所有这 3 个合理度条件都会在这 3 个区组中得以同等表征。这 3 个区组的呈现顺序在不同的被试之间被抵消平衡。

同时，除了 270 个实验句外，根据词汇和句法结构，实验又加入了区别于实验句的 90 个填充句（filler sentence）。填充句包含 60 个真词句和 30 个假词句。真词句包含形容词和副词。36 个真词填充句以无生命性名词开始，一半是过去时，并且／或是被动语态，并且／或是不正确的过去时和被动语态。同时，为了避免被试预测到第一个名词的生命性，一半正确的真词填充句以无生命性名词开始，一半不正确的真词填充句以生命性名词开始。

实验 360 个句子拉丁方后，每位被试需要做 180 个句子，分为 4 个区组休息。

8.3.4　实验程序

实验在 ERP 技术实验室中的隔音电磁屏蔽室进行。实验中，被试戴耳机坐在离计算机屏幕 100 厘米的沙发上；实验时先在电脑屏幕中央呈现白色注视点"＋"（1 000 毫秒），在阅读语料的过程中，依然可见白色注视点"＋"（3 080 毫秒）；在句子结束后，有额外的 2 000 毫秒间隔，白色注视点"＋"随后由绿色注视点"＋"代替，持续 3 000 毫秒，这样被试对阅读的句子进行"是"或者"否"的句子可接受度按键判断。被试被告知实验过程中的白色注视点"＋"时禁止眨眼并禁止头部及全身的其他运动。

8.3.5　ERP 数据采集和分析

被试佩带 Electro-Cap 64 锡电极帽，采用 Neuroscan Synamps 2 记录脑电，电极与头皮接触电阻保持在 5kΨ 以下。分析时程为 200～1 000 毫秒。在这些分析时段里，10％的伪迹信号被剔除。对所要考察的各类刺激的脑电数据进行叠加平均。为了能够更清楚地观测各类刺激的波形及相互之间的差异，对各类刺激总平均的 ERP 波形进行 25Hz 低通滤波，对于控制句、世界知识违反和生命性违反中的主语名词、动词和宾语名词的平均 ERP 数据进行分析，但是所有用于统计分析的数据都来自未被滤波的 ERP。

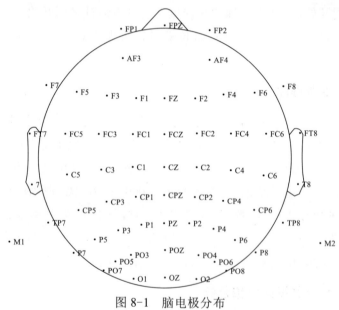

实验过程中采集了 32 通道(国际标准 10—20 系统)的脑电数据。本文选用基于 matlab 的 EEGLAB 和 ERPLAB 工具包对脑电数据进行处理。处理步骤如下:第一步将数据导入,并以 M1 和 M2 作为参考通道完成重参考;第二步,降采样至 500hz;第三步,提取脑电通道的 Fp1、Fpz、Fp2、F7、F3、Fz、F4、F8、FC5、FC1、FC2、FC6、C3、CZ、C4、CP5、CP1、CP2、CP6、P3、PZ、P4、POZ、O1、O2 电极数据(见图 8-1 脑电极分布(electrode configuration));第四步,对脑电信号采用 0.1～30Hz 的 butter 滤波器完成带通滤波;第五步,对滤波后的脑电数据按照事件标签完成分段提取,即提取事件标签 200～1 000 毫秒的信号;第六步,提取后的 1 200 毫秒信号采用 ERPLab 的眨眼伪迹去除眼动干扰。

图 8-1 脑电极分布

脑电数据依据实验进行分组,分为高容量组和低容量组。每组被试均完成语料,均为控制句、世界性知识违反句、生命性违反句。每组语句可分为主语、谓语和宾语。综上,实验将每组被试的任务区分为 9 种状态,列表 8-2 如下。

表 8-2　任务区

打码（mark）	对照组	世界知识违反	生命性违反
主语	11	12	13
谓语	21	22	23
宾语	31	32	33

实验提取了每种状态的脑电 ERP 数据（N400 和 P600），即 300～600 毫秒的 ERP 响应平均幅值和 600～900 毫秒的 ERP 响应平均幅值，并将任务之前的 200 毫秒作为基线值。

实验对脑电数据采用重复测量方差分析进行处理，分别按照世界知识违反相对于控制组、生命性知识违反相对于控制组两种模式完成重复测量方差分析、ANOVA 统计分析。相对于 100 毫秒前刺激基线，分别在 N400（300～600 毫秒）和 P600（600～900 毫秒）时间窗口，对 25 个电极的每个点对关键词的 ERP 成分进行平均波幅测量。同时，对每个时间窗口和每个题元操纵进行方差分析，分别对主语名词、动词和宾语名词进行了方差分析。所有方差分析包括了小组（高工作记忆广度对比低工作记忆广度）、合理性（世界知识违反，控制句；生命性违反，控制句）和电极（25 个点）。

实验分别显示了高工作记忆广度、低工作记忆广度的被试对于控制条件、世界知识违反条件和生命性违反条件在 Fz、Cz 和 Pz3 个电极位置主语名词、动词和宾语名词时间锁定的总平均 ERP 结果。测量结果采用 SPSS19 统计分析软件包进行三因素重复测量方差分析，统计结果进行 Greenhouse-Geisser 校正。

8.4　讨论与结论

8.4.1　行为数据（behavioral data）

被试回答理解问题的平均准确率是 68.5％，这说明两组被试的准确率显著（高容量被试组＝75.3％；低容量被试组＝61.7％；p＝0.008）。行为数据分析表明高容量被试组和低容量被试回答理解问题时，确实存在准确率的主效应（F（1，38）＝7.945，p＝0.008），这反映了高容量被试组正确率显著高于低容量被试组。

8.4.2 EEG 数据

实验对高和低工作记忆容量被试分别在 300～600 毫秒和 600～900 毫秒的 ERP 数据进行了分析，ERP 数据结果下文将列出。

8.4.2.1 300～600 毫秒的 N400 平均幅值

（1）低容量组

① 世界知识违反相对于控制句

电极之间平均幅值存在显著主效应（$F_{(1.71, 32.48)} = 4.97, p = 0.017$）。语义合理度与电极区的交互效应（interactions of plausibility × electrode site）不显著（$F_{(24, 456)} = 1.119, p = 0.31$），主谓宾组（sentence constituent: noun vs. verb vs. object）与电极区的交互效应（interactions of sentence constituent × electrode）不显著（$F_{(1.76, 33.44)} = 2.045, p = 0.015$）。主谓宾组与语义合理度的交互效应（interaction of sentence constituent × plausibility）不显著（$F_{(1.10, 20.98)} = 0.935, p = 0.35$）。主谓宾组、语义合理度和电极区的交互效应（interaction of sentence constituent × plausibility × electrode）不显著（$F_{(2.14, 40.76)} = 1.791, p = 0.178$）。

② 生命性违反相对于控制句

电极之间平均幅值存在显著主效应（$F_{(2.06, 39.19)} = 4.15, p = 0.022$）。语义合理度与电极区的交互效应不显著（$F_{(2.43, 46.21)} = 1.329, p = 0.27$），主谓宾组与电极区的交互效应显著（$F_{(2.41, 45.87)} = 4.047, p = 0.018$）。主谓宾组与语义合理度的交互效应不显著（$F_{(1.23, 23.36)} = 0.40, p = 0.575$）。主谓宾组、语义合理度和电极区的交互效应不显著（$F_{(3.09, 58.84)} = 0.689, p = 0.56$）。

（2）高容量组

① 世界知识违反相对于控制句

电极之间平均幅值存在显著主效应（$F_{(1.677, 31.85)} = 17.086, p < 0.001$）。语义合理度与电极区的交互效应不显著（$F_{(1.386, 26.35)} = 0.83, p = 0.407$），主谓宾组与电极区的交互效应显著（$F_{(1.609, 30.57)} = 4.443, p = 0.027$）。主谓宾组与语义合理度的交互效应不显著（$F_{(48, 912)} = 1.578, p = 0.22$）。主谓宾组、语义合理度和电极区的交互效应不显著（$F_{(3.39,}$

$64.46) = 1.286, p = 0.286$）。

② 生命性违反相对于控制句

电极之间平均幅值存在显著主效应（$F(1.685, 32.017) = 15.68$，$p < 0.001$）。语义合理度与电极区的交互效应不显著（$F(1.46, 27.743) = 0.813$，$p = 0.419$），主谓宾组与电极区的交互效应显著（$F(1.546, 29.379) = 4.194$，$p = 0.034$）。主谓宾组与语义合理度的交互效应不显著（$F(48, 912) = 0.813$，$p = 0.72$）。主谓宾组、语义合理度和电极区的交互效应不显著（$F(2.496, 47.42) = 0.318$，$p = 0.776$）。

8.4.2.2　600～900 毫秒的 P600 平均幅值：

（1）低容量组

① 世界知识违反相对于控制句

语义合理度存在显著主效应（$F(1, 19) = 1.378$，$p = 0.25$）。电极之间存在显著主效应（$F(2.76, 52.455) = 2.989$，$p = 0.043$）。主谓宾组与电极区的交互效应显著（$F(3.811, 72.412) = 2.941$，$p = 0.028$）。主谓宾组与语义合理度的交互效应不显著（$F(1.259, 23.92) = 0.977$，$p = 0.353$）。主谓宾组、语义合理度和电极区的交互效应不显著（$F(2.248, 42.714) = 0.836$，$p = 0.452$）。

② 生命性违反相对于控制句

电极之间不存在显著主效应（$F(3.17, 60.36) = 1.816$，$p = 0.151$）。语义合理度与电极区的交互效应不显著（$F(2.64, 50.25) = 1.675$，$p = 0.189$），主谓宾组与电极区的交互效应显著（$F(3.489, 66.29) = 2.386$，$p = 0.068$）。主谓宾组与语义合理度的交互效应不显著（$F(2, 38) = 0.344$，$p = 0.711$）。主谓宾组、语义合理度和电极区的交互效应不显著（$F(3.09, 58.7) = 2.642$，$p = 0.056$）。

（2）高容量组

① 世界知识违反相对于控制句

语义合理度存在显著主效应（$F(1, 19) = 6.67$，$p = 0.018$）。电极之间存在显著主效应（$F(1.36, 25.88) = 13.13$，$p < 0.001$）。主谓宾组与电极区的交互效应显著（$F(1.98, 37.70) = 3.47$，$p = 0.042$）。主谓宾组与语义合理度的交互效应不显著（$F(48, 912) = 1.61$，$p = 0.213$）。主谓宾组、语义合理度和电极区的交互效应不显著（$F(2.05, 39.06) = 0.746$，$p = 0.899$）。

② 生命性违反相对于控制句

主谓宾组与语义合理度的交互效应不显著（$F_{(48, 912)} = 0.344$, $p = 0.711$）。主谓宾组、语义合理度和电极区的交互效应不显著（$F_{(2.607, 49.53)} = 2.065$, $p = 0.125$）。

（3）600～900 毫秒生命性违反相对于控制句

① 主效应

根据小组（2）×语义合理度（animacy violation vs. control）×电极区（25）×主谓宾组的多重测量方差分析可知，小组（2）存在主效应（$F_{(1, 38)} = 4.18$, $p = 0.048$）。电极区存在主效应（$F_{(2.624, 99.716)} = 10.257$, $p < 0.001$）。

② 交互效应分析

小组×电极区存在交互效应（$F_{(24, 912)} = 3.913$, $p < 0.001$）。主谓宾组×电极区存在交互效应（$F_{(3.138, 119.23)} = 4.63$, $p = 0.004$）。

小组（2）×主谓宾组×电极区存在交互效应（$F_{(48, 1824)} = 1.446$, $p = 0.025$）。语义合理度×主谓宾组×电极区存在交互效应（$F_{(3.93, 149.49)} = 0.2.82$, $p < 0.001$）。

③ 简单效应分析

小组（2）×电极区（25）存在交互效应。在电极（如下表）位置，高容量组和低容量组存在简单效应（$P < 0.05$）：

FC6	C3	CZ	C4	CP5	CP1	CP2
CP6	P3	PZ	P4	POZ	O1	O2

主谓宾组×电极区（25）存在交互效应。小组（2）×主谓宾组×电极区（25）存在交互效应。主语词句情形下，Fz、FC1、CP5、P3、PZ、P4、POZ、O1、O2 电极的低容量组和高容量组之间存在简单效应（$p < 0.05$）。宾语情形下，电极 CP2、P3、P4、POZ 的低容量组与高容量组存在简单效应（$p < 0.05$）；语义合理度×主谓宾组×电极区存在交互效应。宾语情形下，电极 Fp1、Fpz、Fp2、F7、F3、Fz、F4、F8、FC5、FC1、FC2、FC6、C3、CZ、C4、CP5、CP1、CP2、CP6、P3、POZ、O1 存在简单效应（$p < 0.05$）。

图 8-2 的 ERP 结果显示了高容量被试（上）和低容量被试（下）3 个中线电极区（Fz, Cz, 和 Pz）并分别涉及在控制条件（粗实线）、世界知识违反条件

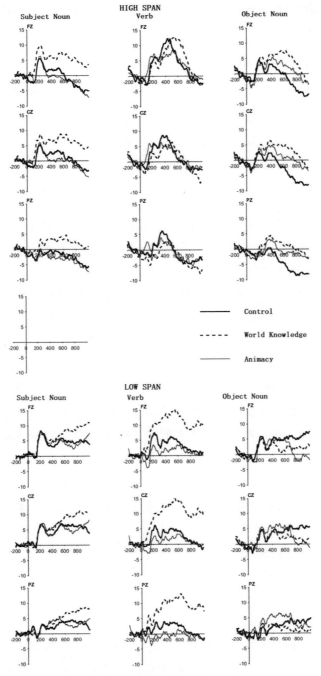

图 8-2　高容量被试(上)和低容量被试(下)的 ERP 结果

（点线）和生命性违反条件（细实线）中主语名词（左栏）、动词（中栏）和宾语名词（右栏）。

8.4.3　相关分析（correlation analyses）

通过对 P600 平均振幅（每位被试）的回归分析，本研究进一步探讨了工作记忆容量与生命性违反条件（相对于控制条件）中的主语名词合理性效应之间的关系。实验数据表明更高的工作记忆分数与更大的 P600 效应相关（r = 0.216，p = 0.0389）。

8.4.4　讨论

尽管大量本族语研究涉及工作记忆容量的个体差异对句法上非歧义句结构的影响，然而，对二语学习者在简单、主动句中加工题元关系时的工作记忆所扮演角色的研究却少之又少。由于加工简单的非歧义句时，被试似乎并不需要具备特别大的工作记忆容量。然而一些实验数据说明在线句子理解过程中，二语高广度个体比低广度个体更可能运用生命性信息。

本实验的目的是探讨是否由阅读广度测试和听力广度测试评估的二语个体工作记忆容量差异会制约简单、主动英语句子中题元关系的在线加工。实验数据表明句子题元加工过程时，具备高和低容量的二语被试实时运用生命性信息，而不是世界知识信息时存在着显著质的差异。

在控制条件和生命性违反条件间的比较中（例如，"The dog/cup is biting the milkman."），二语高容量和低容量被试都对于句子中第一个无生命名词显示出加工负荷，引发了 P600 效应；而二语高容量被试的 P600 振幅更大。在二语高容量被试中获得的 ERP 生命性效应可以说明，与二语低容量被试相比，由于二语高容量被试具有大的工作记忆容量，当阅读句子中第一个名词时，他们会利用这种生命性信息在句子中委派临时的题元角色。在相关分析中，更大的工作记忆容量与更大的 P600 振幅相关。未来研究还需要进一步测试这一种假设的有效性。

同时，在世界知识违反条件和控制条件的比较中（例如，"The cook/dog is biting the milkman."），实验数据没有发现二语高和低广度被试之间存在着显著差异。在此类情形下，动词是一种可能的但更不合理的施事行为。实验数据表明，作为一种工作记忆容量的功能，二语高和低容量被试句子加工过程中在线利用世界知识信息时并不存在差异。然而,生命性信息在句子题元加工过程中扮演着不同寻常的角色,因此,二语高和低广度被试提取和整合与主语名词的生命性相关的题元组合信息时,可能比他们提取词汇—语义信息和世界知识信息需要更多的加工资源。

二语高和低容量被试句子加工过程中在线利用生命性信息的显著差异,反映了工作记忆容量确实影响二语学习者对简单、主动句子的加工。

第九章

任务复杂度和工作记忆容量
对二语写作表现的影响
——学习者情感因素的作用

9.1 引言

写作是一种复杂的心理认知活动,语言的加工、理解和产出过程受到多种因素的影响,其中包括任务因素和学习者因素。

任务复杂度是任务因素的主要特点之一,主要与完成任务所需要的认知需求有关。相关研究表明,由于语言学习者认知资源的局限性,复杂度的增加会显著影响语言的产出(Skehan, 1998; Robinson, 2001a, 2001b; Zalbidea, 2017)。任务复杂度的增加对学习者构建和重组中介语起着关键作用。近年来,记忆与语言理解的关系越来越受到人们的关注,较为普遍的研究领域是工作记忆在处理认知任务中的作用。写作过程中的能力限制问题有必要在记忆理论的影响下加以考虑。语言研究者指出,信息在加工过程中存储于工作记忆中,工作记忆在写作等复杂任务中具有协调作用(Baddeley, 1986, 2003; Daneman & Carpenter, 1980; Kellogg, 1996; Grundy & Timmer, 2017)。由于工作记忆控制语言产出过程的各个层次,决定了一个人能够处理的输入、处理和输出需求的数量。考虑到这些资源限制时,工作记忆容量对任务表现也会产生一定的影响。为了了解任务复杂度和工作记忆容量对写作产出的影响,本章还试图分析情感因素作为中介学习变量的潜在作用。研究发现,影响二语学习的因素不仅包括认知水平,还包括学习者内部的情感因素(Bandura,1977;Spaulding,1992;Swain & Lapkin,1998;Arnold,2000;Brown,2002;Sucuolu,2017;张凯,2021)。目前,很多研究都将"情感过滤假说"用于英语教学。Dulay & Burt(1977)针对二语习得的表现提出了"情感过滤假说",旨在探讨语言习得过程中的情感因素。基于该假说,学习者在接受语言输入时,受不同情感因素的影响会发生不同程度的情感过滤,语言产出会有不同的表现。由此可以得出,情感因素一定程度上在任务特征与工作记忆之间起着中介的作用。Swain & Lapkin(1998)分析了影响二语写作的因素,指出写作水平一定程度上与学习者的认知能力、思维差异、情感因素等有联系。总而言之,二语写作表现要综合考查多方面的因素。

　　Skehan(1998)从语言产出的复杂度、准确度和流利度来综合衡量学习者的二语写作水平。这三个方面从不同角度反映了学习者在写作过程中注意力资源的分配问题。在写作过程中,学习者需要充分利用注意和记忆等认知资源以及情感因素,促进中介语的发展和第二语言体系的重构,从而提高写作产出的质量。本文探讨了任务复杂度和工作记忆容量对二语写作产出的影响,并探讨了情感因素的个体差异对这些影响的调节机制。

9.2　二语写作中的任务复杂度和工作记忆容量

　　"任务"特征对学习者第二语言产出的影响是语言研究和语言教学中理解语言习得过程的基础。因此,对于任务复杂度的理解一直是二语研究中的一个重要的环节。工作记忆容量是一种重要的认知因素,由于工作记忆容量的有限性,语言产出在三个维度之间会有不同的表现。因此,不同工作记忆容量的学习者在任务复杂度不同的情况下对二语写作产出有不同的影响。

9.2.1　二语写作中的任务复杂度

　　认知心理学视角下,学习者任务的完成与个人的认知加工能力相关。研究发现,不同的任务设计对语言产出的影响不同(Skehan & Foster,1999;Robinson,2001a,2001b;Brown,2002)。在二语习得领域,任务复杂度作为主要特点引起了广泛关注。Robinson(2001b)指出,任务复杂度是任务结构对语言学习者的注意力、记忆、推理和其他信息处理要求的结果。这些认知需求的差异是由任务设计的不同而形成的。也就是说，与复杂的任务相比，认知上更简单、资源需求更少的任务具有更低的错误率，能更快地被完成，因而不容易受到竞争任务的干扰。韩亚文、刘思（2019）同样认为，任务复杂度是任务结构要素施加给学习者的认知负荷，会影响学习者的认知加工过程。因此，任务复杂度可以解释学习者在成功完成两个不同任务时的内在差异，即内在语言系统的变化。比如，一些任务可能会让学习者优先考虑语言产出的流利性，其他任务则会让学习者优先考虑产出的复杂性或准确性。关于认知复杂度如何影响第二语言学习者的注意力分配，进而影响语言的产出，主要存在两种对立的理论解释：Robinson & Foster（1999，2001）的多重注意资源模型及 Skehan（1998，2001）和 Skehan & Foster（2001）的有限注意力模型。

多重注意资源模型，又称认知假说，认为学习者可以进入多个非竞争性资源池，只要不占用相同的认知资源，语言产出就不会受到影响。也就是说，结构复杂性和功能复杂性是相互关联的。基于此，Robinson（2001a）把影响任务复杂度的因素分为资源指引型和资源消耗型。资源指引维度下，学习者试图映射任务中不断增加的概念和功能要求，注意力资源倾向于写作产出的形式，语言的复杂度和准确度会随之提高，但会对流利度产生负面影响。这种情况下，语言表现被预测为不那么流利，但更准确和复杂。相比之下，通过操控资源分散变量来增加任务的复杂性时，复杂任务对注意力和工作记忆的需求更大，学习者已有的知识会受限，写作产出的三个维度都会受到制约。这种类型的任务复杂性被假设为有助于加工过程的自动化，最终产出更流畅的语言。更重要的是，认知假说声称，当任务同时在两个维度上变得复杂时，可能会对语言产生协同效应。总之，不同维度下任务复杂度的增加对写作产出的影响不同。

基于信息加工理论和工作记忆理论的有限注意力模型，又称竞争假说，认为对认知任务要求或语言表现的关注可以被视为一组有限的心理资源，必须由各种处理活动共享。Skehan & Foster（2001）指出，由于工作记忆容量和注意资源的有限性，增加任务的认知需求会越来越多地占用认知资源。在这种情况下，学习者会对写作输出的某一方面给予更多的关注和修改，如复杂度、准确度和流利度。因此，语言产出存在两方面的竞争：一是形式和意义的竞争;二是准确度和复杂度的竞争。当面对一个认知要求较高的任务时,学习者会首先注意传达意义,最后注意输出语言的复杂性和准确性。由此可以得出,意义优先于形式;流利度优先于复杂度和准确度。因此,为了使写作语言发展达到最佳水平,学习者需要在这三个维度之间建立平衡。

　　简而言之,两种认知模型均充分肯定学习者在任务完成过程中注意力资源投入量的重要性。由于两种模型对注意力资源分配的理解不同,因而对语言输出的预测存在着显著差异。显然,两者的理论都对二语写作表现有一定的影响。然而,对语言产出的预测不仅局限于任务因素方面,学习者因素与任务因素相互作用,从而决定上述预测效果的程度。

9.2.2　二语写作中的工作记忆容量

　　虽然任务复杂度会影响二语写作表现,但注意力资源、记忆和处理能力等认知能力的个体差异也会影响任务表现。工作记忆是一项被广泛研究的认知学习变量,它关系到个体对语言信息的存储、检索和加工能力。工作记忆最主要的特点是短时存储和有限的容量,反映的是我们在短期内将信息储存在记忆中的能力。在此基础上,Daneman & Carpenter(1980)提出了工作记忆容量,指出工作记忆具有有限的容量,由于系统内整体资源限制,工作记忆的存储和处理之间存在权衡。也就是说,用于处理功能的资源越多,用于储存信息的资源就越少。这种概念更好地反映了人类认知中存储和加工之间的动态关系。基于此,Grundy & Timmer(2017)研究发现,工作记忆广度较大的人能够更好地处理需要复杂认知能力的任务,语言产出水平较高。考虑到这些资源限制,工作记忆对写作复杂过程的影响就变得更加明显了。

　　基于 Baddeley(1986)的工作记忆模型,Kellogg(1996)将写作过程分为形成、执行和监察。形成包括两部分:一是产生和组织思想;二是翻译,指的是学习者把自己的思想转换成有意义、语法正确的句子。形成过程的目的是产生想法,构建写作框架,需要工作记忆的参与,也需要更多的认知努力;因此,中央执行器和视觉空间模板被激活。执行指句子的实际产出,中央执行器和语音循环参与其中。监察包括阅读文本之后编辑文中的语言错误或结构,这就涉及语音循环和中央执行系统。写作模型明确指出了不同工作记忆成分是如何跟写作产出的三个阶段联系在一起的。写作过程理论上是递归性的,而不是线性的。学习者在写作加工过程中需要同时激活这三个子过程,激活的程度取决于工作记忆容量,这就对中央执行系统提出了重要的要求。因此,部分写作过程需要达到一种自动化的状态,从而促进写作过程的同步协调。除认知因素以外,学习者的情感因素这一变量也在任务复杂度和工作记忆容量之间起到中介的作用。

9.3　二语写作中的情感过滤假说

Krashen(1982)提出了一套完整的二语习得模式,该模式对二语习得有着重要影响,其中情感过滤假说对习得效率起着关键作用,一定程度上会影响二语写作产出。

9.3.1　二语写作中的情感过滤假说

Dulay & Burt(1977)提出情感过滤说,认为情感过滤是一种内在的处理系统,通过情感因素来控制语言的吸收。在此基础上,Krashen总结了为什么所有的学习者不能在同样的条件下很好地习得第二语言。Krashen认为,习得过程中只有输入是不够的,需将输入转化为吸收,形成语言习得机制,从而习得语言。Krashen进一步提出了情感过滤假说,认为情感过滤起着干扰和限制语言输入的作用。也就是说,情感因素起着过滤器的作用,它减少了学习者能够理解的语言输入量。不同情感学习态度的学习者对语言学习输入有不同的过滤能力:拥有积极情绪态度的学习者对语言学习输入的过滤能力较低,促进了语言输入的高效加工;相反,拥有消极情绪态度的学习者对语言学习输入的过滤能力较强,阻碍了语言输入的高效加工。因此,情感过滤并不直接影响二语学习的效果,但是可以阻止可理解性输入到达习得机制。

从情感过滤假说的角度讲,情感因素强烈影响学习者的输入量和多少输入转化为吸收。因此,学习者语言能力差异的一个重要原因就是学习者在语言转换过程中受到的情感过滤的影响不同。因此,在二语写作过程中,学习者应该适度地调整情绪,为语言输出提供可理解性输入。

9.3.2　二语写作中情感过滤假说的三要素

情感因素影响第二语言的学习,尤其是学习速度,而不是学习路径和方向。基于此,Krashen 确定了三种情感因素:动机、焦虑和自信心。

动机是影响语言习得的一个重大因素。Brown(2002)指出,动机是学习者对目标做出选择的程度,以及为追求目标所付出的努力。动机是引起和维持学习者某项行为并促使行为朝着一个方向前进的一种力量。二语习得过程中,主要的动机为学习动机。从心理学角度讲,学习动机指的是激励学习者不断追求上进的一种心理状态,具有驱动和指导的作用。适度的学习动机可以提高学习者的信息加工水平,对学习有积极的影响。Saulding(1992)的研究表明,动机直接而深刻地影响着学习者使用外语学习策略的频率,决定着学习者在语言学习中接受了多少输入。

焦虑是另一个特殊的因素。根据 Arnold(2000)的说法,焦虑是学习者学习时担心犯错而产生的焦急情绪。在二语习得领域中,情境型焦虑受到了广泛关注,其从某种程度上讲也是一种驱动力。也就是说,部分学习者倾向于与其他学习者比较,发现有较大差距时,会产生焦虑,这种焦虑会促使学习者为缩小差距而努力学习;反之,如果学习者焦虑过高,语言在大脑中的加工转换一定程度上会受到影响,从而会阻碍语言的输入和产出。只有那些输出焦虑较低的学习者,才会通过产出越来越复杂的语言来响应复杂的推理任务要求。因此,在二语写作过程中,学习者要尽可能地将焦虑情绪控制在一个合理的范围内,确保语言的输入被大脑所吸收,从而确保写作产出的质量。

自信心是指学习者是否相信自己能完成某一学习目标的心理状态。自信心强的学生由于学习动机明确,对学习语言的能力有信心,从而能更快地提高二语学习水平。学习者自身的自信程度与自我效能感的强弱有关。Bandura(1977)指出,自我效能感是个体对自身是否能完成某一任务的信念。也就是说,如果学习者有信心完成某一项任务,那么其自我效能感就较强;反之,自我效能感就弱。因此,自信心的强弱也会影响写作语言的输入与输出。

情感过滤假说表明,在二语写作过程中,如果写作动机高、自信心和焦虑感程度低,过滤能力就弱。因此,可理解性的语言输入就会经过"情感过滤器"顺利进入语言习得机制,促进写作的进程;反之,情感过滤强的情况下,会形成心理障碍,并阻碍语言输入,因此,二语写作产出就会受到影响。

9.4 结论

二语写作是一个复杂的认知过程,语言的产出质量受多方面因素综合的影响。总体而言,任务复杂度、工作记忆容量与学习者的情感因素一定程度上都会影响二语写作的产出质量。随着任务复杂性的增加,任务的认知需求和情感因素的个体差异有望越来越多地区分基于任务的语言产出的表现。语言产出过程中,当学习者拥有满足复杂任务要求所需的认知资源和情感因素时,语言产出就会有积极的效果;反之,则会产生消极影响。但是,由于任务类型、写作策略和写作环境等其他变量,对写作语言表现的三个维度可能会产生不同的影响,人们可能会更一致地倾向于支持或不支持某一假设。因此,未来关于这方面的研究可以从不同的角度去进一步考察,例如,任务复杂度的设定、工作记忆容量的测量方法以及其他情感因子。

通过对多种因素的综合分析,本研究可以进一步验证和完善认知假说和竞争假说,并且帮助教师合理设计教学任务。首先,教师在课堂中可以通过不同的方式提高学生的工作记忆容量,使学生在写作过程中合理利用资源,从而产出高质量的语言。其次,教师可以使教学模式从传统的英语写作模式向以"任务"为中心的写作模式转变。教师可以利用任务复杂度框架设计不同难度的写作任务,使学习者根据任务的认知要求合理分配注意力资源。例如,在最初的写作教学时,可以设计复杂度低的任务,提高写作的准确度和流利度,从而减少学习者写作的焦虑情绪;然后循序渐进地增加任务的复杂度,提高语言产出的复杂性。按照认知复杂性的顺序能有效地促进第二语言的发展,重构现有的第二语言表征。最后,单纯地运用认知理论进行教学是不够的,情感是影响语言学习和教学的重要因素;教学过程中要使学生达到一个相对平衡的心理状态,降低情感过滤。因此,写作教学过程中,要综合考查多方面的因素,通过提供最大程度的可理解性输入,从而产出高质量的写作。

附　录

附录 1

阅读广度测试

1. The nurse left the patient and refused to help him in <u>emergency</u>.

2. The burglar schemed to steal the money and prepared the <u>map</u>.

3. The student forgot to do the assignment and failed the <u>exam</u>.

4. The athlete trained himself very hard and injured his leg <u>unluckily</u>.

5. The artist declined to sell the painting and made a living by <u>begging</u>.

6. The politician gave a wonderful speech and won the loud <u>applause</u>.

7. The scientist aspired to win the prize and worked hard in the <u>lab</u>.

8. The nephew borrowed money from his uncle and refused to pay <u>back</u>.

9. The tailor sewed the worn suit and repaired the broken <u>zipper</u>.

10. The singer received the flowers from the girls and began to <u>sing</u>.

11. The conductor gave the audience a deep bow and then turned <u>around</u>.

12. The chairman entered the room and shook hands with everyone <u>warmly</u>.

13. The boy took off his shoes and began to climb up the <u>tree</u>.

14. The pilot hesitated to fly the plane and left the <u>airport</u>.

15. The child refused to clean the room and fell asleep <u>instead</u>.

16. The shopper bought the expensive coat and was given a discount.

17. The criminal escaped from the jail and killed two innocent persons.

18. The secretary made the coffee for the chairman and attended the meeting.

19. The typist typed the paper and submitted it to the boss.

20. The waitress walked into the noisy lobby and served the banquet.

21. The two robbers broke into the shop and stole the necklace.

22. The wise policeman arrested the thief and began to interrogate him.

23. The milkman accepted the money from the lady and delivered the milk.

24. The boy bought a bunch of roses and sent them to his girlfriend.

25. The father went to the hospital and saw the son in surgery.

26. The mother baked some bread and drank some coffee in the kitchen.

27. The hunter put on his fur coat and walked into the forest.

28. The couple booked a cruise and planned to travel the following day.

29. The passenger fastened his seat belt and turned off his mobile phone.

30. The detective followed the tricky suspect and lost the trail unexpectedly.

31. The manager decided to hire the man and by impressed his courage.

32. The driver was stopped the taxi and threaten by the passenger.

33. The model posed for the company without reward and to sign contract.

34. The engineer built the bridge and paying very well by the government.

35. The spy started to tell the truth and was lied for years.

36. The florist decorated the big church and good at many weddings.

37. The repairman was fix the television and was removing bad parts.

38. The librarian refusing to lend the books and was closed the library.

39. The prince yearning to marry the pretty girl and was proposed.

40. The writer was edited the detective novel and requesting more money.

41. The clerk helped collecting the money in the store and firing for theft.

42. The woman agreed to seeing the play and enter the theatre.

43. The baby permitted to touch the vase and is put flowers into it.

44. The worker went on vacation and given a raise after the journey.

45. The schoolgirl recited the poem and be very nervous in the public.

46. The astronomer attempted to watch the comet and too busy <u>reading</u>.

47. The musician joined the orchestra and not very good at <u>cooperation</u>.

48. The judge have to stop the trial and asking to <u>resign</u>.

49. The activitist addressed the audience and was prepared to all <u>night</u>.

50. The soldier watched residents crossing the bridge and into the <u>distance</u>.

51. The referee making the decision to stopping the basketball game at <u>once</u>.

52. The mother looked after the children after school and up the <u>dishes</u>.

53. The sailor set sail and through a new route of India and <u>Asia</u>.

54. The man set the table to distributing the forks and <u>knives</u>.

55. The conscientious accountant discovering the error and to balance the <u>books</u>.

56. The actress struggled to remember her lines and ready to <u>quit</u>.

57. The photographer took the beautiful pictures and to up the <u>hill</u>.

58. The babysitter pat the baby on the back and singing the <u>song</u>.

59. Tom win the first prize in the competition and off the <u>campus</u>.

60. Mary marry with John at last and happily live <u>together</u>.

听力广度测试

1. A watermelon is a large fruit with green skin, pink flesh and black <u>seeds</u>. （True）

2. Newton was inspired by an apple falling down from the <u>tree</u>. （True）

3. Air is very essential and important for human being's <u>life</u>. （True）

4. Kentucky Fried chicken is a fast-food restaurant chain that specializes in fried <u>chicken</u>. （True）

5. The formal and standard language for Korean is <u>Japanese</u>. （False—Korean）

6. Beijing, in the southern part of China, is the <u>capital</u>. （False—Northern）

7. Water is a kind of solid which forms the world's streams, lakes and <u>oceans</u>. （False—substance）

8. Alfred Nobel, for whom the Nobel Prizes were named, invented <u>radio</u>. （False—dynamite）

9. Mosquito is a small flying insect that sucks the blood of people and <u>animals</u>.

（True）

10. The Titanic didn't have enough lifeboats to save almost everyone on <u>board</u>. （True）

11. Ears are the most important auditory organ of human <u>being</u>.（True）

12. A boy is a child who will grow up to be a <u>woman</u>.（False—man）

13. There are ten zeros in the number one <u>million</u>.（False—six）

14. The Great Wall is one of American key scenic <u>spots</u>.（False—Chinese）

15. A sheep is a farm animal which is covered with thick hair called <u>wool</u>. （True）

16. An island is a piece of land that is completely surrounded by <u>water</u>.（True）

17. A mobile phone can make and receive telephone calls over a radio <u>link</u>. （True）

18. There are altogether 5 stars on Chinese national <u>flag</u>.（True）

19. On Oct. 10, 1949, People's Republic of China was <u>founded</u>.（False—Oct.1, 1949）

20. In September, 2018, terrorists crashed two planes into New York's World Trade <u>Centre</u>.（False—2001）

21. Scotland is the most northern state in the United <u>States</u>.（False—United Kingdom）

22. The People's Republic of China has the smallest population in <u>Asia</u>. （False—largest）

23. The first president of the United States is President <u>Obama</u>.（False—Washington）

24. There are 52 weeks and 11 months in a <u>year</u>.（False—12）

25. A dog is often kept by people as a pet or to <u>guard</u>.（True）

26. A classroom is a room in a school where lessons take <u>place</u>.（True）

27. When the weather gets colder, the snow will begin to <u>melt</u>.（False—warmer）

28. Basketball is a kind of game played between two <u>teams</u>.（True）

29. The sun rises from the west in the <u>morning</u>.（False—east）

30. The person who navigates the ship is called cook. (False—captain)

31. A clock is an instrument that shows what time of day it is. (True)

32. Both prince and princess belong to a royal family. (True)

33. The smallest country in the world is the United Kingdom. (False—Vatican)

34. The moon is the object that you often see in the sky at night. (True)

35. The 2008 summer Olympic Games was held in Beijing. (True)

36. A rose is a flower, often with a pleasant smell. (True)

37. Summer is the season between spring and fall. (True)

38. Snow falls from the sky in the cold winter. (True)

39. The most southern country in Africa is South Africa. (True)

40. You can find the country of United States in Pacific Ocean. (True)

41. On the eve of Spring Festival, Chinese usually watch spring festival program. (True)

42. Apple is a company that sells laptops and smart phones. (True)

43. Harvard University is a university in the city of Paris. (False—New Haven)

44. For a normal person, we usually have two arms and two legs. (True)

45. Shakespeare is famous for his sonnets and four tragedies. (True)

46. The most sensitive organ in our body is hands. (False—skin)

47. The animal referred as the ship of the desert is dog. (False—camel)

48. The coldest continent in the world is South Asia. (False—Antarctica)

49. In the United States, American people usually speak American English. (True)

50. Edison was the first person who invented the light bulb. (True)

51. Lu Xun is a very famous writer in American literature. (False—Chinese)

52. A university is an institution in which students study for degrees. (True)

53. Ernest Hemingway won Nobel Prize for his contribution to Chemistry. (False—literature)

54. A year usually has four seasons and 365 days. (True)

55. Beijing University is a famous university in New York. (False—China)

56. The Battle of Waterloo marked American emperor Napoleon's final <u>defeat</u>. （False—French）

57. Winston Churchill was the important leader of the Soviet <u>Union</u>. （False—United Kingdom）

58. The largest coffee growing country in the world is <u>Japan</u>. （False—Brazil）

59. August 15 of every year is a traditional Chinese festival—the Mid-Autumn <u>Festival</u>. (True）

60. The White House is the official residence of British Prime <u>Minister</u>. （False—American）

附录 2

Comparative Analysis of News Discourse on Public Health Emergencies from the Perspective of Proximization Theory

Yingchan Yan, Fang Xu

College of Foreign Languages, Qingdao University of Science and Technology,
No. 99, Songling Road, Laoshan District, Qingdao, Shandong, 266061, China

Abstract: This paper builds a small corpus based on *China Daily's* coverage of SARS and COVID-19 and analyses the proximization strategies and metonymic words used on the spatial, temporal and axiological axes. The study finds that the two public health emergencies' coverage at different times utilizes plenty of proximization strategies and metonymic words. The difference is that the COVID-19 news draws upon significantly more proximization strategies than the SARS news. The findings suggest that from SARS to COVID-19, Chinese media have accumulated substantial experience in practice and become increasingly professional. Specifically, during the COVID-19 outbreak, they can more skillfully employ discursive strategies to guide the public to respond to the central government's call for anti-epidemic actively and capitalize on discursive strategies to establish a harmonious atmosphere for all individuals to combat the epidemic and enhance the determination and cohesion in the fight.

Keywords: *China Daily*; SARS; COVID-19; proximization strategies; metonymic words

1. Introduction

According to *Regulation on Preparedness for and Response to Emergent Public Health Hazards* (2003), a public health emergency refers to a contagious disease or large-scale event that suddenly poses a public health concern and requires urgent measures. SARS and COVID-19 are two representative major public health emergencies in China. In 2003, SARS was spread throughout China, which is the seriously devastating epidemic of the 21st century. The second public health emergency is COVID-19. During the epidemic phase, numerous media actively guide social opinion while conveying information to the public. In short, the discourse on epidemic prevention and control has shown rich discourse characteristics (Zhang & Wang, 2020: 115). As a result, the study of epidemic-related discourse has become an important area of interest for linguistic scholars, such as news narrative (Zhang & Ji, 2021), social media discourse (Yao et al., 2021), heroic discourse (Shan et al., 2021), and metadiscourse (Yang, 2021). However, few studies have explored changes in the cognition of epidemic-related news discourse from a macro-temporal perspective.

Proximization Theory can be loosely described as a discursive strategy that ultimately legitimizes the speaker's defence. This legitimization comes from a process wherein an entity with opposite values is constantly approaching the speaker. The addressees perceive this approach and thus believe that the speaker is acting in the right way. It has been applied to discourse studies on various subjects, such as war discourse (Cap, 2013), non-traditional security discourse (Zhao & Zhao, 2021), immigration discourse (Wu & Niu, 2018), and so-called "Huawei threat" discourse (Zhou, 2021). The above studies have confirmed the effectiveness of Proximization Theory in the Critical Discourse Analysis, but most of them have only been taken using Proximization Theory alone, thus lacking a broader theoretical framework. Although some scholars (Hart, 2010; Zhang, 2016; Li & Pan, 2021) have attempted to combine Proximization Theory with other theories from Cognitive Linguistics such as metaphor and categorization, the combination with metonymy remains unclear.

Given this, this paper employs Critical Cognitive Linguistics as a theoretical framework. It develops two small corpora to compare and contrast the proximization strategies and metonymic words used in SARS and COVID-19 news in an attempt to depict a convergent path while exploring the parallels and distinctions in the proximization strategies drawn upon by the media in response to public health emergencies in different periods.

2. Background on Proximization Theory and Metonymy

2.1 Proximization Theory

Chilton (2004) emphasizes that in conversation, we map out the mental space in which the world portrayed by the discourse is conceptually represented in our thinking, which is the Discourse Space. It is a three-dimensional space where the spatial, temporal and modal axes intersect at the deictic center.

The theory of proximization proposed by Cap (2013) is a further development of the Discourse Space Theory. It is a discursive strategy that presents events and states being distant in space, time and value at the lexico-grammatical level and having an imminent negative impact on the speaker and his or her addressees so that addressees perceive the threat posed by entities outside the deictic center (ODCs), which causes the addressees to be alerted and thus to take precautionary actions to avoid the expected impact. The underlying purpose of this strategy is to legitimize the speaker's actions. It can be argued that proximization is a strategically planned cognitive and pragmatic construal operation in which the speaker organizes his or her speech (Cap, 2017a: 24).

More specifically, this construal operation could be divided into spatial proximization, temporal proximization and axiological proximization. The threat can come from these three axes that intersect at the deictic center. (1) The first axis is spatial proximization, where the ODCs are perceived by the addressees as encroaching on the IDCs at the level of physical space. At the lexical-grammatical level, there are six modes of expression: noun phrases denoting elements of the deictic center (IDCs), noun phrases denoting elements ODCs, motion and directionality verb phrases referring to the movement of ODCs towards IDCs, action verb phrases referring to the influence exerted by the ODCs on IDCs, abstract noun phrases indicating the anticipation due to the influence of ODCs on IDCs, and abstract noun phrases indicating the result due to the influence of ODCs on IDCs (Cap, 2013: 75-109). (2) The second axis is temporal proximization which means that the threat is approaching. Thus, it is so urgent that the addressees must take immediate precautions. At the lexico-grammatical level, temporal proximization can be expressed in five forms: indefinite noun phrases constructing the impact of ODCs in other temporal frames, the simultaneous use of the general past tense and the present perfect constructing an infinite extension of the threat of past events to the future, nominalized noun phrases presupposing the conditions about ODCs impact to occur at any moment in the future, modal verb phrases constructing continuous ODCs impact between the present and the future, and parallel contrastive sentence forms constructing oppositional and privileged futures extending from the now (Cap, 2013: 111-126). (3) The third axis is axiological proximization, which is used to identify the conflict between the values of IDCs and ODCs. There are three types of expression at the lexico-grammatical level: noun phrases denoting positive values or ideologies of IDCs, noun phrases denoting negative values or ideologies of ODCs, and linear arrangements of lexico-grammatical phrases constructing materialization of the ODCs' negative values in the IDCs' space (Cap, 2013: 119-122). The three aspects of the proximization strategy drive the ODC entities closer to the addresser-addressees territory with adverse effects. Therefore, addresser and addressees are forced to adopt relevant measures to avoid harm so that the discursive strategy of proximization becomes one of the main legitimizing tools in political discourse (Cap, 2008: 39).

The main purpose of the public discourse on the epidemic is to provide information and explain the current situation promptly to remind the addresses about the destructiveness of the virus. Eventually, the public will comply with the government's appeal to take precautionary steps in a positive and orderly manner. This intention is consistent with the essence of Proximization Theory. Consequently, epidemic discourse is suitable to be analyzed by Proximization Theory.

2.2 Metonymy

Metonymy is a fundamental cognitive and linguistic process (Nerlich, 2006: 109) in which one entity represents the other based on relations of contiguity (Evans & Green, 2015: 311). One is the cognitive reference point, whereas the other is the goal. In this way, the addressees are guided to perceive the target domain from the perspective of cognitive reference point (Langacker, 2008: 69). Many studies have explored the cognitive mechanisms of language from the perspective of metonymy. Wang (2014), for example, provides a unified explanation for Referentialism based on the metonymy theory. Wei (2019) explores the metonymic mechanism of Chinese idioms. Apart from that, many scholars have conducted metonymic studies from the perspective of Critical Discourse Analysis. For example, Li & Wang (2015) attempt to set a theoretical framework for critical metonymy analysis. Later, Hu (2019) further refines the research framework of critical metonymy analysis and applies it to a specific corpus to explore the metonymic words in courtroom discourse. Mclachlan (2021) takes multimodal discourse as the research object to analyze the role of metonymy in high school web page narrative and reveals the neoliberal ideology in it. These empirical studies amply confirm that metonymic analysis is a crucial component of Critical Discourse Analysis because of its mighty explanatory power in the cognitive model and ideological study of texts (Zhang & Zhang, 2012). Therefore, it is an inevitable trend to use metonymy to conduct critical cognition research.

Metonymy and Proximization Theory have the basis for building a framework for integration. First, both theories complement Critical Discourse Analysis from a cognitive perspective. In relation to theoretical foundations, both of them focus on the cognitive construal of texts. Secondly, in terms of research methodology, they are both based on the text for the identification, description and interpretation of discursive strategies. Thus, Proximization Theory can combine with metonymy to better understand the ideology behind the language.

3. Methods

3.1　The Corpus

The corpus for this study was collected from news articles during the early stages of SARS and COVID-19: (1) A search was conducted on the official website of *China Daily* (http://www. chinadaily. com. cn/) using *SARS* and *atypical pneumonia* as the keyword and being limited to the period from November 2002 to May 2003. Forty-five reports were randomly selected to form a corpus totaling 20,397 words in SARS reports. (2) Regarding the corpus of COVID-19, a search was conducted on the official website of *China Daily* using *COVID-19* and *novel coronavirus* as keywords, with the dates being limited to between December 2019 and June 2020. Forty-five randomly selected news articles were used as the content to constitute the corpus with 20,912 words in COVID-19 reports. This news reports cover the economy, politics, life and other topics concerning the epidemic.

3.2　Research Instruments

The corpus annotation software used in this study was UAM Corpus Tool 3.3x, which was developed for the study of Systematic-Functional Grammar, allowing for automatic annotation of content in it. In addition to this, the software had a manual annotation function. Therefore, UAM Corpus Tool 3.3x was perfectly suited to other corpus studies. The process of using the software could be divided into three parts. Above all, the corpora were input. Then, the theoretical framework (called "layers" in UAM Corpus Tool 3.3x) was listed in the software. In the end, the corpora were annotated. This meant that the lexico-grammatical item to be annotated was selected in the corpus, and the category to which the item belonged was then clicked in the theoretical framework. It was very convenient for corpus-based Critical Cognitive Linguistic analysis.

In addition, after deriving the relevant data for the two corpora through the UAM Corpus Tool 3.3x, we compared in a statistically significant way using SPSS 20.

3.3　Procedure

The study could be broken down into three sections. (1) Firstly, the news was retrieved from the *China Daily's* official website and picked out to form the corpus. And then, the irrelevant information such as headlines and photo descriptions were deleted. (2) In the second stage, the corpus was manually annotated and counted with the help of the UAM Corpus Tool 3.3x to obtain statistical data for each lexical-grammatical item. It should be noted that the adaptability of Proximization Theory varies with different types of discourse (Cap, 2017b: 17). In the corpus of this study, few abstract nouns were indicating the result due to the influence of ODCs on IDCs, but many concrete nouns indicating the result due to the influence of ODCs on IDCs were involved. Therefore, based on the characteristics of the present corpus, this study made a small adjustment to the lexico-grammatical forms reflecting the proximization strategies: the abstract noun phrases indicating the influence of ODCs on IDCs were expanded to noun phrases. Besides, the statistics followed the 0.1% threshold principle. That is, the lexico-grammatical items counted should occur at least once in every 1,000 words on average (Cap, 2013: 108-109). Tables were then plotted based on the statistical results. (3) Finally, a comparative analysis was conducted to illustrate the commonalities and differences in the frequency of relevant wordings to characterize the two corpora in terms of the usage of proximization strategies and metonymic words. At this stage, comparisons between the two groups were made using chi-square tests.

4. Results and Discussion

4.1　Analysis of the Proximization in SARS News Discourse

4.1.1　Analysis of the Spatial Proximization Strategies

According to statistics, the lexico-grammatical items belonging to the spatial proximization and their frequency in the reports on SARS are shown in Table 1.

Table 1 The Use of Spatial Proximization Strategies in SARS-Related Reports

Category	The Lexico-Grammatical items	Number of Times	Frequency
Noun Phrases Denoting IDCs	doctor/expert/scientist/hospital/researcher/ medical personnel/medical staff	283	13.87
	China/the Chinese government/the Chinese Ministry of Health/the State Council	276	13.53
	travel agency/hotel/bus/market/shopping company/college/spending/universitycampus/ school/kindergarten/economy/Shenzhou V/ investment/holiday/examination/The 93rd China Export Commodities Fair	184	9.02
	Beijing/Guangdong/Taiwan Province/rural area/ Chinese mainland/village/Macao/SARS-stricken area/North China's Shanxi Province/central and western regions/China's Hong Kong Special Administrative Region	176	8.63
	people/the public/we/resident/passenger/ visitor/traveler/tourist	167	8.19
	patient/people in close contact with the sick/pupil or staff infected with SARS	131	6.42
	WHO/WHO official/Japan/some countries	84	4.12
Total		1,301	63.78
Noun Phrases Denoting ODCs	disease/coronavirus/epidemic/severe acute respiratory syndrome (SARS)/origin of the disease/atypical pneumonia	463	22.70
Total		463	22.70
Motion and Directionality Verb Phrases Referring to the Movement of ODCs Towards IDCs	climb/increase/soar/rise/surge	33	1.62
Total		33	1.62
Action Verb Phrases Referring to the Influence Exerted by the ODCs on IDCs	die/contract/infect/diagnose	82	4.02
	cancel/delay/postpone/close/trigger/ discourage/affect/damage/hit/dip/drop/drag	80	3.92
Total		162	7.94

(to be continued)

Category	The Lexico-Grammatical items	Number of Times	Frequency
Noun Phrases Indicating the Anticipation Due to the Influence of ODCs on IDCs	possibility/risk/uncertainty/further spread/ forecast for China's trade growth/China's trade deficit this year	42	2.06
Total		42	2.06
Noun Phrases Indicating the Result Due to the Influence of ODCs on IDCs	case/death	160	7.84
	cough/sneeze/fever/diarrhea/symptom/ shortness of breath	42	2.06
	impact/effect/slump/the drastic fall/trade deficit	33	1.62
Total		235	11.52
The Totality of Spatial Proximization		2, 236	109.62

It can be learned from the data in Table 1 that the core members of the IDC elements in the news about SARS are expressions such as *doctor*, *expert* and *hospital* (13.87). The emergence of SARS has had great influence on the lives of healthcare professionals. Hospitals and healthcare personnel served as the last line of defense between SARS and the general public, meaning that health personnel sacrificed their time to help fight the virus in the front lines. Placing health care workers at the deictic center gives the public a concrete perception of their commitment, which in turn leads to greater understanding and support for anti-epidemic measures. In other words, this positive guidance can increase public participation in the fight against the epidemic. The expressions such as *doctor*, *expert* and *hospital* are followed by a high proportion of expressions in the category of *China, the Chinese government* and relevant agencies and departments (13.53), all representing the interests of the general public. After SARS was confirmed to be infectious, the Chinese government was active in responding and implementing laws to prevent it from spreading further. A responsible image is brought into focus, which helps to gain popular support and increase cooperation with the call to fight the epidemic. In addition, ordinary institutions and organizations such as *school, travel agency* (9.02) and the general public as well as every ordinary person in society (8.19) frequently appear in the coverage, on account of the fact that SARS affected everyone in society and no one or organization could be left out of the prevention and control of the epidemic. This kind of emphasis forms a sense of urgency among the people to obey the call to fight the epidemic. There are also names of various places in China (8.63) in the IDC camp, such as *Beijing, Guangdong, Macao,* in which SARS cases have been reported. The diverse use of place names highlights the widespread nature of the epidemic infestation and conveys the mighty spreading and killing power of the virus in order to stress the perniciousness of SARS and prevent the public from thinking that SARS has nothing to do with them, or that their geographical area is safe. Ultimately, it makes the government's epidemic prevention policy necessary. The most frequently mentioned place name is *Beijing* (2.16), which accounts for a quarter of all place names. Although the first case of SARS appeared in Guangdong Province, the epidemic became more and more severe in Beijing as it spread. The repeated emphasis on the areas hardest hit by the epidemic is another way of unveiling the destructive nature of the virus to the public, which justifies the need to fight the epidemic.

The use of names concerning some places and agencies in these IDC entities involves metonymy (10.83), i.e., the names of locations to refer to residents and those of the agencies to refer to officials or staff.

(1) More progress is needed to assist China's fight against an epidemic that had claimed the lives of 64 people on the Chinese mainland by Tuesday. (Apr. 17, 2003)

In example (1), *China's fight* actually refers to the resistance of all Chinese people. Based on the affiliation between the source and target domain, this metonymy cognitively focuses on China as a whole. The implication is that the whole country unites in the fight against the epidemic, which further suggests the determination to win in the context of proximization strategies paying attention to the malignancy of SARS.

The ODC elements in SARS-related reports are the SARS-related expressions (22.70). SARS not only is dangerous to people's health, but also affects the normal life of the general public. The placement of SARS as the sole entity at the periphery implies, on the one hand, that the primary entity we fight against is SARS. On the other hand, it is underlined that SARS is so aggressive that so many IDC entities (63.78) are needed to defend against ODC entities. The perniciousness of SARS is highlighted. In these expressions about SARS, "whole-for-part metonymy" is involved, namely *the disease* referring to SARS (4.36). SARS is one of the diseases. Relatively speaking, the public would be familiar with the term *disease* rather than SARS because SRAS is the newer thing. Therefore, it is more cognitively economical to put *the disease* in the semantic focus. That is, *disease* activates SARS destructiveness directly in the public perception and is a direct basis for confirming the harmfulness of SARS.

On the basis of IDCs and ODCs, the media also use action verb phrases referring to the influence exerted by the ODCs on IDCs (7.94) and noun phrases indicating the result due to the influence of ODCs on IDCs (11.52) many times to construct the imminence of the risk of SARS:

(2) The unprecedented measure underlined tough actions taken by governments to break the chain of transmission for the mysterious disease, which has killed 17 people and infected more than 450 around the world, most of them in Asia, in the past two weeks. (Mar. 26, 2003)

(3) Many exhibitions, trade fairs and other trade-promotion activities have been cancelled or postponed due to fears over SARS. (May 8, 2003)

The successive use of two verbs denoting infection in Example (2) gives the reader a more tangible and visual sense of the spread of SARS. This is a concrete manifestation of the negative behavior of SARS, which causes a fear of SARS in the population and legitimizes the fight against the epidemic to raise awareness of precautions. In Sentence (3), many events such as exhibitions and trade fairs had to be cancelled because of the potential danger of SARS, which reflects the epidemic's impact on the normal functioning of society. This language strategy aims to lead the public to believe that SARS is extremely destructive. At the same time, it suggests that it is difficult for the general public to have a normal life during the epidemic. Under the circumstances, people who want to return to their previous state of life would proactively take effective measures to join in preventing and controlling the epidemic.

(4) As of yesterday, 2,722 cases, including 106 deaths, have been reported by 16 countries. This represents an increase of 51 cases and 3 deaths when compared with the previous day's totals. (Apr. 11, 2003)

(5) Cut any journey or travel plans if you or your travelling companions begin to show signs of any of the following-fever, coughing, diarrhea or shortness of breath. Avoid contact with others if you have any of these symptoms and seek immediate medical help. (Apr. 16, 2003)

The number of confirmed *cases* and *deaths* in Example (4) presents the most severe consequences of SARS to alert readers. This emphasizes the damaging consequences of the virus on the IDCs and shapes the public's negative perception of the virus. As a result, the public will support outbreak prevention and control emotionally and behaviourally. At the same time, the *case* in (4) originally refers to the example of occurrence of something. However, here *case* belongs to "event-for-person metonymy". Specifically, it literally refers to 2,722 SARS cases but essentially refers to the number of people suffering from the infection. Similarly, *death* originally refers to the event of dying or departure from life, but here it is turned into the number of people who died of the disease. This type of metonymy (7.35) occurs several times in SARS-related reports, where euphemisms are used to show respect for the patients and the deceased. In Example (5), the symptoms of SARS are specifically listed to demonstrate in detail the negative consequences of SARS and reinforce the legitimaization and necessity of epidemic prevention and control.

4.1.2　Analysis of the Temporal Proximization Strategies

According to statistics, the lexico-grammatical items belonging to the temporal proximization and their frequency in the reports on SARS are represented in Table 2.

Table 2　The Use of Temporal Proximization Strategies in SARS-Related Reports

Category	The Lexico-Grammatical Items	Number of Times	Frequency
Nominalized Noun Phrases Presupposing the Conditions about ODCs Impact to Occur at Any Moment in the Future	spread/increase/risk	38	1.86
Total		38	1.86
Modal Verb Phrases Constructing Continuous ODCs Impact Between the Present and the Future	will/may/might/could/would	30	1.47
Total		30	1.47
The Totality of Temporal Proximization		68	3.33

As shown in Table 2, nominalized noun phrases presupposing the conditions about ODCs' impact to occur at any moment in the future (1.86) and modal verb phrases constructing continuous ODCs' impact between the present and the future (1.47) are frequently used in all temporal proximization strategies in SARS-related reports.

(6) And so long as China takes effective measures in treating SARS patients and prevents the further spread of the disease, the country is capable of maintaining the growth advantages of its economy, said Wang. (Apr. 29, 2003)

(7) Presently, the disease outbreak will not have a large negative effect on investment, but it will have some effect on domestic spending, especially the tourism and catering industry. (Apr. 29, 2003)

In Example (6), the phrase *the further spread* presupposes the possibility of further spread of SARS and suggests no fixed point at which such spread will occur. In this situation, the dangers posed by SARS can appear at any moment, and thus the public cannot take it lightly. In short, the use of *the further spread* exploits people's fear of the uncertainty of potential danger. Through this psychology, the general public become aware of the necessity of taking defensive measures and become more alert to the spread of the virus. In Example (7), the word *will* demonstrates the negative impact of the epidemic on social life and enhances the legitimization of the fight against the epidemic through its negative effects.

4.1.3　Analysis of the Axiological Proximization Strategies

According to statistics, the lexico-grammatical items belonging to the axiological proximization and their frequency in the reports on SARS are demonstrated in Table 3.

Table 3　The Use of Axiological Proximization Strategies in SARS-Related Reports

Category	The Lexico-Grammatical Items	Number of Times	Frequency
Noun Phrases Denoting Positive Values or Ideologies of IDCs	investigation/findings/treatment/ researchmeasure/precautions/test reagent/test kit/vaccine/fund	252	12.35
	responsibility/respect/gratitude/devotion/ reverence/appreciation/dedication/co-operation/ support	39	1.91
	fight/frontline/day and night/victory/war/ campaign/brunt/battle/defense/struggle	31	1.52
Total		322	15.79
Noun Phrases Denoting Negative Values or Ideologies of ODCs	virus/coronavirus	103	5.05
	fear/concern/worry	27	1.32
Total		130	1.32
The Totality of Axiological Proximization		452	22.16

From the data in Table 3, it is apparent that the media use various noun phrases to construct positive values of the IDC entities in the news related to SARS. Specifically speaking, a lot of terms show measures taken by the government, experts, healthcare personnel and the public to actively respond to the outbreak of SARS (12.35), such as *investigation, findings, treatment, research*. These words suggest that entities inside the deictic center do not give up in the face of threats from ODC entities and work hard to take steps to defend against entities outside the deictic center, which builds a positive image of IDCs. Many nouns that express good qualities of people (1.91), such as *responsibility, respect, gratitude, devotion, reverence, appreciation*, are frequently employed. Through these terms, readers are aware of the government's duty in response to the epidemic, the medical personnel's selflessness, and the public's regard and admiration for the hospital staff. What's more, many non-hospital workers contribute to the battle in other areas. In this way, a positive and active atmosphere is created to fight the war. In addition to this, noun phrases connoting battles (1.52), such as *fight, frontline, day and night, war, battle* and *defense*, are frequently utilized in the SARS-related news. Such terms construct the response to the outbreak of a war. In this war, health care workers are the warriors in the front line of the fight, which increases the public's aversion to ODCs and enables them to support epidemic prevention and control.

Meanwhile, the media capitalize on noun phrases to construct negative values of peripheral entities as well. The most frequently used expressions are the *virus* and *coronavirus* (5.05). The virus is responsible for the emergence of the outbreak. At the same time, the word virus itself has a negative connotation. Firstly, the virus is a type of microorganism that can cause disease in people. Therefore, in the popular conception, it is a substance of an injurious nature. Secondly, some viruses are strongly contagious and thus are capable of eliciting even more negative evaluations, which further stimulates the negative image of SARS. For these reasons, the virus is both an ODC entity and a noun denoting the negative values of ODC when referring to the harm-maker in the corpus. The conflict of values is utilized to raise public awareness of the need to combat SARS.

4.2　Analysis of the Proximization in COVID-19 News Discourse

4.2.1　Analysis of the Spatial Proximization Strategies

According to statistics, the lexico-grammatical items belonging to the spatial proximization and their frequency in the reports on COVID-19 are manifested in Table 4.

Table 4　The Use of Spatial Proximization Strategies in COVID-19-Related Reports

Category	The Lexico-Grammatical items	Number of Times	Frequency
Noun Phrases Denoting IDCs	WHO/World Health Organization/Europe/EU/ Africa/world/Kinshasa/the Democratic Republic of Congo/Peru/Syria/the United States/international community	583	27.88
	China/the Chinese government/Wuhan Municipal Health Commission/Red Cross Society of China	336	16.07
	the public/the masses/people/we/netizen/ customer/tourist/vendor	292	13.96
	medical institution/medial worker/medical researcher/doctor/professional/expert/hospital	227	10.86
	meeting/school/kindergarten/university/flight/ private organization/private sector/company/ economy/social development/food production/ transport/investment/market	178	8.51
	Wuhan/Beijing/Chaoyang/Guilin/Hong Kong/ Sichuan Province/Hebei Province/Tianjin/heavily stricken or remote area/Langfang city of Hebei	175	8.37
	patient/suspect/those who were in close contact with them	97	4.64
Total		1,888	90.28
Noun Phrases Denoting ODCs	outbreak/pneumonia/epidemic/cause of infection/ new coronavirus/new virus	485	23.19
	claim/scam/misinformation/sanction/conspiracy/ false theory	56	2.68
	bacterial lung infection/HIV/malaria/tuberculosis/ Ebola virus disease/SARS/MERS/the Spanish fever/Marburg virus infection/snake flu	53	2.53
Total		594	28.40
Motion and Directionality Verb Phrases Referring to the Movement of ODCs Towards IDCs	spread/transmit/import/expand	28	1.34
	increase/rise/raise/climb	21	1.00
Total		49	2.34

(*to be continued*)

Category	The Lexico-Grammatical items	Number of Times	Frequency
Action Verb Phrases Referring to the Influence Exerted by the ODCs on IDCs	infect/sicken/die/confirm/contract	90	4.30
	close/suspend/postpone/cancel/ban/cause/spark/ hit/affect/undermine/distract/reduce/apply/ swindle/fall/establish	79	3.78
Total		169	8.08
Noun Phrases Indicating the Anticipation Due to the Influence of ODCs on IDCs	risk/chance/transmission/spread/potential victim	78	3.73
Total		78	3.73
Noun Phrases Indicating the Result Due to the Influence of ODCs on IDCs	fatality/case/death toll/death	148	7.08
	emergency/spread/high-risk area/low-risk/ medium risk	52	2.49
	symptom/fever/cough/sign/sore throat	29	1.39
	isolation/quarantine/observation	24	1.15
Total		253	12.10
The Totality of Spatial Proximization		3,001	144.94

Through observing Table 4, it can be revealed that the media make substantial use of the spatial proximization strategies (144.94) when reporting news about COVID-19. Multiple noun phrases are identified as the IDC entities. (1) Firstly, the most frequently utilized noun phrases are international organizations and some international place names (27.88). International organizations are dominated by *WHO*. International place names include *Europe*, *Africa*, *Congo*, *Kinshasa*, etc. They are all victims of COVID-19. The extensive employment of names of organizations and places outside of China intangibly broadens the scope of COVID-19's impact and builds a horizontal perception of the new coronavirus among the general public. It also emphasizes that COVID-19 is not just a disease that spreads in China but a disease that spreads worldwide, which increases the harmful effect of the new coronavirus. Ultimately, it highlights the severity of the situation. On this basis, the legitimization of anti-epidemic measures has been realized, which further enhances the general public's knowledge and implementation of these measures. (2) Secondly, China and its government agencies (16.07) appear frequently in the IDC camp, which suggests that the government, being fully committed to serving its people, is a crucial role in response to the epidemic. COVID-19 was spread from person to person. The masses were more conscious of the dangers. The legitimization of epidemic prevention and control is guaranteed. (3) Thirdly, the general public (13.96) and some fields, institutions and conferences (8.51) are located in the deictic center. They are representatives of ordinary people and affairs and thus can form a community of interest with readers, implying that the epidemic is relevant to everyone and that it is not advisable to consider it personally. This discursive strategy creates a sense of fear in the minds of the public, which reinforces their vigilance against external dangers. (4) Lastly, medical professionals and medical institutions (10.86) in the IDC camp contribute the most to the fight against the epidemic. The advent of COVID-19 has greatly affected their lives and work. They work day and night in their inconvenient protective clothing to save the lives of infected people. A positive image of health care can lead to better public support for the call to fight the epidemic.

The IDC entities are also involved with metonymy to employ location names to refer to citizens and to employ government agency names to refer to authorities or personnel (12.24). In this type of metonymy, the individual characteristics of humankind are backgrounded, whereas the group characteristics of humanity are brought to the fore at a cognitive reference point, which allows people to relax when they recognize the seriousness of the situation and to be confident that they can defeat the epidemic under the leadership of the central government.

In the ODC camp, the expressions occurring most frequently are associated with COVID-19 (23.19), which reflects the antagonism to the public. In the ODC entities, the metonymy of the *disease* to refer to COVID-19 (1.96) is used to place the dangerousness of the new coronavirus in the perceived focus and to make people aware of the seriousness of the epidemic. After the general public learn that COVID-19 poses a direct threat to their lives, they will take active action against the epidemic. In addition to the new coronavirus, a common enemy faced by the whole world, some countries created certain negative words about China and spread rumors during the present pandemic. These terms (2.68) likewise appear several times in the ODC camp. The construction of such terms as the ODC entities not only clarifies China's innocence but also cautions the public against believing and spreading rumors. It is noteworthy that there are several references to other diseases in the reports on COVID-19. Such a discursive strategy reminds the masses of the negative impact of the disease outbreaks on their lives and conveys the harmfulness of COVID-19.

The media also frequently take advantage of the action verb phrases referring to the influence exerted by ODCs on IDCs (8.08) and noun phrases indicating the result due to the influence of ODCs on IDCs (12.10) in coverage.

(8) He was sent to the hospital, where he was confirmed to have contracted COVID-19. (Apr. 22, 2020)

(9) Yoweri Museveni, Uganda's president has announced a raft of measures, including sealing off borders and banning all public transport, to contain the outbreak. (Mar. 7, 2020)

(10) On April 14, Beijing reported an imported case that resulted in three more confirmed cases among family members. It is categorized as a concentrated case, which is why Chaoyang was listed as a high-risk area, Pang said. (Apr. 22, 2020)

Example (8) uses verbs to express the effect of the new coronavirus on the patient in order to emphasize its influence on the lives of people. Likewise, Example (9) utilizes verb phrases that influence daily life to emphasize the impact of the new coronavirus on the functioning of society. The employment of verbs visualizes the harm brought by the ODC to people's lives, which makes readers feel the imminence of the ODC more intensely and warn reader against ODC. The negative image of COVID-19 is presented to the public. In Example (10), the juxtaposition of the four noun phrases is used to make the sentence more powerful and influential, foreshadowing the imminence of danger. It also projects the patients' experience into the readers' mental space to arouse the readers' awareness to protect themselves, which reinforces the harmfulness of COVID-19. The use of *case* here is also the metonymy of event to refer to human (4.11).

4.2.2 Analysis of the Temporal Proximization Strategies

According to statistics, the lexico-grammatical items belonging to the temporal proximization and their frequency in the reports on COVID-19 are shown in Table 5.

Table 5　The Use of Temporal Proximization Strategies in COVID-19-Related Reports

Category	The Lexico-Grammatical Items	Number of Times	Frequency
Nominalized Noun Phrases Presupposing the Conditions about ODCs Impact to Occur at Any Moment in the Future	risk/transmission/threat/spread	77	3.68
Total		77	3.68
Modal Verb Phrases Constructing Continuous ODCs Impact Between the Present and the Future	will/could/would/might	31	1.48
Total		31	1.48
The Totality of Temporal Proximization		108	5.16

As seen in Table 5, nominalized noun phrases presupposing the conditions about ODCs' impact to occur at any moment in the future (3.68) and modal verb phrases constructing continuous ODCs impact between the present and the future (1.48) are capitalized on by the media in COVID-19-related reports.

(11) The World Health Organization (WHO) director-general said on Wednesday that measures being taken in the Chinese city of Wuhan to close down transport to limit spread of the new coronavirus showed commitment to minimizing risks locally and abroad. (Jan. 23, 2020)

(12) If we don't invest in both, we will face not just health consequences but the social, economic and political fallout that we're already experiencing in this pandemic. (May 14, 2020)

In Example (11), drawing on the abstract noun *risk* leaves room for the readers' imagination. In fact, the new coronavirus is still spreading. It presupposes that the infection may occur at any time and is likely to be ongoing if nothing is done to counteract it. Thus, this potential threat can make the general public aware of the need to respond positively to prevention and control of outbreak. The word *will*, in Example (12), shortens the time distance between the hazards posed by COVID-19 and the IDCs, which presents a trend of ODCs constantly looming towards the general public and provokes them to be alerted to COVID-19.

4.2.3   Analysis of the Axiological Proximization Strategies

According to statistics, the lexico-grammatical items belonging to the axiological proximization and their frequency in the reports on COVID-19 are displayed in Table 6.

Table 6   The Use of Axiological Proximization Strategies in COVID-19-Related Reports

Category	The Lexico-Grammatical Items	Number of Times	Frequency
Noun Phrases Denoting Positive Values or Ideologies of IDCs	notice/sanitizer/investigation/study/treatment/ evidence/face mask/prevention/vaccine/measure/ action/equipment/funding/preparedness/step	406	19.41
	commitment/praise/credit/ solidarity/coordination/ support/ unity/ assistance	121	5.79
	health/human right/peace/stability/safety/dignity	49	2.34
	front line/fight/struggle/weapon	42	2.01
Total		618	29.55
Noun Phrases Denoting Negative Values or Ideologies of ODCs	virus/coronavirus	200	9.56
	risk/challenge/threat/crisis/severity/difficult times/trouble/shock/cost/uncertainty/stigma/ hate/confusion/disruption/prejudice/enemy	90	4.30
Total		290	13.87
The Axiological Proximization Total		908	43.42

From Table 6, it can be seen that the media draw on a variety of noun phrases to construct values and ideologies of IDC entities and ODC entities. Among the values of the entities inside the deictic center, the words indicating measures appear most frequently (19.41), which suggests that the IDC entities are actively taking steps to undermine the intrusion by ODC entities. These words create a positive atmosphere for the prevention and control of the epidemic and make the public more willing to participate. Also, words indicating the good qualities of the IDC entities (5.79) and indicating the original state of IDC entities (2.34) are frequently employed. In the face of overwhelming epidemic violence, individuals unite together and help each other in unison. Words indicating the original situation of IDCs, such as *health, peace*, and *stability*, are utilized to contrast with the current condition. These words emphasize the magnitude and severity of the coronavirus' impact on the global and national societies, which further highlights the dichotomy between IDCs and ODCs.

While a large number of positive values are applied to describe IDCs, negative terms are also utilized to construct the values of ODCs. The most frequently used words to denote the values of the ODC entities are *virus* and *coronavirus* (9.56). The coronavirus is the cause of all misfortunes. In addition, the word virus highlights the pejorative character of the ODC. Thus, consistent with the SARS corpus, the term virus belongs to both the ODCs and the words indicating the negative values of the ODC when referring to the emitter of the danger. There are also a variety of derogatory terms (4.30), such as *crisis, trouble, enemy*. These terms allude to the negative characteristics and mighty destructive power of the ODCs. The negative image created by the frequent utilization of these phrases contrasts sharply with the image by the IDCs, which implies that the ODCs could pose a severe threat to the IDCs and increase readers' hatred and enmity toward coronavirus. The foundation is laid to improve the need for epidemic prevention and control.

4.3　Comparative Analysis of Proximization Strategies

4.3.1　Overall Comparative Analysis

From the statistical results, we can see that both SARS-related and COVID-19-related reports draw upon spatial proximization strategies, temporal proximization strategies and axiological proximization strategies. Spatial proximization strategies followed by axiological proximization strategies appear most frequently in both reports. In contrast, temporal proximization strategies account for the smallest proportion of these strategies. This reflects the unevenness and consistency in the utilization of proximization strategies. Unevenness refers to the different frequency in the different strategies. Consistency refers to the fact that proximization strategies always are utilized more often in the discourse while temporal proximization strategies are less often. This is in line with Cap (2013), who has suggested that temporal proximization generally accounts for less, with its effect being achieved through perlocutionary effects.

Through the chi-square test, it can be discovered that the frequency of proximization strategies in COVID-19-related news is significantly greater than in SARS-related news ($\chi^2 = 256.063$, $df = 1$, $p < 0.05$). Following public health crises such as SARS and H1N1, the media have gained a deep understanding of applying the news as a channel to make epidemic prevention and control measures indispensable.

Specifically, the spatial proximization strategies show a tremendous difference between COVID-19 and SARS reports ($\chi^2 = 115.770$, $df = 1$, $p < 0.05$), with the former being used more frequently. This demonstrates that media place more emphasis on spatial proximization. The reason for this may be that spatial proximization itself is a three-dimensional space that allows readers to feel the imminence and threat of the ODCs, which produces a more pronounced legitimization and persuasive effect. Regarding the occurrence of temporal proximization strategies, there is a significant difference in the two corpora ($\chi^2 = 8.157$, $df = 1$, $p < 0.05$), which displays an upward tendency. The temporal proximization strategies reduce the temporal distance between the virus and the masses, which moderately evokes fear in the general public and reflects the delegitimization of COVID-19 behaviour. In terms of the frequency of axiological proximization, there is also a significant difference in the two corpora ($\chi^2 = 146.584$, $df = 1$, $p < 0.05$), which also shows an increasing trend. On the one hand, it unveils that the media increasingly put emphasis on influencing readers unconsciously. On the other hand, it suggests that the public's moral quality has improved, and the media are more confident in guiding readers in this subtle way.

4.3.2   Comparison and Analysis of Spatial Proximization Strategies

The chi-square tests of the various strategies among spatial proximization reveal that the occurrence of noun phrases denoting IDC entities is significantly different between the two corpora ($\chi^2=101.781$, $df=1$, $p<0.05$), with IDC noun phrases in COVID-19-related reports being significantly used more than those in SARS-related reports. Similarly, there is a significant difference in the utilization of the ODC entities in the two news corpora ($\chi^2=13.480$, $df=1$, $p<0.05$), with the ODC entities appearing more frequent in the COVID-19 news than in the SARS news. This reflects an increasing focus on the construction of images in the space and a growing awareness of the influence concerning the image of the victim at the deictic center and the image of the intruder outside the deictic center in the media so as to establish a spatial opposition between the two. The readers themselves are part of the image, so noun phrases denoting the image of IDCs and ODCs are more familiar to readers than other strategies in the spatial proximization strategies, which ensures the persuasiveness of the content.

After a statistical comparison between metonymic words in IDCs and ODCs, it is exhibited that there is no significant difference in the metonymy of using location to refer to residents and of using agencies to refer to officials or staff ($\chi^2=1.791$, $df=1$, $p>0.05$). The use of the "whole-for-part metonymy" about the disease is significantly different between the two news ($\chi^2=19.003$, $df=1$, $p<0.05$) and exhibits a decline in the frequency of metonymy. It is possible that COVID-19 is preceded by several outbreaks of infectious diseases, and the media attempt to focus on COVID-19 in their coverage by directly mentioning the name of this infectious disease. Moreover, the direct reference to COVID-19 makes it easier to inform the public of its harmful nature. Likewise, there is a significant difference in the metonymy of events referring to people ($\chi^2=19.100$, $df=1$, $p<0.05$), which exhibits a decreasing trend. In fact, reducing the employment of euphemisms in reports is more conducive to the creation of an image of ODCs as a hazard.

The comparison between the verb phrases in the two news corpora reveals that there is no significant difference in the use of motion and directionality verb phrases referring to the movement of ODC towards IDCs ($\chi^2=2.742$, $df=1$, $p>0.05$). In the same way, there is no significant difference in the frequency of action verb phrases referring to the influence exerted by ODCs on IDCs in the news items of the two topics ($\chi^2=0.025$, $df=1$, $p>0.05$). However, in both corpora, the former (motion and directionality verb phrases) is obviously less frequent than the latter (action verb phrases) ($1.62<7.94$, $2.34<8.08$). Compared to motion and directionality verb phrases, action verb phrases would be more specific, giving the readers a precise perception of the damage given to IDCs and an intuitive sense of the harms caused by ODCs. Therefore, the action verb is more likely to increase the tension of the public about the threat from the virus.

In relation to the noun phrases indicating the anticipation due to the influence of ODCs on IDCs and indicating the result due to the influence of ODCs on IDCs, a comparison reveals that noun phrases indicating the anticipation due to the influence in COVID-19 reports are used more frequently than those in SARS reports ($\chi^2=9.951$, $df=1$, $p<0.05$). However, the noun phrases indicating the result due to the influence are not significantly different between the two news ($\chi^2=0.294$, $df=1$, $p>0.05$). In essence, the noun phrases indicating the anticipation due to the influence construct the imminence of ODCs on IDCs from a dual perspective (spatial and temporal perspective) to more effectively present the harmfulness of the virus.

4.3.3   Comparison and Analysis of Temporal Proximization Strategies

By comparing the temporal proximization strategies in the two news corpora, it is unveiled that the occurrence of nominalized noun phrases presupposing the conditions about ODCs' impact to occur at any moment in the future is significantly different ($\chi^2=12.308$, $df=1$, $p<0.05$). On the contrary, there is no significant difference in the modal verb phrases constructing continuous ODCs' impact between the present and the future ($\chi^2=0.001$, $df=1$, $p>0.05$). It is more likely to arouse the public's vigilance by reminding them of the potential dangers.

4.3.4   Comparison and Analysis of Axiological Proximization Strategies

By comparison, it is demonstrated that the noun phrases denoting positive values or ideologies of the entities inside the deictic center present a significant difference between the reports of the two themes ($\chi^2=87.990$, $df=1$, $p<0.05$), so do the noun phrases denoting negative values or ideologies of the entities outside the deictic center ($\chi^2 = 57.623$, $df = 1$, $p < 0.05$). What's more, both noun phrases are more frequently presented in COVID-19 reports. In this indirect way, the media make the readers feel the opposition between the values of IDCs and those of ODCs. Through such a strong contrast, readers with the right values will inevitably accept the positive values of the deictic center and resist the negative values of the ODCs, thus responding positively to the situation against the epidemic and achieving the purpose of news reports.

5. Conclusion

Based on a small self-built corpus, this paper has presented a comparative study of the proximization discourse strategies and metonymy in the news articles on SARS and COVID-19. The findings reveal that both proximization strategies and metonymic words are used in the coverage of public health emergencies across time, with spatial proximization strategies being the most prevalent and temporal proximization strategies being the least prevalent. The difference is that COVID-19 news coverage draws upon more proximization strategies, which suggests that the media are more skillful at guiding the public during public health emergencies effectively. In general, COVID-19-related news makes greater use of spatial proximization strategies. Specifically, in the spatial proximization strategies, the COVID-19-related news discourse makes significantly more use of nouns that denote entities inside the deictic center and entities outside the deictic center. Besides, there is significant more employment of noun phrases indicating the result because of the influence of the ODC entities on the IDC entities. Among the expressions of the spatial proximization strategies, metonymic words are less employed in COVID-19-related news discourse. Regarding the temporal proximization strategies, their number is even more in COVID-19 reports. In the axiological proximization strategies, the COVID-19 news articles make significantly more use of noun phrases denoting the positive values of the entities inside the deictic center and the negative values of the entities outside the deictic center.

These results suggest that the media are much more proficient during the

COVID-19 period, as seen by their capacity to effectively take advantage of discursive strategies in the fight against the epidemic through the Press and to reasonably persuade the public to heed the government's call for more prevention and control. Furthermore, utilizing these discursive strategies in news reporting has created an image of China as a responsible power in the international community. Overall, the proximization strategies and metonymy have positively contributed to this public health emergency.

References

Cap, P. Towards the Proximization Model of the Analysis of Legitimization in Political Discourse[J]. *Journal of Pragmatics*, 2008, *40*(1): 17-41.

Cap, P. *Proximization: The Pragmatics of Symbolic Distance Crossing*[M]. Amsterdam: John Benjamins, 2013.

Cap, P. Studying Ideological Worldviews in Political Discourse Space: Critical-Cognitive Advances in the Analysis of Conflict and Coercion[J]. *Journal of Pragmatics*, 2017a(108): 17-27.

Cap, P. *The Language of Fear: Communicating Threat in Public Discourse*[M]. Amsterdam: John Benjamins, 2017b.

Chilton, P. *Analysing Political Discourse: Theory and Practice*[M]. London: Routledge, 2004.

Evans, V. & Green, M. *Cognitive Linguistics: An Introduction*[M]. Beijing: World Publishing Corporation, 2015.

Hart, C. *Critical Discourse Analysis and Cognitive Science: New Perspectives on Immigration Discourse*[M]. Berlin: Springer, 2010.

Hu, X. A Study of Courtroom Discourse from the Perspective of Critical Metonymy Analysis[D]. Jinan: Shandong University, 2019.

Langacker, R. W. *Cognitive Grammar: A Basic Introduction*[M]. Oxford: Oxford University Press, 2008.

Li, K. & Wang, X. A Study of Critical Metonymy Analysis from the Perspective of Rhetorical Criticism[J]. *Modern Foreign Languages*, 2015, *38*(2): 183-193.

Li, Y. & Pan, F. A Cognitive Contrastive Study of News Discourse of Covid-19 from *China Daily* and *The Guardian* from the Perspective of Proximization Theory[J]. *Journal of Tianjin Foreign Studies University*, 2021, *28*(4): 60-73.

Mclachlan, M. Neoliberal Rules: A Critical Multimodal Analysis of Metonymy on High School Webpages[J]. *Linguistics and Education*, 2021(65): 100957.

Mohammed, S., Peter, E., Kikkackey, T. & Maciver, J. The 'Nurse as Hero' Discourse in the COVID-19 Pandemic: A Poststructural Discourse Analysis[J]. *International Journal of Nursing Studies*, 2021(117): 103887.

Nerlich, B. *Encyclopedia of Language and Linguistics*[M]. Oxford: Elsevier, 2006.

Regulation on Preparedness for and Response to Emergent Public Health Hazards[EB/OL]. (2011-01-08) [2022-08-10]. http://www.gov.cn/gongbao/content/2011/content_1860801.htm.

Wang, Y. A New Understanding of Argument on Referentialism: Metonymy View[J]. *Foreign Language Teaching and Research*, 2014, *46*(5): 711-722.

Wei, Z. A Metonymic Study of Chinese Idioms: Embodied-Cognitive Linguistics Perspective[J]. *Foreign Languages in China*, 2019, *16*(6): 26-33.

Wu, J. & Niu, Z. Analyzing Legitimization in Political Discourse from the Perspective of Proximization Theory: A Case Study of Trump's Immigration Policy[J]. *Foreign Languages in China*, 2018, *15*(6): 48-53.

Yao, L. & Cindy, S. Engaging Social Media Users with Attitudinal Messages during Health Crisis Communication[J]. *Lingua*, 2022(268): 103-199.

Yang, N. Engaging Readers across Participants: A Cross-Interactant Analysis of Metadiscourse in Letters of Advice during the COVID-19 Pandemic[J]. *Journal of Pragmatics*, 2021(186): 181-193.

Zhang, T. A Study of Discourse System Construction in Politicians' Speech: A Case Study from Proximization Theory Approach[J]. *Foreign Language in China*, 2016, *13*(5): 28-35.

Zhao, W. & Wang, S. The Cognitive Power of Deliberate Metaphors in the Reports of COVID-19 Outbreak[J]. *Journal of Tianjin Foreign Studies University*, 2020, *27*(2): 114-127.

Zhang, H. & Ji, X. A Critical Cognitive Linguistic Approach to COVID-19 News Narratives from Chinese and American Media[J]. *Contemporary Rhetoric*, 2021(4): 42-56.

Zhang, H. & Zhang, T. Cognitive Metonymy Approach to Critical Discourse Analysis[J]. *Foreign Language and Literature*, 2012, *28*(3): 41-46.

Zhao, X. & Zhao, L. The Explanatory Power of Proximization Theory to Non-traditional Security Discourse: A Case Study[J]. *Journal of Tianjin Foreign Studies University*, 2021, *28*(3): 63-77.

Zhou, B. A Study on News Media Stance from the Perspective of Proximization: A Corpus-Based Analysis on Reports About "Huawei Threat" in German Media[J]. *Journal of Foreign Languages*, 2021, *44*(3): 71-81.

参考文献

Abbott, G. & Wingard, P. *The Teaching of English as an International Language: A Practical Guide* [M]. Collins: Glasgow and London, 1981.

Abu-Rabia, S. The influence of working memory on reading and creative writing processes in a second language [J]. *Educational Psychology*, 2003, *23*(2): 209–222.

Alain, C., Woods, D. L. & Knight, R. T. A distributed cortical network for auditory sensory memory in humans [J]. *Brain Research*, 1998, *812*(1–2): 23–37.

Alloway T. P. & Alloway R. G. Investigating the predictive roles of working memory and IQ in academic attainment [J]. *Journal of Experimental Child Psychology*, 2010, *106*(1): 20–29.

Alloway, T. P., Gathercole, S. E., Kirkwood, H. & Elliott, J. The cognitive and behavioral characteristics of children with low working memory J]. *Child Development*, 2009, *80*(2): 606–621.

Alloway, T. & Gathercole, S. Working memory and short-term sentence recall in young children [J]. *European Journal of Cognitive Psychology*, 2005, *17*(2): 207–220.

Alloway, T. Working memory, but not IQ, predicts subsequent learning in children with learning difficulties [J]. *European Journal of Psychological Assessment*, 2009, *25*(2): 92–98.

Alloway, T. *Improving Working Memory: Supporting Students' Learning* [M]. London: SAGE Publications, 2010.

Altmann, G. & Steedman, M. Interaction with context during human sentence processing [J]. *Cognition*, 1988(30): 191–238.

Alvarez, J. A. & Emory, E. Executive function and the frontal lobes: a meta-analytic review [J]. *Neuropsychology Review*, 2006, *16*(1): 17–42.

Andersson, U. Working memory as a predictor of written arithmetical skills in children: The importance of central executive functions [J]. *British Journal of Educational Psychology*, 2010, *78*(2): 181–203.

Ardila, A. Language representation and working memory with bilinguals [J]. *Journal of Communication Disorders*, 2003(36): 233–240.

Arnold, A. *Affect in Language Learning* [M]. Beijing: Foreign Language Teaching and Research Press, 2000.

Arnsten, A. F., Paspalas, C. D., Gamo, N. J., Yang, Y. & Wang, M. Dynamic network connectivity: a new form of neuroplasticity [J]. *Trends in Cognitive Sciences*, 2010, *14*(8): 365–375.

Atkinson, R. C. & Juola, J. F. *Attention and Performance, IV* [M]. New York: Academic Press, 1973.

Atkinson, R. C. & Shiffrin, R. M. *Mathematical Models for Memory and Learning. Technical Report 79* [M]. Institute for mathematical studies in social sciences, Stanford University, 1965.

Atkinson, R. C. & Shiffrin, R. M. Storage and retrieval processes in long-term memory [J]. *Psychological Review*, 1969, *76*(2): 179–193.

Atkinson, R. C. & Shiffrin, R. M. Human memory: A proposed system and its control processes [M] // Spence, K. W. & Spence, J. T. *The Psychology of Learning and Motivation: Advances in Research and Theory*. London: Academic Press, 1968: 89–195.

Atkinson, R. C. & Shiffrin, R. M. The control of short-term memory [J]. *Scientific American*, 1971(225): 82–90.

Baddeley A. & Wilson, B. A. Prose recall and amnesia: implications for the structure of working memory [J]. *Neuropsychologia*, 2002, *40*(10): 1737-1743.

Baddeley, A. Working memory: looking back and looking forward [J]. *Nature Reviews Neuroscience*, 2003, *4*(10): 829-839.

Baddeley, A., Logie, R., Nimmo-Smith, I. & Brereton, N. Components of fluent reading [J]. *Journal of Memory and Language*, 1985(24): 119-131.

Baddeley, A, Gathercole, S. & Papagno, C. The phonological loop as a language learning device [J]. *Psychological Review*, 1998, *105*(1): 158-173.

Baddeley, A. Working memory [J]. *Science*, 1992, *255*(5044): 556-559.

Baddeley, A. The episodic buffer: A new component of working memory? [J]. *Trends in Cognitive Sciences*, 2000(4): 417-423.

Baddeley, A. *Working Memory, Thought, and Action* [M]. Oxford: Oxford University Press, 2007.

Baddeley, A. Working memory [J]. *Current Biology*, 2010(20): R136-R140.

Baddeley, A. Exploring the central executive [J]. *Quarterly Journal of Experimental Psychology*, 1996(49A): 5-28.

Baddeley, A. & Hitch, G. J. Working memory [M]// Bower, G. A. *The Psychology of Learning and Motivation*. New York: Academic Press, 1974: 47-89.

Baddeley, A. & Logie, R. H. Working memory: The multicomponent model [M]// Miyake, A. & Shah, P. *Models of Working Memory: Mechanisms of Active Maintenance and Executive Control*. New York: Cambridge University Press, 1999: 28-61.

Baddeley, A. Working memory and language: An overview [J]. *Journal of Communication Disorders*, 2003, *36*(3): 189-208.

Baddeley, A. *Working Memory* [M]. Oxford: Oxford University Press, 1986.

Baddeley, A., Hitch, G. & Allen, R. Working memory and binding in sentence recall [J]. *Journal of Memory and Language*, 2009, *61*(3): 438-456.

Baddeley, A. & Jarrold, C. Working memory and down syndrome [J]. *Journal of Intellectual Disability Research*, 2007(51): 925-931.

Baddeley, A. D. Is working memory still working? [J]. *American Psychologist*, 2001, *56*(11): 851-864.

Baddeley, A., Eysenck, M, W. & Anderson, M. C. *Memory* [M]. New York: Psychology Press, 2009.

Badre, D., Kayser, A. S. & D'Esposito, M. Frontal cortex and the discovery of abstract action rules [J]. *Neuron*, 2010, *66*(2): 315-326.

Bancroft, T. & Servos, P. Distractor frequency influences performance in vibrotactile working memory [J]. *Experimental Brain Research*, 2011, *208*(4): 529-532.

Bandura, A. Self-efficacy: toward a unifying theory of behavioral change [J]. *Psychological Review*, 1977(84): 191-215.

Barbey, A. K., Koenigs, M. & Grafman, J. Dorsolateral prefrontal contributions to human working memory [J]. *Cortex*, 2013, *49*(5): 1195-1205.

Barrouillet, P., Bernardin, S. & Camos, V. Time constraints and resource sharing in adults' working memory spans [J]. *Journal of Experimental Psychology, General*, 2004, *133*(1): 83-100.

Bates, E. & MacWhinney, B. Functionalism and the competition model [M]// MacWhinney, B. & Bates, E. *A Cross-linguistic Study of Sentence Processing*. Cambridge: Cambridge University Press, 1989: 3-73.

Berry, A. S., Zanto, T. P., Rutman, A. M., Clapp, W. C. & Gazzaley, A. Practice-related improvement in working memory is modulated by changes in processing external interference [J]. *Journal of Neurophysiology*, 2009, *102*(3): 1779-1789.

Berwick, R. C., Friederici, A. D., Chomsky, N. & Bolhuis, J. J. Evolution, brain, and the nature of language [J]. *Trends in Cognitive Sciences*, 2013, *17*(2): 89-98.

Bever, T. B. The ascent of the specious, or there's a lot we don't know about mirrors [M]// Cohen, D. *Explaining Linguistic Phenomena*. Washington: Hemisphere, 1974: 173-200.

Bever, T. G. The cognitive basis for linguistic structure [M]// Hayes, J. R. *Cognitive Development of Language*. New York: Wiley, 1970.

Bever, T. G. & McElree, B. Empty categories access their antecedents during comprehension [J]. *Linguistic Inquiry*, 1988(19): 35-43.

Bever, T. G., Sanz, M. & Townsend, D. J. The emperor's psycholinguistics [J].
 Journal of Psycholinguistic Research, 1998(27): 261–284.

Bialystok, E. & Hakuta, K. Confounded age: Linguistic and cognitive factors in
 age differences for second language acquisition [M] // Birdsong, D. *Second
 Language Acquisition and the Critical Period Hypothesis*. Mahwah: Lawrence
 Erlbaum Associates, 1999: 161–181.

Bledowski, C., Kaiser, J. & Rahm, B. Basic operations in working memory:
 Contributions from functional imaging studies [J]. *Behavioural Brain
 Research*, 2010, *214*(2): 172–179.

Bledowski, C., Rahm, B. & Rowe, J. B. What "works" in working memory?
 Separate systems for selection and updating of critical information [J]. *The
 Journal of Neuroscience*, 2009, *29*(43): 13735–13741.

Bock, J. K. Syntactic persistence in language production [J]. *Cognitive Psychology*,
 1986(18): 355–387.

Bookheimer, S. Functional MRI of language: New approaches to understanding
 the cortical organization of semantic processing [J]. *Annual Review of
 Neuroscience*, 2002(25): 151–188.

Bornkessel, I. D., Fiebach, C. & Friederici, A. D. On the cost of syntactic ambiguity
 in human language comprehension: An individual differences approach [J].
 Cognitive Brain Research, 2004(21): 11–21.

Bornkessel, I., McElree, B., Schlesewsky, M. & Friederici, A. D. Multi-dimensional
 contributions to garden path strength: Dissociating phrase structure from case
 marking [J]. *Journal of Memory and Language*, 2004(51): 495–522.

Bornkessel-Schlesewsky, I. & Schlesewsky, M. An alternative perspective on
 "semantic P600" effects in language comprehension [J]. *Brain Research
 Reviews*, 2008(59): 55–73.

Broadway, J. M. & Engle, R. W. Validating running memory span: Measurement
 of working memory capacity and links with fluid intelligence [J]. *Behavior
 Research Methods*, 2010(42): 563–570.

Brothers, T., Hoversten, L. J. & Traxler, M. J. Bilinguals on the garden-path:

Individual differences in syntactic ambiguity resolution [J]. *Bilingualism: Language and Cognition*, 2021, *24*(4): 612-627.

Brown, H. D. *Principles of Language Learning and Teaching* [M]. Beijing: Foreign Language Teaching and Research Press, 2002.

Brown, J. Some tests of the decay theory of immediate memory [J]. *Quarterly Journal of Experimental Psychology*, 1958(10): 12-21.

Bue-Estes, C. L., Willer, B., Burton, H., Leddy, J. J., Wilding, G. E. & Horvath, P. J. Short-Term Exercise to Exhaustion and its Effects on Cognitive Function in Young Women [J]. *Perceptual and Motor Skills*, 2008, *107*(3): 933-945.

Call, M. E. Auditory short-term memory, listening comprehension, and the input hypothesis [J]. *TESOL Quarterly*, 1985, *19*(4): 765-781.

Camblin, C. C., Gordon, P. C. & Swaab, T. Y. The interplay of discourse congruence and lexical association during sentence processing: Evidence from ERPs and eye tracking [J]. *Journal of Memory and Language*, 2007(56): 103-128.

Caplan, D., Alpert, N. & Waters, G. Effects of syntactic structure and propositional number on patterns of regional blood flow [J]. *Journal of Cognitive Neuroscience*, 1998(10): 541-552.

Caplan, D. & Waters, G. S. Working memory and connectionist models of parsing: A response to MacDonald and Christiansen [J]. *Psychological Review*, 2002(109): 66-74.

Caplan, D. & Waters, G. S. Memory mechanisms supporting syntactic comprehension [J]. *Psychonomic Bulletin & Review*, 2013, *20*(2): 243-268.

Caplan, D. & Waters, G. S. Short-term memory and verbal comprehension: A critical view of the neuropsychological literature [M]// Vallar, G. & Shallice, T. *Neuropsychological Impairments of Short-term Memory*. Cambridge: Cambridge University Press, 1990: 337-389.

Caplan, D. & Waters, G. S. Aphasic disorders of syntactic comprehension and working memory capacity [J]. *Cognitive Neuropsychology*, 1995(12): 637-649.

Caplan, D. & Waters, G. S. Verbal working memory and sentence comprehension

[J]. *Behavioral and Brain Sciences*, 1999(22): 77-94.

Carpenter, P. A., Miyake, A. & Just, M. A. Working memory constraints in comprehension: evidence from individual differences in aphasia, and aging [M]// Gernsbacher, M. A. *Handbook of Psycholinguistics*. New York: Academic Press, 1994: 1075-1122.

Carreiras, M., Salillas, E. & Barber, H. Event-related potentials elicited during parsing of relative clauses in Spanish [J]. *Cognitive Brain Research*, 2004(20): 98-105.

Caspari, I., Parkinson, S. R., LaPointe, L. L. & Katz, R. C. Working memory and aphasia [J]. *Brain and Cognition*, 1998(37): 205-223.

Chiappe, P., Hasher, L. & Siegel, L. S. Working memory, inhibitory control, and reading disability [J]. *Memory & Cognition*, 2000(28): 8-17.

Christianson, K. When language comprehension goes wrong for the right reasons: Good-enough, underspecified, or shallow language processing [J]. *The Quarterly Journal of Experimental Psychology*, 2016, *69*(5): 817-828.

Christianson, K., Williams, C., Zacks, R. & Ferreira, F. Younger and older adults' good enough interpretations of garden-path sentences [J]. *Discourse Processes*, 2006(42): 205-238.

Christianson, K., Hollingworth, A., Halliwell, J. F. & Ferreira, F. Thematic roles assigned along the garden path linger [J]. *Cognitive Psychology*, 2001, *42*(4): 368-407.

Christianson, K. Sensitivity to changes in garden path sentences [J]. *Journal of Psycholinguistic Research*, 2008(37): 391-403.

Clahsen, H. & Felser, C. How native-like is non-native language processing? [J]. *Trends in Cognitive Sciences*, 2006a(10): 564-570.

Clahsen, H. & Felser, C. Grammatical processing in language learners [J]. *Applied Psycholinguistics*, 2006b(27): 3-42.

Clark, H. H. & Clark, E. V. *Psychology and Language: An Introduction to Psycholinguistics* [M]. New York: Harcourt Brace Jovanovich Inc., 1977.

Clifton Jr., C., Traxler, M. J., Mohamed, M. T., Williams, R. S., Morris, R. K.

& Rayner, K. The use of thematic role information in parsing: Syntactic processing autonomy revisited [J]. *Journal of Memory and Language*, 2003(49): 317–334.

Collette, F., Hogge, M., Salmon, E. & Van der Linden, M. Exploration of the neural substrates of executive functioning by functional neuroimaging [J]. *Neuroscience*, 2006, *139*(1): 209–221.

Coltheart, M. What has functional neuroimaging told us about the mind (so far)? [J]. *Cortex*, 2006, *42*(3): 323–331.

Conway, A. R., Kane, M. J. & Engle R. W. Working memory capacity and its relation to general intelligence [J]. *Trends in Cognitive Sciences*, 2003, *7*(12): 547–552.

Cook, V. *Linguistics and Second Language Acquisition* [M]. Beijing: Foreign Language Teaching and Research Press, 2000.

Coulson, S., King, J. W. & Kutas, M. Expect the unexpected: Event-related brain response to morphosyntactic violations [J]. *Language and Cognitive Processes*, 1998(13): 21–58.

Cowan, N. The magical number 4 in short-term memory: A reconsideration of mental storage capacity [J]. *Behavioral and Brain Sciences*, 2001(24): 87–185.

Cowan, N. *Attention and Memory: An Integrated Framework* [M]. Oxford: Oxford University Press, 1995.

Cowan, N. Evolving conceptions of memory storage, selective attention, and their mutual constraints within the human information processing system [J]. *Psychological Bulletin*, 1988(104): 163–191.

Cowan, N. What are the differences between long-term, short-term, and working memory? [J]. *Progress in Brain Research*, 2008, *169*(169): 323–338.

Craik, F. I. M. & Lockhart, R. S. Levels of processing: A framework for memory research [J]. *Journal of Verbal Learning and Verbal Behavior*, 1972(11): 671–684.

Crowder, R. G. The demise of short-term memory [J]. *Acta Psychologica*,

1982(50): 291–323.

Cunnings, I. Parsing and working memory in bilingual sentence processing [J].
Bilingualism: Language and Cognition, 2016, *20*(4): 659–678.

Curtis, C. E. & D'Esposito, M. Persistent activity in the prefrontal cortex during
working memory [J]. *Trends in Cognitive Sciences*, 2003, *7*(9): 415–423.

Czerlinski, J. G., Gigerenzer, G. & Goldstein, D. G. How good are simple
heuristics? [M]// Gigerenzer, G., Todd, P. M. & the ABC Research Group.
Simple Heuristics that Make us Smarter. New York: Oxford University Press,
1999: 97–118.

Chiappe, Dan L. & Chiappe, P. The role of working memory in metaphor production
and comprehension [J]. *Journal of Memory and Language*, 2007(56): 172–
188.

Daneman, M. & Merikle, P. M. Working memory and language comprehension: A
meta-analysis [J]. *Psychonomic Bulletin & Review*, 1996(3): 422–433.

Daneman, M. & Carpenter, P. A. Individual difference in working memory and
reading [J]. *Journal of Verbal Learning & Verbal Behavior*, 1980, *19*(4): 450–
466.

Dapretto, M. & Bookheimer, S. Y. Form and content: Dissociating syntax and
semantics in sentence comprehension [J]. *Neuron*, 1999(24): 427–432.

de Swart, P., Lamers, M. & Lestrade, S. Animacy, argument structure, and argument
encoding [J]. *Lingua*, 2008(118): 131–140.

Dempster, F. & Cooney, J. B. Individual differences in digit span, susceptibility to
proactive interference, and aptitude/achievement test scores [J]. *Intelligence*,
1982(6): 399–416.

Dempster, F. The rise and fall of the inhibitory mechanism: Toward a unified theory
of cognitive development and aging [J]. *Developmental Review*, 1992(12):
45–75.

Desimone, R. & Duncan, J. Neural mechanisms of selective visual attention [J].
Annual Review of Neuroscience, 1995(18): 193–222.

DeYoung, C. G., Hirsh, J. B., Shane, M. S., Papademetris, X., Rajeevan, N. & Gray,

J. R. Testing predictions from personality neuroscience. Brain structure and the big five [J]. *Psychological Science*, 2010, *21*(6): 820-828.

Diamond, A. Executive functions [J]. *Annual Review of Psychology*, 2013(64): 135-168.

Dorph-Petersen, K. A., Pierri, J. N., Perel, J. M., Sun, Z., Sampson, A. R. & Lewis, D. A. The influence of chronic exposure to antipsychotic medications on brain size before and after tissue fixation: a comparison of haloperidol and olanzapine in macaque monkeys [J]. *Neuropsychopharmacology*, 2005, *30*(9): 1649-1661.

Dulay, H. & Burt, M. *Remarks on Creativity in Language Acquisition* [M]. New York: Regents, 1977.

Dussias, P. E. & Pinar, P. Effects of reading span and plausibility in the reanalysis of wh-gaps by Chinese-English second language speakers [J]. *Second Language Research*, 2010(26): 443-473.

Ellis, N. C. & Sinclair, S. G. Working memory in the acquisition of vocabulary and syntax: Putting language in good order [J]. *The Quarterly Journal of Experimental Psychology*, 1996, *49A*(1): 234-250.

Ellis, R. *The Study of Second Language Acquisition* [M]. 上海：上海外语教育出版社, 1994.

Elvira, V. M. & Susan, E. G. Contrasting contributions of short-term memory and long-term memory to vocabulary learning in a foreign language [J]. *Memory*, 2005, *13*(3/4): 422-429.

Engelhardt, P. E., Ferreira, F. & Patsenko, E. G. Pupillometry reveals processing load during spoken language comprehension [J]. *Quarterly Journal of Experimental Psychology*, 2010(63): 639-645.

Engle, R. W. Working memory and retrieval: An inhibition-resource approach [M]// Richardson, J. T. E., Engle, R. W., Hasher, L., Logie, R. H., Stoltzfus, E. R. & Sacks, R. T. *Working Memory and Human Cognition*. New York: Oxford University Press, 1996: 89-119.

Engle, R. D., Kane, M. J. & Tuholski, S. W. Individual differences in working memory capacity and what they tell us about controlled attention, general fluid intelligence, and functions of the prefrontal cortex [M]// Miyake, A. & Shah, P. *Models of Working Memory: Mechanism of Active Maintenance and Executive Control*. New York: Cambridge University Press, 1999: 102-134.

Engle, R. W. & Oransky, N. Multi-store versus dynamic models of temporary storage in memory [M]// Sternberg, R. J. *The Nature of Cognition*. Massachusetts Institute of Technology, 1999.

Engle, R. W. Working memory capacity as executive attention [J]. *Current Directions in Psychological Science*, 2002(11): 19-23.

Engle, R. W. & Kane, M. J. Executive attention, working memory capacity, and a two-factor theory of cognitive control [M]// Ross, B. *The Psychology of Learning and Motivation*. New York: Elsevier, 2004: 145-199.

Engle, R. W., Tuholski, S. W., Laughlin, J. E. & Conway, A. R. Working memory, short-term memory, and general fluid intelligence: a latent-variable approach [J]. *Journal of Experimental Psychology: General*, 1999, *128*(3): 309-331.

Ericsson, K. A. & Kintsch, W. Long-term working memory [J]. *Psychological Review*, 1995, *102*(2): 211-245.

Eysenck, M. W. *Human Memory* [M]. Oxford: Pergamon Press, 1977.

Faust, M. E. & Gernsbacher, M. A. Cerebral mechanisms for suppression of inappropriate information during sentence comprehension [J]. *Brain Language*, 1996(53): 234-259.

Fedorenko, E. The role of domain-general cognitive control in language comprehension [J]. *Frontiers in Psychology*, 2014(5): 1-17.

Fedorenko, E., Gibson, E. & Rohde, D. The nature of working memory capacity in sentence comprehension: Evidence against domain-specific resources [J]. *Journal of Memory and Language*, 2006(54): 541-553.

Fedorenko, E. & Thompson-Schill, S. L. Reworking the language network [J]. *Trends Cognitive Science*, 2014, *18*(3): 120-126.

Felser, C. & Roberts, L. Processing wh-dependencies in a second language: A cross-modal priming study [J]. *Second Language Research*, 2007, *23*(1): 9-36.

Felser, C., Marinis, T. & Clahsen, H. Children's processing of ambiguous sentences: A study of relative clause attachment [J]. *Language Acquisition: A Journal of Developmental Linguistics*, 2003a(11): 127–163.

Felser, C., Roberts, L., Marinis, T. & Gross, R. The processing of ambiguous sentences by first and second language learners of English [J]. *Applied Psycholinguistics*, 2003b(24): 453–489.

Ferreira, F. & Henderson, J. M. Use of verb information in syntactic parsing: Evidence from eye movements and word-by-word self-paced reading [J]. *Journal of Experimental Psychology: Learning, Memory, and Cognition*, 1990, *16*(4): 555–568.

Ferreira, F. The misinterpretation of noncanonical sentences [J]. *Cognitive Psychology*, 2003(47): 164–203.

Ferreira, F. & Clifton, C. E. The independence of syntactic processing [J]. *Journal of Memory and Language*, 1986(25): 348–368.

Ferreira, F. & Patson, N. D. The "Good Enough" approach to language comprehension [J]. *Language and Linguistics Compass*, 2007, *1*(1–2): 71–83.

Ferreira, F., Bailey, K. G. D. & Ferraro, V. Good enough representations in language comprehension [J]. *Current Directions in Psychological Science*, 2002(11): 11–15.

Ferreira, F., Christianson, K. & Hollingworth, A. Misinterpretations of garden-path sentences: Implications for models of reanalysis [J]. *Journal of Psycholinguistic Research*, 2001(30): 3–20.

Ferreira, F., Engelhardt, P. E. & Jones, M. W. Good enough language processing: A satisficing approach [C]// Taatgen, N., Rijn, H., Nerbonne, J. & Schomaker, L. *Proceedings of the 31st Annual Conference of the Cognitive Science Society*. Austin: Cognitive Science Society, 2009: 413–418.

Ferrier, D. The Croonian lectures on cerebral localisation. Lecture II [J]. *The British Medical Journal*, 1890, *1*(1537): 1349–1355.

Fiebach, C. J., Schlesewsky, M., Lohmann, G., von Cramon, D. Y. & Friederci, A. D. Revisiting the role of Broca's area in sentence processing: syntactic integration versus syntactic working memory [J]. *Human Brain Mapping*, 2005(24): 79–91.

Fischler, I., Bloom, P., Childers, D., Roucos, S. & Perry, N. Brain potentials related to stages of sentence verification [J]. *Psychophysiology*, 1983(20): 400–409.

Fitch, W. T. *The Evolution of Language* [M]. Cambridge: Cambridge University Press, 2010.

Fodor, Janet D. Prosodic disambiguation in silent reading [C]// Hirotani, M. *Proceedings of the North East Linguistic Society*. Amherst: GLSA Publications, 2002(32): 113–132.

Frazier, L. & Clifton, C. *Construal* [M]. Cambridge: MIT Press, 1996.

Frazier, L. & Rayner, K. Making and correcting errors during sentence comprehension: Eye movements in the analysis of structurally ambiguous sentences [J]. *Cognitive Psychology*, 1982(14): 178–210.

Frazier, L. *On Comprehending Sentences: Syntactic Parsing Strategies* [D]. Storrs: University of Connecticut, 1979.

Frazier, L. Sentence processing: A tutorial review [M]// Coltheart, M. *Attention and Performance XII. The Psychology of Reading*. Hillsdale: Erlbaum, 1987a: 559–586.

Frazier, L. Syntactic processing: Evidence from Dutch [J]. *Natural Language and Linguistic Theory*, 1987b, 5(4): 519–559.

Frazier, L. Against lexical generation of syntax [M]// Marslen-Wilson, W. *Lexical Representation and Process*. Cambridge: MIT Press, 1989.

Frazier, L. Constraint satisfaction as a theory of sentence processing [J]. *Journal of Psycholinguistic Research*, 1995(24): 437–468.

Frazier, L. & Fodor, J. A. The sausage machine: A new two-stage parsing model [J]. *Cognition*, 1978(6): 291–325.

French, L. M. *Phonological Working Memory and Second Language Acquisition: A Developmental Study of Francophone Children Learning English in Quebec* [M]. Lewiston: Edwin Mellen Press, 2006.

French, L. M. & O'Brien, I. Phonological memory and children's second language grammar learning [J]. *Applied Psycholinguistics*, 2008(29): 463–487.

Frenck-Mestren, C. & Pynte, J. Syntactic ambiguity resolution while reading in second and native languages [J]. *The Quarterly Journal of Experimental Psychology*, 1997(50A): 119–148.

Friederici, A. D. The time course of syntactic activation during language processing: A model based on neuropsychological and neurophysiological data [J]. *Brain and Language*, 1995(50): 259–281.

Friederici, A. D. Towards a neural basis of auditory sentence processing [J]. *Trends in Cognitive Sciences*, 2002, 6(2): 78–84.

Friederici, A. D., Hahne, A. & Mecklinger, A. Temporal structure of syntactic parsing: Early and late event-related brain potential effects [J]. *Journal of Experimental Psychology: Learning, Memory, and Cognition*, 1996(22): 1219–1248.

Friederici, A. D., Mecklinger, A., Spencer, K. M., Steinhauer, K. & Donchin, E. Syntactic parsing preferences and their on-line revisions: A spatio temporal analysis of event-related brain potentials [J]. *Cognitive Brain Research*, 2001(11): 305–323.

Friederici, A. D., Steinhauer, K., Mecklinger, A. & Meyer, M. Working memory constraints on syntactic ambiguity resolution as revealed by electrical brain responses [J]. *Biological Psychology*, 1998(47): 193–221.

Friederici, Angela D. Towards a neural basis of auditory sentence processing [J]. *Trends in Cognitive Sciences*, 2002(6): 78–84.

Friederici, Angela D., Hahne, A. & Saddy, D. Distinct neurophysiological patterns reflecting aspects of syntactic complexity and syntactic repair [J]. *Journal of Psycholinguistic Research*, 2002(31): 45–62.

Friedman, N. P. & Miyake, A. The relations among inhibition and interference control functions: a latent-variable analysis [J]. *Journal of Experimental Psychology: General*, 2004, 133(1): 101–135.

Friedman, N. P. & Miyake, A. Differential roles for visuospatial and verbal working memory in situation model construction [J]. *Journal of Experimental*

Psychology: General, 2000(129): 61-83.

Friedman, N. P. & Miyake, A. The reading span test and its predictive power for reading comprehension ability [J]. *Journal of Memory and Language*, 2004, *51*(1): 136-158.

Frisson, S. Semantic underspecification in language processing [J]. *Language and Linguistics Compass*, 2009, *3*(1): 111-127.

Fukuda, K. & Vogel, E. K. Human variation in overriding attentional capture [J]. *The Journal of Neuroscience*, 2009, *29*(27): 8726-8733.

Funahashi, S., Bruce, C. J. & Goldman-Rakic, P. S. Dorsolateral prefrontal lesions and oculomotor delayed-response performance: Evidence for mnemonic "scotomas" [J]. *The Journal of Neuroscience: The Official Journal of the Society for Neuroscience*, 1993, *13*(4): 1479-1497.

Fuster, J. M., Bodner, M. & Kroger, J. K. Cross-modal and cross-temporal association in neurons of frontal cortex [J]. *Nature*, 2000, *405*(6784): 347-351.

Fuster, J. M. *The Prefrontal Cortex* [M]. 4th ed. Oxford: Elsevier, 2008.

Fuster, J. M. *The Prefrontal Cortex: Anatomy, Physiology, and Neuropsychology of the Frontal Lobe* [M]. Philadelphia: Lippincott-Raven, 1997.

Garnsey, S., Tanenhaus, M. K. & Chapman, R. M. Evoked potentials and the study of sentence comprehension [J]. *Journal of Psycholinguistic Research*, 1989(IS): 51-60.

Gass, S. M. *Input, Interaction, and the Second Language Learner* [M]. Mahwah: Lawrence Erlbaum Associates, 1997.

Gathercole, S. E. & Baddeley, A. *Working Memory and Language* [M]. Hove: Lawrence Erlbaum Associates, 1993.

Gathercole, S. E. & Alloway, T. P. *Working Memory and Learning: A Practical Guide for Teachers* [M]. London: SAGE Publications, 2008.

Gathercole, S. E. & Pickering, S. J. Working memory deficits in children with low achievements in the national curriculum at 7 years of age [J]. *British Journal of Educational Psychology*, 2000, *70*(2): 177-194.

Gernsbacher, M. A. & Faust, M. E. The mechanism of suppression: A component of general comprehension skill [J]. *Journal of Experimental Psychology: Learning, Memory, and Cognition*, 1991, *17*(2): 245-262.

Gernsbacher, M. A. *Language Comprehension as Structure Building* [M]. Hillsdale: Lawrence Erlbaum Associates, 1990.

Gernsbacher, M. A. Cognitive processes and mechanisms in language comprehension: the structure building framework [M]//Bower, G. H. *The Psychology of Learning and Motivation*. New York: Academic Press, 1991: 217-263.

Gernsbacher, M. A. & St. John, M. F. Modeling suppression in lexical access [M]// Gorfein, D. S. *On the Consequences of Meaning Selection: Perspectives on Resolving Lexical Ambiguity*. Washington: American Psychological Association, 2001: 47-65.

Gibson, E. Syntactic prediction locality theory [J]. *Cognition*, 1998(68): 1-76.

Gibson, E. The dependency locality: A distance-based of linguistic complexity [M]// Miyashita, Y., Marantz, A. & O'Neil, W. *Image, Language, Brain*. Cambridge: MIT Press, 2000: 95-126.

Gibson, E. A. *A Computational Theory of Human Linguistic Processing: Memory Limitations and Processing Breakdown* [D]. Pittsburgh: Carnegie Mellon University, 1991.

Gibson, E., Hickok, G. & Schütze, C. Parsing empty categories: A parallel approach [J]. *Journal of Psycholinguistic Research*, 1994(23): 381-405.

Gibson, E., Pearlmutter, N. J., Canseco-Gonzalez, E. & Hickok, G. Recency preference in the human sentence processing mechanism [J]. *Cognition*, 1996(59): 23-59.

Gigerenzer, G. Why heuristics work [J]. *Perspectives on Psychological Science*, 2008(3): 20-29.

Gigerenzer, G. & Goldstein, D. G. Reasoning the fast and frugal way: Models of bounded rationality [J]. *Psychological Review*, 1996(103): 650-669.

Gigerenzer, G. & Selten, R. *Bounded Rationality: The Adaptive Toolbox* [M].

Cambridge: MIT Press, 2001.

Gillon Dowens, M., Barber, H., Guo, J., Guo, T. & Carreiras, M. ERP correlates of automatic syntactic processing in highly proficient L1 Chinese-L2 Spanish late learners [C]. Paper presented at the 17th Annual Cognitive Neuroscience Society Meeting, San Francisco, 2008.

Gillon Dowens, M., Guo, T., Guo, Jingjing, Barber, H. & Carreiras, M. Gender and number processing in Chinese learners of Spanish-evidence from event related potentials [J]. *Neuropsychologia*, 2011(49): 1651-1659.

Gillon Dowens, M., Vergara, M., Barber, H. A. & Carreiras, M. Morphosyntactic processing in late second-language learners [J]. *Journal of Cognitive Neuroscience*, 2010, 8(22): 1870-1887.

Glass, E., Sachse, S. & Suchodoletz, W. Development of auditory sensory memory from 2 to 6 years: an MMN study [J]. *Journal of Neural Transmission*, 2008, 115(8): 1221-1229.

Gluck, M. A., Mercado, E. & Myers, C. E. *Learning and Memory: From Brain to Behavior* [M]. New York: Worth Publishers, 2008.

Goad, H., Guzzo, N. B. & White, L. Parsing ambiguous relative clauses in L2 English learner sensitivity to prosodic cues [J]. *Studies in Second Language Acquisition*, 2021, 43(1): 83-108.

Gobet, F. Some shortcomings of long-term working memory [J]. *British Journal of Psychology*, 2000, 91(Pt 4): 551-570.

Goldman-Rakic, P. S. Topography of cognition: parallel distributed networks in primate association cortex [J]. *Annual Review of Neuroscience*, 1988(11): 137-156.

Goldman-Rakic, P. S. The prefrontal landscape: implications of functional architecture for understanding human mentation and the central executive [J]. *Philosophical Transactions of the Royal Society of London. Series B, Biological Sciences*, 1996, 351(1346): 1445-1453.

Gordon, P. C., Hendrick, R., Johnson, M. & Lee, Y. Similarity-based interference during language comprehension: Evidence from eye tracking during reading

[J]. *Journal of Experimental Psychology: Learning, Memory and Cognition*, 2006(32): 1304-1321.

Gorenflo, D. & McConnell, J. The most frequently cited journal articles and authors in introductory psychology textbooks [J]. *Teaching of Psychology*, 1991(18): 8-12.

Gorrell, P. G. *Syntax and Parsing* [M]. Cambridge: Cambridge University Press, 1995.

Gorrell, P. G. *Studies of Human Syntactic Processing: Ranked-parallel versus Serial Models* [D]. Storrs: University of Connecticut, 1987.

Graham, S. Executive control in the revising of students with writing and learning difficulties [J]. *Journal of Educational Psychology*, 1997(89): 223-234.

Green, D. W. The neural basis of the lexicon and the grammar in L2 acquisition [M]// van Hout, R., Hulk, A., Kuiken, F. & Towell, R. *The Interface Between Syntax and the Lexicon in Second Language Acquisition*. Amsterdam: John Benjamins, 2003.

Greenberg R. & Underwood, B. J. Retention as a function of stage of practice [J]. *Journal of Experimental Psychology*, 1950(40): 452-457.

Greenhouse, S. & Geisser, S. On methods in the analysis of profile data [J]. *Psychometrika*, 1959(24): 95-112.

Grundy. J. G. & Timmer, K. Bilingualism and working memory capacity: a comprehensive meta-analysis [J]. *Second Language Research*, 2017, *33*(3): 325-340.

Guida, A., Gobet, F., Tardieu, H. & Nicolas, S. How chunks, long-term working memory and templates offer a cognitive explanation for neuroimaging data on expertise acquisition: A two-stage framework [J]. *Brain and Cognition*, 2012, *79*(3): 221-244.

Guida, A. & Tardieu, H. Is personalisation a way to operationalise long-term working memory? [J]. *Current Psychology Letters: Behaviour, Brain & Cognition*, 2005, *15*(1): 1-15.

Guida, A., Tardieu, H. & Nicolas, S. The personalisation method applied to a

working memory task: Evidence of long-term working memory effects [J].
European Journal of Cognitive Psychology, 2009, *21*(6): 862–896.

Gunter, T. C., Friederici, A. D. & Schriefers, H. Syntactic gender and semantic
expectancy: ERPs reveal early autonomy and late interaction [J]. *Journal of
Cognitive Neuroscience*, 2000(12): 556–568.

Gunter, T. C., Wagner, S. & Friederici, A. D. Working memory and lexical ambiguity
resolution as revealed by ERPs: A difficult case for activation theories [J].
Journal of Cognitive Neuroscience, 2003, *15*(5): 643–657.

Gunter, T. C., Wagner, S. & Friederici, A. D. Working memory and processing
ambiguous words: Inhibition or activation? [C]// Friederici, A. D. & von
Cramon, D. Y. *Annual Report 1998*. Max-Planck-Institute of Cognitive
Neuroscience, 1999: 31–33.

Hagoort, P. Broca's complex as the unification space for language [M]// Cutler,
A. *Twenty-First Century Psycholinguistics: Four Cornerstones*. Mahwah:
Lawrence Erlbaum Associates, 2005.

Hagoort, P., Brown, C. M. & Groothusen, J. The syntactic positive shift (SPS) as an
ERP measure of syntactic processing [J]. *Language and Cognitive Processes*,
1993(8): 439–483.

Hagoort, P., Brown, C. & Swaab, T. Y. Lexical-semantic event-related potential
effects in patients with left hemisphere lesions and aphasia, and patients with
right hemisphere lesions without aphasia [J]. *Brain*, 1996(119): 627–649.

Hagoort, P., Hald, L., Bastiaansen, M. & Petersson, K. M. Integration of word
meaning and world knowledge in language comprehension [J]. *Science*,
2004(304): 438–441.

Hahne, A. & Friederici, A. D. Electrophysiological evidence for two steps in
syntactic analysis: Early automatic and late controlled processes [J]. *Journal
of Cognitive Neuroscience*, 1999, *11*(2): 193–204.

Hahne, A., Mueller, J. L. & Clahsen, H. Morphological processing in a second
language: Behavioral and event-related brain potential evidence for storage and
decomposition [J]. *Journal of Cognitive Neuroscience*, 2006(18): 121–134.

Halsband, U., Krause, B. J., Sipila, H., Teras, M. & Laihinen, A. PET studies on the memory processing of word pairs in bilingual Finnish-English subjects [J]. *Behavioural Brain Research*, 2002, *132*(1): 47-57.

Hambrick, D. Z. & Engle, R. W. Effects of domain knowledge, working memory capacity, and age on cognitive performance: An investigation of the knowledge-is-power hypothesis [J]. *Cognitive Psychology*, 2002(44): 339-387.

Hanten, G. & Martin, R. C. Contributions of phonological and semantic short-term memory to sentence processing: Evidence from two cases of closed head injury in children [J]. *Journal of Memory and Language*, 2000(43): 335-361.

Hanten, G. & Martin, R. C. A developmental phonological short-term memory deficit: A case study [J]. *Brain and Cognition*, 2001(45): 164-188.

Hasegawa, M., Carpenter, P. A. & Just, M. A. An fMRI study of bilingual sentence comprehension and workload [J]. *NeuroImage*, 2002(15): 647-660.

Haupt, F. S., Schlesewsky, M., Roehm, D., Friederici, A. D. & Bornkessel-Schlesewsky, I. The status of subject-object reanalyses in the language comprehension architecture [J]. *Journal of Memory and Language*, 2008, *59*(1): 54-96.

Havik, E., Roberts, L., van Hout, R., Schreuder, R. & Haverkort, M. Processing subject-object ambiguities in L2 Dutch: A self-paced reading study with German L2 learners of Dutch [J]. *Language Learning*, 2009(59): 73-112.

Haynes, M. Patterns and perils of guessing in second language reading [M]// Huckin, T., Haynes, M. & Coady, J. *Second Language Reading and Vocabulary Learning*. Norwood: Ablex, 1993: 46-64.

Heitz, R. P., Redick, T. S., Hambrick, D. Z., Kane, M. J., Conway, A. R. A. & Engle, R. W. Working memory, executive function, and general fluid intelligence are not the same [J]. *Behavioral and Brain Sciences*, 2006(29): 135-136.

Hernandez, A., Hofmann, J. & Kotz, S. A. Age of acquisition modulates neural activity for both regular and irregular syntactic functions [J]. *NeuroImage*, 2007(36): 912-923.

Hernandez, A., Li, Ping & Whinney, B. M. The emergence of competing modules in bilingualism [J]. *Trends in Cognitive Sciences*, 2005(9): 220–225.

Hickok, G. Parallel parsing: Evidence from reactivation in garden-path sentences [J]. *Journal of Psycholinguistic Research*, 1993(22): 239–250.

Hoeks, J. C. J., Stowe, L. A. & Doedens, G. Seeing words in context: The interaction of lexical and sentence level information during reading [J]. *Cognitive Brain Research*, 2004(19): 59–73.

Honey, G. D., Fu, C. H. & Kim, J. Effects of verbal working memory load on corticocortical connectivity modeled by path analysis of functional magnetic resonance imaging data [J]. *NeuroImage*, 2002, *17*(2): 573–582.

Hopp, H. Syntactic features and reanalysis in near-native processing [J]. *Second Language Research*, 2006(22): 369–397.

Hopp, H. Ultimate attainment in L2 inflectional morphology: Performance similarities between non-native and native speakers [J]. *Lingua*, 2010(120): 901–931.

Hopp, H. Working memory effects in the L2 processing of ambiguous relative clauses [J]. *Language Acquisition*, 2014(21): 250–278.

Hopp, H. Individual differences in the second language processing of object-subject ambiguities [J]. *Applied Psycholinguistics*, 2015, *36*(2): 129–173.

Hsu, N. S., Jaeggi, S. M. & Novick, J. M. A common neural hub resolves syntactic and non-syntactic conflict through cooperation with task-specific networks [J]. *Brain and Language*, 2017(166): 63–77.

Izumi, S. Processing difficulty in comprehension and production of relative clauses by learners of English as a second language [J]. *Language Learning*, 2003(53): 285–323.

Jacobsen, C. F. Functions of frontal association area primates [J]. *Archives of Neurology and Psychiatry*, 1935, *33*(3): 558–569.

Jacobsen, C. F. Studies of cerebral function in primates. I. The functions of the frontal association areas in monkeys [J]. *Comparative Psychology Monographs*, 1936(13): 3–60.

Jaeggi, S. M., Buschkuehl, M., Jonides, J. & Perrig, W. J. Improving fluid intelligence with training on working memory [C]. Proceedings of the National Academy of Sciences of the United States of America, 2008, *105*(19): 6829–6833.

Jeon, H.-A. & Friederici, A. D. Two principles of organization in the prefrontal cortex are cognitive hierarchy and degree of automaticity [J]. *Nature Communications*, 2013, *4*(3): 20–41.

Jeon, H.-A. & Friederici, A. D. Degree of automaticity and the prefrontal cortex [J]. *Trends in Cognitive Sciences*, 2015(19): 244–250.

Jeon, H.-A. Hierarchical processing in the prefrontal cortex in a variety of cognitive domains [J]. *Frontiers in Systems Neuroscience*, 2014, *223*(8): 1–8.

Jeong, H., Sugiura, M., Sassa, Y., Haji, T., Usui, N., Taira, M., Horie, K., Sato, S. & Kawashima, R. Effect of syntactic similarity on cortical activation during second language processing: A comparison of English and Japanese among native Korean trilinguals [J]. *Human Brain Mapping*, 2007(28): 194–204.

Juffs, A. The influence of first language on the processing of wh-movement in English as a second language [J]. *Second Language Research*, 2005(21): 121–151.

Juffs, A. Representation, processing and working memory in a second language [J]. *Transactions of the Philological Society*, 2004(102): 199–226.

Juffs, A. Some effects of first language and working memory on the processing of wh-movement in English as a second language [J]. *Second Language Research*, 2006(21): 121–151.

Just, M. A. & Carpenter, P. A. A capacity theory of comprehension: Individual differences in working memory [J]. *Psychological Review*, 1992(99): 122–149.

Just, M. A. & Varma, S. A hybrid architecture for working memory: Reply to MacDonald and Christiansen (2002) [J]. *Psychological Review*, 2002, *109*(1): 55–65.

Just, M. A. & Varma, S. The organization of thinking: What functional brain imaging reveals about the neuroarchitecture of complex cognition [J]. *Cognitive,*

Affective, & Behavioral Neuroscience, 2007, *7*(3): 153-191.

Just, M. A., Carpenter, P. A. & Keller, T. The capacity theory of comprehension: new frontiers of evidence and arguments [J]. *The Psychological Review*, 1996(103): 773-780.

Kaan, E. & Swaab, T. Repair, revision, and complexity in syntactic analysis: An electrophysiological differentiation [J]. *Journal of Cognitive Neuroscience*, 2003(15): 98-110.

Kaan, E., Harris, A., Gibson, E. & Holcomb, P. The P600 as an index of syntactic integration difficulty [J]. *Language and Cognitive Processes*, 2000(15): 159-201.

Kane, M. J., Hambrick, D. Z., Wilhelm, O., Payne, T., Tuholski, S. & Engle, R. W. The generality of working memory capacity: A latent variable approach to verbal and visuospatial memory span and reasoning [J]. *Journal of Experimental Psychology: General*, 2004(133): 189-217.

Kane, M. J. & Engle, R. W. The role of prefrontal cortex in working-memory capacity, executive attention, and general fluid intelligence: an individual-differences perspective [J]. *Psychonomic Bulletin & Review*, 2002, *9*(4): 637-671.

Karimi, H. & Ferreira, F. Good-enough linguistic representations and online cognitive equilibrium in language processing [J]. *Quarterly Journal of Experimental Psychology*, 2016, *69*(5): 1013-1040.

Kellogg, R. A model of working memory in writing [M]// Levy, C. M. & Ransdell, S. *The Science of Writing: Theories, Methods, Individual Differences and Applications*. Mahwah: Lawrence Erlbaum, 1996.

Kemper, S., Crow, A. & Kemtes, K. Eye-fixation patterns of high-and low-span young and older adults: down the garden path and back again [J]. *Psychology and Aging*, 2004(19): 157-170.

Kemtes, K. A. & Kemper, S. Younger and older adults' on-line processing of syntactically ambiguous sentences [J]. *Psychology and Aging*, 1997, *12*(2): 362-371.

Keppel, G. & Underwood, B. J. Proactive inhibition in the short-term retention of single items [J]. *Journal of Verbal Learning and Verbal Behavior*, 1962(2): 153–161.

Keppel, G., Postman, L. & Zavortink, B. Studies of learning to learn: VIII. The influence of massive amounts of training upon the learning and retention of paired-associate lists [J]. *Journal of Verbal Learning and Verbal Behavior*, 1968(7): 790–796.

Kidd, E., Donnelly, S. & Christiansen, M. H. Individual differences in language acquisition and processing [J]. *Trends in Cognitive Sciences*, 2018, *22*(2): 154–169.

Kim, A. & Osterhout, L. The independence of combinatory semantic processing: Evidence from event-related potentials [J]. *Journal of Memory and Language*, 2005(52): 205–225.

Kim, J. H. & Christianson, K. Sentence complexity and working memory effects in ambiguity resolution [J]. *Journal of Psycholinguistics Research*, 2012(42): 393–411.

Kim, J. H. *Working Memory Effects on Bilingual Sentence Processing* [D]. Urbana-Champaign: University of Illinois, 2008.

Kim, J., Kim, M., Lee, J., Lee, D., Lee, M. & Kwon, J. Dissociation of working memory processing associated with native and second languages: PET investigation [J]. *NeuroImage*, 2002(15): 879–891.

Kim, J. H. & Christianson, K. Working memory effects on L1 and L2 processing of ambiguous relative clauses by Korean L2 learners of English [J]. *Second Language Research*, 2017, *33*(3): 365–388.

Kimball, J. Seven principles of surface structure parsing in natural language [J]. *Cognition*, 1973(2): 15–47.

Kimball, J. *Syntax and Semantics. Volume 4* [M]. New York: Academic Press, 1975.

King, J. W. & Kutas, M. Who did what and when? Using word and clause-level ERPs to monitor working memory usage in reading [J]. *Journal of Cognitive Neuroscience*, 1995(7): 376–395.

King, J. & Just, M. A. Individual differences in syntactic processing: The role of working memory [J]. *Journal of Memory and Language*, 1991(30): 580-602.

Kintsch, W. & Cacioppo, J. T. Introduction to the 100th anniversary issue of the Psychological Review [J]. *Psychological Review*, 1994, *101*(2): 195-199.

Kintsch, W., Patel, V. L. & Ericsson, K. A. The role of long-term working memory in text comprehension [J]. *Psychologia*, 1999, *42*(4): 186-198.

Klauer, K. C. & Zhao, Z. Double dissociations in visual and spatial short-term memory [J]. *Journal of Experimental Psychology: General*, 2004(133): 355-381.

Klimesch, W. Binding principles in the theta frequency range [M]// Zimmer, H. D., Mecklinger, A. & Lindenberger, U. *Handbook of Binding and Memory*. Oxford: Oxford University Press, 2006: 115-144.

Klingberg, T. *The Overflowing Brain: Information Overload and the Limits of Working Memory* [M]. Oxford: Oxford University Press, 2009.

Kluender, R. & Kutas, M. Bridging the gap: Evidence from ERPs on the processing of unbounded dependencies [J]. *Journal of Cognitive Neuroscience*, 1993(5): 196-214.

Kluender, R. & Münte, T. F. Subject/object asymmetries: ERPs to grammatical and ungrammatical wh-questions [C]. Poster presented at the 11 Annual CUNY Conference on Human Sentence Processing. New Brunswick, 1998.

Knoesche, T. R., Maess, B. & Friederici, A. D. Processing of syntactic information monitored by brain surface current density mapping based on MEG [J]. *Brain Topography*, 2000(12): 75-87.

Koechlin, E. & Jubault, T. Broca's area and the hierarchical organization of human behavior [J]. *Neuron*, 2006(50): 963-974.

Koechlin, E., Ody, C. & Kouneiher, F. The architecture of cognitive control in the human prefrontal cortex [J]. *Science*, 2003(302): 1181-1185.

Kolk, H. H., Chwilla, D. J., van Herten, M. & Oor, P. J. Structure and limited capacity in verbal working memory: A study with event-related potentials [J]. *Brain and Language*, 2003(85): 1-36.

Kondo, H., Osaka, N. & Osaka, M. Cooperation of the anterior cingulate cortex and dorsolateral prefrontal cortex for attention shifting [J]. *NeuroImage*, 2004, *23*(2): 670–679.

Kormos, J. & S'af'ar, A. Phonological short-term memory, working memory and foreign language performance in intensive language learning [J]. Bilingualism: *Language and Cognition*, 2008(11): 261–271.

Kotz, S. A., Holcomb, P. J. & Osterhout, L. ERPs reveal comparable syntactic sentence processing in native and non-native readers of English [J]. *Acta Psychologica*, 2008, *128*(3): 514–527.

Krashen, S. D. *Second Language Acquisition and Second Language Learning* [M]. Oxford: Pergamon Press, 1981.

Krashen, S. D. *Principles and Practice in Second Language Acquisition* [M]. Oxford: Pergamon Press, 1982.

Krashen, S. D., Terrell, T. D., Ehrman, M. E. & Herzog, M. A theoretical basis for teaching the receptive skills [J]. *Foreign Language Annals*, 1984, *17*(4): 261–275.

Kuno, S. The position of relative clauses and conjunctions [J]. *Linguistic Inquiry*, 1974(5): 117–136.

Kuperberg, G. R. Neural mechanisms of language comprehension: Challenges to syntax [J]. *Brain Research*, 2007(1146): 23–49.

Kuperberg, G. R., Kreher, D. A., Sitnikova, T., Caplan, D. & Holcomb, P. J. The role of animacy and thematic relationships in processing active English sentences: Evidence from event-related potentials [J]. *Brain and Language*, 2007(100): 223–238.

Kuperberg, G. R., Sitnikova, T., Caplan, D. & Holcomb, P. J. Electrophysiological distinctions in processing conceptual relationships within simple sentences [J]. *Cognitive Brain Research*, 2003(17): 117–129.

Kurthen, I., Meyer, M., Schlesewsky, M. & Bornkessel-Schlesewsky, I. Individual differences in peripheral hearing and cognition reveal sentence processing differences in healthy older adults [J]. *Frontiers in Neuroscience*, 2020(14):

1-20.

Kurtzman, H. *Studies in Syntactic Ambiguity Resolution* [D]. Bloomington: Indiana University Linguistics Club, 1985.

Kutas, M. & Federmeier, K. D. Electrophysiology reveals semantic memory use in language comprehension [J]. *Trends in Cognitive Sciences*, 2000(4): 463-470.

Kutas, M. & Federmeier, K. D. Thirty years and counting: Finding meaning in the N400 component of the event-related brain potential (ERP) [J]. *Annual Review of Psychology*, 2011(62): 621-647.

Kutas, M. & Hillyard, S. A. Reading senseless sentences: Brain potentials reflect semantic anomaly [J]. *Science*, 1980a(207): 203-205.

Kutas, M. & Hillyard, S. A. Event-related brain potentials to semantically inappropriate and surprisingly large words [J]. *Biological Psychology*, 1980b(11): 99-116.

Kutas, M. & Hillyard, S. A. Reading between the lines: Event-related brain potentials during natural sentence processing [J]. *Brain and Language*, 1980c(11): 354-373.

Kutas, M. & Hillyard, S. A. Event-related brain potentials to grammatical errors and semantic anomalies [J]. *Memory and Cognition*, 1983(11): 539-550.

Kutas, M. & Hillyard, S. A. Brain potentials reflect word expectancy and semantic association during reading [J]. *Nature*, 1984(307): 161-163.

Kutas, M., & van Petten, C. Psycholinguistics electrified: Event-related brain potential investigations [M]// Gernsbacher, M. A. *Handbook of Psycholinguistics*. San Diego: Academic Press, 1994: 83-143.

Kwon, H., Reiss, A. L. & Menon, V. Neural Basis of Protracted Developmental Changes in Visuo-Spatial Working Memory [J]. *Proceedings of the National Academy of Sciences*, 2002, *99*(20): 13336-13341.

Lebedev, M. A., Messinger, A., Kralik, J. D. & Wise, S. P. Representation of Attended Versus Remembered Locations in Prefrontal Cortex [J]. *PLoS Biology*, 2004, *2*(11): e365.

Ledoux, K., Camblin, C. C., Swaab, T. Y. & Gordon, P. C. Reading words in discourse: The modulation of intralexical priming effects by message-level context [J]. *Behavioral and Cognitive Neuroscience Reviews*, 2006(5): 107–127.

Leeser, M. J. Learner-based factors in L2 reading comprehension and processing grammatical form: Topic familiarity and working memory [J]. *Language Learning*, 2007(57): 229–270.

Lehto, J. Are executive function tests dependent on working memory capacity? [J] *The Quarterly Journal of Experimental Psychology Section A*, 1996(49): 29–50.

Lenneberg, E. *Biological Foundations of Language* [M]. New York: Wiley, 1967.

Levin, E. S. *Working Memory: Capacity, Developments and Improvement Techniques* [M]. New York: Nova Science Publishers, Inc., 2011.

Lewis, R. L. & Vasishth, S. An activation-based model of sentence processing as skilled memory retrieval [J]. *Cognitive Science*, 2005(29): 375–419.

Lewis, R. L., Vasishth, S. & van Dyke, J. A. Computational principles of working memory in sentence comprehension [J]. *Trends in Cognitive Sciences*, 2006(10): 44–54.

Linck, J. A., Hughes, M. M., Campbell, S. G., Silbert, N. H., Tare, M., Jackson, S. R. & Doughty, C. J. Hi-LAB: A new measure of aptitude for high-level language proficiency [J]. *Language Learning*, 2013(63): 530–566.

Logačev, P. & Vasishth, S. Understanding underspecification: A comparison of two computational implementations [J]. *Quarterly Journal of Experimental Psychology*, 2016, *69*(5): 996–1012.

Long, D. L. & Prat, C. Individual differences in syntactic ambiguity resolution: Readers vary in their use of plausibility information [J]. *Memory and Cognition*, 2008(36): 375–391.

MacDonald, M. C. & Christiansen, M. H. Reassessing working memory: Comment on Just and Carpenter (1992) and Waters and Caplan (1996) [J]. *Psychological Review*, 2002(109): 35–54.

MacDonald, M. C., Just, M. A. & Carpenter, P. A. Working memory constraints on the processing of syntactic ambiguity [J]. *Cognitive Psychology*, 1992(24): 56–98.

MacDonald, M. C., Pearlmutter, N. J. & Seidenberg, M. S. The lexical nature of syntactic ambiguity resolution [J]. *Psychological Review*, 1994(101): 676–703.

Mander, B. A., Rao, V. & Lu, B. Prefrontal atrophy, disrupted NREM slow waves and impaired hippocampal-dependent memory in aging [J]. *Nature Neuroscience*, 2013, *16*(3): 357–364.

Marcus, M. P. *A Theory of Syntactic Recognition for Natural Language* [M]. Cambridge: MIT Press, 1980.

Marian, V. & Spivey, M. Bilingual and monolingual processing of competing lexical items [J]. *Applied Psycholinguistics*, 2003, *24*(2): 173–193.

Markowitsch, H. J. & Pritzel, M. The prefrontal cortex: Projection area of the thalamic mediodorsal nucleus? [J]. *Physiological Psychology*, 1979, *7*(1): 1–6.

Markus, P., Bornkessel-Schlesewsky, I., Bisang, W. & Schlesewsky, M. The role of animacy in the real time comprehension of Mandarin Chinese: Evidence from auditory event-related brain potentials [J]. *Brain and Language*, 2008(105): 112–133.

Marslen-Wilson, W. & Tyler, L. K. The temporal structure of spoken language understanding [J]. *Cognition*, 1980(8): 1–71.

Martin, R. C. Working memory doesn't work: A critique of Miyake et al.'s capacity theory of aphasic comprehension deficit [J]. *Cognitive Neuropsychology*, 1995(12): 623–636.

Martin, R. C. & Feher, E. The consequences of reduced memory span for the comprehension of semantic versus syntactic information [J]. *Brain and Language*, 1990(38): 1–20.

Martin, R. C. & He, T. Semantic short-term memory and its role in sentence processing: A replication [J]. *Brain and Language*, 2004(89): 76–82.

Martin, R. C. & Lesch, M. F. Correspondences and dissociations between single word processing and short-term memory [J]. *Brain and Language*, 1995(51): 220–223.

Martin, R. C. & Romani, C. Verbal working memory and sentence comprehension: A multiple-components view [J]. *Neuropsychology*, 1994(8): 506–523.

Martin, R. C., Shelton, J. R. & Yaffee, L. S. Language processing and working memory: Neuropsychological evidence for separate phonological and semantic capacities [J]. *Journal of Memory and Language*, 1994(33): 83–111.

Martin, C. D., Thierry, G., Kuipers, J.-R., Boutonnet, B., Foucart, A. & Costa, A. Bilinguals reading in their second language do not predict upcoming words as native readers do [J]. *Journal of Memory and Language*, 2013(69): 574–588.

Mazuka, R., Jincho, N. & Oishi, H. Development of executive control and language processing [J]. *Language and Linguistics Compass*, 2009, *3*(1): 59–89.

McCabe, D. P., Roediger, H. L., McDaniel, M. A., Balota, D. A. & Hambrick, D. Z. The relationship between working memory capacity and executive functioning: Evidence for a common executive attention construct [J]. *Neuropsychology*, 2010(24): 222–243.

McCarthy, R. A. & Warrington, E. K. *Cognitive Neuropsychology: A Clinical Introduction* [M]. London: Academic Press, 1990.

McDonald, J. Beyond the critical period: Processing-based explanations for poor grammaticality judgment performance by late second language learners [J]. *Journal of Memory and Language*, 2006(55): 381–401.

McElree, B. Accessing recent events [M] // Ross, B. *The Psychology of Learning and Motivation, Volume 46*. San Diego: Academic Press, 2006.

McElree, B., Foraker, S. & Dyer, L. Memory structures that subserve sentence comprehension [J]. *Journal of Memory and Language*, 2003(48): 67–91.

McKinnon, R. & Osterhout, L. Constraints on movement phenomena in sentence processing: Evidence from event-related brain potentials [J]. *Language and Cognitive Processes*, 1996(11): 495–523.

McNab, F., Varrone, A. & Farde, L. Changes in cortical dopamine D1 receptor binding associated with cognitive training [J]. *Science*, 2009, *323*(5915): 800–

802.

McRae, K., Spivey-Knowlton, M. J. & Tanenhaus, M. K. Modeling the influence of thematic fit (and other constraints) in on-line sentence comprehension [J]. *Journal of Memory and Language*, 1998(38): 283-312.

Mecklinger, A., Schriefers, H., Steinhauer, K. & Friederici, A. D. Processing relative clauses varying on syntactic and semantic dimensions: An analysis with event-related potentials [J]. *Memory and Cognition*, 1995(23): 477-494.

Mendelsohn, A., & Pearlmutter, N. J. Individual differences in relative clause attachment ambiguities [C]. Poster presented at the 12th Annual CUNY Conference on Human Sentence Processing, City University of New York, 1999.

Miller, E. K., Freedman, D. J. & Wallis, J. D. The prefrontal cortex: categories, concepts and cognition [J]. *Philosophical Transactions: Biological Sciences*, 2002, *357*(1424): 1123-1136.

Miller, G. A. The magical number seven, plus or minus two: Some limits on our capacity for processing information [J]. *Psychological Review*, 1956, *63*(2): 81-97.

Mitchell, J. P., Heatherton, T. F. & Macrae, C. N. Distinct neural systems subserve person and object knowledge [J]. Proceedings of the National Academy of Sciences of the United States of America, 2002, *99*(23): 15238-15243.

Mitchell, D. C. Sentence parsing [M]// Gernsbacher, M. A. *Handbook of Psycholinguistics*. San Diego: Academic Press, 1994: 375-409.

Miyake, A. & Friedman, N. Individual differences in second language proficiency: Working memory as language aptitude [M]// Healy, A. & Bourne, L. *Foreign Language Learning: Psycholinguistic Studies on Training and Retention*. Mahwah: Lawrence Erlbaum, 1998: 339-364.

Miyake, A. & Friedman, N. P. The nature and organization of individual differences in executive functions: Four general conclusions [J]. *Current Directions in Psychological Science*, 2012(21): 8-14.

Miyake, A., Carpenter, P. A. & Just, M. A. A capacity approach to syntactic comprehension disorders: Making normal adults perform like aphasic patients [J]. *Cognitive Neuropsychology*, 1994(11): 671-717.

Miyake, A., Carpenter, P. A. & Just, M. A. Reduced resources and specific impairments in normal and aphasic sentence comprehension [J]. *Cognitive Neuropsychology*, 1995(12): 651-679.

Miyake, A., Friedman, N. P., Emerson, M. J., Witzki, A. H., Howerter, A. & Wager, T. D. The unity and diversity of executive functions and their contributions to complex "frontal lobe" tasks: A latent variable analysis [J]. *Cognitive Psychology*, 2000, *41*(1): 49-100.

Miyake, A., Just, M. A. & Carpenter, P. A. Working memory constraints on the resolution of lexical ambiguity: maintaining multiple interpretation in neutral contexts [J]. *Journal of Memory and Language*, 1994(33): 175-202.

Miyake, A. & Shah, P. Toward unified theories of working memory [C] // Miyake, A. *Models of Working Memory: Mechanism of Active Maintenance and Executive Control*. Cambridge: Cambridge University Press, 1999.

Moody, D. E. Can intelligence be increased by training on a task of working memory? [J] *Intelligence*, 2009, *37*(4): 327-328.

Muente, T. F., Heinze, H. J., Matzke, M., Wieringa, B. M. & Johannes, S. Brain potentials and syntactic violations revisited: No evidence for specificity of the syntactic positive shift [J]. *Neuropsychologia*, 1998(36): 217-226.

Müller, Ralph-Axel & Basho, S. Are nonlinguistic functions in "Broca's area" prerequisites for language acquisition? FMRI findings from an ontogenetic viewpoint [J]. *Brain and Language*, 2004(89): 329-336.

Münte, T. F., Schiltz, K. & Kutas, M. When temporal terms belie conceptual order [J]. *Nature*, 1998(395): 71-73.

Murray, E., Wise, S. & Graham, K. *Chapter 1: The History of Memory Systems. The Evolution of Memory Systems: Ancestors, Anatomy, and Adaptations* [M]. 1st ed. Oxford: Oxford University Press, 2016: 22-24.

Myles, F., Mitchell, R. & Hooper, J. Interrogative chunks in French L2: A basis for creative construction [J] *Studies in Second Language Acquisition*, 1999(21):

49-80.

Näätänen, R. & Escera, C. Mismatch negativity: clinical and other applications [J]. *Audiology and Neurotology*, 2000, *5*(3-4): 105-110.

Nakano, Y. & Wang, M. Relative-clause attachments in L1 and L2 English of Japanese Learners: An Offline Questionnaire and Eye-Tracking Studies [C]. Poster presented at Architectures and Mechanisms for Language Processing (AMLaP), York, 2011: 19-23.

Nee, D. E., Brown, J. W., Askren, M. K., Berman, M. G., Demiralp, E., Krawitz, A. & Jonides, J. A meta-analysis of executive components of working memory [J]. *Cerebral Cortex*, 2012, *23*(2): 264-282.

Nee, D. E., Wager, T. D. & Jonides, J. Interference resolution: Insights from a meta-analysis of neuroimaging tasks [J]. *Cognitive, Affective, & Behavioral Neuroscience*, 2007, *7*(1): 1-17.

Neville, H. J., Mills, D. B. & Lawson, D. S. Fractionating language: Different neural subsystems with different sensitive periods [J]. *Cerebral Cortex*, 1992(2): 244-258.

Newport, E. L. Maturational constraints on language learning [J]. *Cognitive Science*, 1990(14): 11-28.

Newport, E. L., Bavelier, D. & Neville, H. J. Critical thinking about critical periods: Perspectives on a critical period for language acquisition [M] // Dupoux, E. *Language, Brain and Cognitive Development: Essays in Honor of Jaques Mehler*. Cambridge: MIT Press, 2001: 481-502.

Nieuwland, M. S. & van Berkum, J. J. A. Individual differences and contextual bias in pronoun resolution: Evidence from ERPs [J]. *Brain Research*, 2006(1118): 155-167.

Novick, J. M., Trueswell, J. C. & Thompson-Schill, S. L. Cognitive control and parsing: Reexamining the role of Broca's area in sentence comprehension [J]. *Cognitive, Affective, & Behavioral Neuroscience*, 2005, *5*(3): 263-281.

Novick, J. M., Trueswell, J. C. & Thompson-Schill, S. L. Broca's area and language processing: Evidence for the cognitive control connection [J]. *Language and*

Linguistics Compass, 2010, *4*(10): 906–924.

Novick, J. M., Hussey, E., Teubner-Rhodes, S., Harbison, J. I. & Bunting, M. F. Clearing the garden-path: Improving sentence processing through cognitive control training [J]. *Language, Cognition and Neuroscience*, 2014, *29*(2): 186–217.

O' Malley, J. M. & Chamot, A. U. *Learning Strategies in Second Language Acquisition* [M]. Cambridge: Cambridge University Press, 1990.

Oberauer, K. Access to information in working memory: exploring the focus of attention [J]. *Journal of Experimental Psychology. Learning, Memory, and Cognition*, 2002, *28*(3): 411–421.

Oberauer, K., Sus, H.-M., Schulze, R., Wilhelm, O. & Wittmann, W. W. Working memory capacity—facets of a cognitive ability construct [J]. *Personality and Individual Differences*, 2000, *29*(6): 1017–1045.

Oberauer, K. & Kliegl, R. A formal model of capacity limits in working memory [J]. *Journal of Memory and Language*, 2006, *55*(4): 601–626.

Omaki, A. *Working Memory and Relative Clause Attachment in First and Second Language Processing* [D]. Honolulu: University of Hawaii, 2005.

O' Reilly, R. C., Busby, R. S. & Soto, R. Three forms of binding and their neural substrates: Alternatives to temporal synchrony [M] // Cleeremans, A. *The Unity of Consciousness: Binding, Integration, and Dissociation*. Oxford: Oxford University Press, 2003: 168–190.

Osaka, N., Osaka, M., Kondo, H., Morishita, M., Fukuyama, H. & Shibasaki, H. The neural basis of executive function in working memory: an fMRI study based on individual differences [J]. *NeuroImage*, 2004, *21*(2): 623–631.

Osterhout, L. & Holcomb, P. Event-related potentials and syntactic anomaly: Evidence of anomaly detection during the perception of continuous speech [J]. *Language and Cognitive Processes*, 1993(8): 413–437.

Osterhout, L. & Holcomb, P. J. Event-related brain potentials elicited by syntactic anomaly [J]. *Journal of Memory and Language*, 1992(31): 785–806.

Osterhout, L. & Nicol, J. On the distinctiveness, independence, and time course of the brain responses to syntactic and semantic anomalies [J]. *Language and Cognitive Processes*, 1999(14): 283–317.

Osterhout, L., Holcomb, P. J. & Swinney, D. A. Brain potentials elicited by garden-path sentences: Evidence of the application of verb information during parsing [J]. *Journal of Experimental Psychology: Learning, Memory, and Cognition*, 1994(20): 786–803.

Owen, A. M. The functional organization of working memory processes within human lateral frontal cortex: the contribution of functional neuroimaging [J]. *The European Journal of Neuroscience*, 1997, 9(7): 1329–1339.

Pan, H. & Felser, C. Referential context effects in L2 ambiguity resolution: Evidence from self-paced reading [J]. *Lingua*, 2011(121): 221–236.

Pan, H., Schimke, S. & Felser, C. Referential context effects in non-native relative clause ambiguity resolution [J]. *International Journal of Bilingualism*, 2015(19): 298–313.

Papadopoulou, D. & Clahsen, H. Parsing strategies in L1 and L2 sentence processing: A study of relative clause attachment in Greek [J]. *Studies in Second Language Acquisition*, 2003(25): 501–528.

Patson, N. D., Darowski, E. S., Moon, N. & Ferreira, F. Lingering misinterpretations in garden-path sentences: Evidence from a paraphrasing task [J]. *Journal of Experimental Psychology: Learning, Memory, & Cognition*, 2009(35): 280–285.

Payne, B. R. & Stine-Morrow, E. A. L. The effects of home-based cognitive training on verbal working memory and language comprehension in older adulthood [J]. *Frontiers in Aging Neuroscience*, 2017(9): 1–20.

Pearlmutter, N. J. & MacDonald, M. C. Individual differences and probabilistic constraints in syntactic ambiguity resolution [J]. *Journal of Memory and Language*, 1995(34): 521–542.

Penfield, W. & Roberts, L. *Speech and Brain Mechanisms* [M]. Princeton: Princeton University Press, 1959.

Perani, D. & Abutalebi, J. The neural basis of first and second language processing

［J］. *Current Opinion in Neurobiology*, 2005(15): 202-206.

Peterson, L. R. & Peterson, M. J. Short-term retention of individual verbal items［J］. *Journal of Experimental Psychology*, 1959(58): 193-198.

Phillips, C., Kazanina, N. & Abada, S. H. ERP effects of the processing of syntactic long-distance dependencies［J］. *Cognitive Brain Research*, 2005(22): 407-428.

Pickering, S. J., Tracy, P. A. & Susan, E. G. *Working Memory in Dyslexia. Working Memory and Neurodevelopmental Disorders*［M］. New York: Psychology Press, 2006.

Postle, B. R. Working memory as an emergent property of the mind and brain［J］. *Neuroscience*, 2006, *139*(1): 23-38.

Potter, M. Very short-term conceptual memory［J］. *Memory and Cognition*, 1993, *21*(2): 156-161.

Preuss, T. M. Do rats have prefrontal cortex? The rose-woolsey-akert program reconsidered［J］. *Journal of Cognitive Neuroscience*, 1995, *7*(1): 1-24.

Pribram, K. H., Mishkin, M., Rosvold, H. E. & Kaplan, S. J. Effects on delayed-response performance of lesions of dorsolateral and ventromedial frontal cortex of baboons［J］. *Journal of comparative and physiological psychology*, 1952, *45*(6): 565-575.

Pribram, K. H., Miller, G. A. & Galanter, E. *Plans and the Structure of Behavior*［M］. New York: Holt, Rinehart and Winston, 1960.

Price, J. L. Prefrontal cortical networks related to visceral function and mood［J］. *Annals of the New York Academy of Sciences*, 1999(877): 383-396.

Pulido, D. C. Modeling the role of second language proficiency and topic familiarity in second language incidental vocabulary acquisition through reading［J］. *Language Learning*, 2003(53): 233-284.

Pulido, D. C. The relationship between text comprehension and second language incidental vocabulary acquisition: A matter of topic familiarity［J］ *Language Learning*, 2004(54): 469-523.

Qian, Z., Garnsey, S. & Christianson, K. A comparison of online and offline measures of good enough processing in garden path sentences [J]. *Language, Cognition and Neuroscience*, 2018(2): 227–254.

Raffone, A. & Wolters, G. A cortical mechanism for binding in visual working memory [J]. *Journal of Cognitive Neuroscience*, 2001, *13*(6): 766–785.

Rayner, K., Carlson, M. & Frazier, L. The interaction of syntax and semantics during sentence processing [J]. *Journal of Verbal Learning and Verbal Behavior*, 1983, *22*(3): 358–374.

Reichle, R. V., Tremblay, A. & Coughlin, C. E. Selected Proceedings of the 2011 Second Language Research Forum: Converging Theory and Practice [C]// Erik Voss, S.-J., Tai, D. & Li, Z. *Cascadilla Proceedings Project Somerville*. Amherst: GLSA Publications, 2013: 115–119.

Richards, J. C., Platt, J. & Platt, H. *Longman Dictionary of Language Teaching & Applied Linguistics* [M]. Beijing: Foreign Language Teaching and Research Press, 2000.

Rivers, W. M. *Interactive Language Teaching* [M]. Cambridge: Cambridge University Press, 1987.

Robbins, T. W. & Arnsten, A. F. The neuropsychopharmacology of fronto-executive function: monoaminergic modulation [J]. *Annual Review of Neuroscience*, 2009(32): 267–287.

Robinson, P. Effects of individual differences in intelligence, aptitude and working memory on adult incidental SLA: A replication and extension of Reber, Walkenfeld and Hernstadt, 1991 [M]// Robinson, P. *Individual Differences and Instructed Language Learning* Amsterdam: John Benjamins, 2002: 211–266.

Robinson, P. Attention, memory, and the "noticing" hypothesis [J]. *Language learning*, 1995(45): 283–331.

Robinson, P. Task complexity, cognitive resources, and syllabus design: A triadic framework for examining task influences on SLA [M]// Robinson, P. *Cognition and Second Language Instruction*. New York: Cambridge University Press, 2001a: 287–318.

Robinson, P. Task complexity, task difficulty, and task production: Exploring interactions in a componential framework [J]. *Applied Linguistics*, 2001b(22): 27–57.

Rodriguez-Fornells, A., Rotte, M., Heinze, H.-J., Nösselt, T. & Münte, T. F. Brain potential and functional MRI evidence for how to handle two languages with one brain [J]. *Nature*, 2002(415): 1026–1029.

Roesler, F., Pechmann, T., Streb, J., Roeder, B. & Hennighausen, E. Parsing of sentences in a language with varying word order: Word-by-word variations of processing demands are revealed by event-related brain potentials [J]. *Journal of Memory and Language*, 1998(38): 150–176.

Roodenrys, S., Alloway, T. P. & Gathercole, S. E. *Working Memory Function in Attention Deficit Hyperactivity Disorder Working Memory and Neurodevelopmental Disorders* [M]. New York: Psychology Press, 2006.

Rosen, V. & Engle, R. W. Working memory capacity and suppression [J]. *Journal of Memory and Language*, 1998(39): 418–436.

Rüschemeyer, Shirley-Ann, Zysset, S. & Friederici, A. D. Native and non-native reading of sentences: An fMRI experiment [J]. *NeuroImage*, 2006(31): 354–365.

Rüschemeyer, Shirley-Ann, Fiebach, C. J., Kempe, V. & Friederici, A. D. Processing lexical semantic and syntactic information in first and second language: fMRI evidence from German and Russian [J]. *Human Brain Mapping*, 2005(25): 266–286.

Rubin, J. A review of second language listening comprehension research [J]. *The Modern Language Journal*, 1994(78): 199–221.

Rudner, M., Fransson, P., Ingvar, M., Nyberg, L. & Rönnberg, J. Neural representation of binding lexical signs and words in the episodic buffer of working memory [J]. *Neuropsychologia*, 2007, *45*(10): 2258–2276.

Rummer, R. & Engelkamp, J. Phonological information contributes to short-term recall of auditorily presented sentences [J]. *Journal of Memory and Language*, 2001, *45*(3): 451–467.

Sabri, M., Kareken, D. A., Dzemidzic, M., Lowe, M. J. & Melara, R. D. Neural correlates of auditory sensory memory and automatic change detection [J]. *NeuroImage*, 2004, *21*(1): 69–74.

Saffran, E. Short-term memory impairment and language processing [M] // Caramazza, A. *Cognitive Neuropsychology and Neurolinguistics: Advances in Models of Cognitive Function and Impairment*. Hillsdale: Erlbaum, 1990: 137–168.

Sagarra, N. Investigation the role of working memory in L2 processing: Methodological issues [M] // Han, Z. *Second Language Processing and Instruction: Broadening the Scope of Inquiry*. Clevedon: Multilingual Matters, 2005: 363–398.

Sanford, A. J. & Sturt, P. Depth of processing in language comprehension: Not noticing the evidence [J]. *Trends in Cognitive Sciences*, 2002(6): 382–386.

Schacter, D. L., Gilbert, D. T. & Wegner, D. M. *Psychology* [M]. 2nd ed. New York: Worth Publishers, 2011: 364–366.

Scheutz, M. & Eberhard, K. Effects of morphosyntactic gender features in bilingual language processing [J]. *Cognitive Science*, 2004, *28*(4): 559–588.

Schlesewsky, M. & Bornkessel, I. On incremental interpretation: degrees of meaning accessed during sentence comprehension [J]. *Lingua*, 2004, *114*(9): 1213–1234.

Schonwiesner, M., Novitski, N., Pakarinen, S., Carlson, S., Tervaniemi, M. & Naatanen, R. Heschl's gyrus, posterior superior temporal gyrus, and mid-ventrolateral prefrontal cortex have different roles in the detection of acoustic changes [J]. *Journal of Neurophysiology*, 2007, *97*(3): 2075–2082.

Schwartz, B. D. & Sprouse, R. A. L2 cognitive states and the full transfer/full access model [J]. *Second Language Research*, 1996(12): 40–72.

Schweickert, R. & Boruff, B. Short-term memory capacity: Magic number or magic spell? [J]. *Journal of Experimental Psychology: Learning, Memory, and Cognition*, 1986, *12*(3): 419–425.

Schweppe, J. Attention, working memory, and long-term memory in multimedia learning: An integrated perspective based on process models of working memory [J]. *Educational Psychology Review*, 2014, *26*(2): 289.

Scoresby-Jackson, R. Case of aphasia with right hemiplegia [J]. *Edinburgh Medical Journal*, 1867(12): 696–706.

Service, E. Phonology, working memory, and foreign-language learning [J]. *Quarterly Journal of Experimental Psychology*, 1992(45): 21–50.

Shallice, T. *From Neuropsychology to Mental Structure* [M]. Cambridge: Cambridge University Press, 1988.

Sharkey, N. E. & Mitchell, D. C. Word recognition in a functional context: The use of scripts in reading [J]. *Journal of Memory and Language*, 1985(24): 253–270.

Shiffrin, R. & Robert, N. Seven plus or minus two: A commentary on capacity limitations [J]. *Psychological Review*, 1994, *2*(101) (Centennial): 357–361.

Shimamura, A. P. The role of the prefrontal cortex in dynamic filtering [J]. *Psychobiology*, 2000(28): 207–218.

Sinai, A. & Pratt, H. Semantic processing of unattended words and studies on the memory processing of word pairs in bilingual Finnish-English subjects [J]. *Behavioural Brain Research*, 2002(132): 47–57.

Sinai, A. & Pratt, H. Semantic processing of unattended words and pseudowords in first and second language: An ERP study [J]. *Journal of Basic and Clinical Physiology and Pharmacology*, 2003, *14*(2): 177–190.

Skehan, P. *A Cognition Approach to Language Learning* [M]. Oxford: Oxford University Press, 1998.

Skehan, P. & Foster, P. Cognition and task [M]// Robinson, P. *Cognition and Second Language Instruction*. Cambridge: Cambridge University Press, 2001.

Skehan, P. & Foster, P. The influence of task structure and processing conditions on narrative retellings [J]. *Language Learning*, 1999, *49*(9): 93–120.

Slattery, T. J., Sturt, P., Christianson, K., Yoshida, M. & Ferreira, F. Lingering misinterpretations of garden path sentences arise from competing syntactic representations [J]. *Journal of Memory and Language*, 2013, *69*(2): 104–120.

Smith, E. E. & Jonides, J. Working memory: a view from neuroimaging [J]. *Cognitive Psychology*, 1997, *33*(1): 5-42.

Smith, E. E. & Jonides, J. Neuroimaging analyses of human working memory [J]. *Proceedings of the National Academy of Sciences of the United States of America*, 1998, *95*(20): 12061-12068.

Smith, E. E. & Jonides, J. Storage and executive processes in the frontal lobes [J]. *Science*, 1999(283): 1657-1661.

Smith, E. E., Jonides, J., Marshuetz, C. & Koeppe, R. A. Components of verbal working memory: evidence from neuroimaging [J]. *Proceedings of the National Academy of Sciences of the United States of America*, 1998, *95*(3): 876-882.

Smith, E. E. & Jonides, J. Working memory: a view from neuroimaging [J]. *Cognitive Psychology*, 1997(33): 5-42.

Snijders, T. M., Vosse, T., Kempen, G., van Berkum, J. J. A., Petersson, K. M. & Hagoort, P. Retrieval and unification of syntactic structure in sentence comprehension: An fMRI study using word-category ambiguity [J]. *Cerebral Cortex*, 2009(19): 1493-1503.

Spaulding, C. L. *Motivation in the Classroom* [M]. New York: McGraw-Hill, 1992.

Speciale, G., Ellis, N. C. & Bywater, T. Phonological sequence learning and short-term store capacity determine second language vocabulary acquisition [J]. *Applied Psycholinguistics*, 2004(25): 293-321.

Spivey, M. J. & Tanenhaus, M. K. Syntactic ambiguity resolution in discourse: Modeling the effects of referential context and lexical frequency [J]. *Journal of Experimental Psychology: Learning, Memory, and Cognition*, 1998(24): 1521-1543.

Spivey-Knowlton, M. J., Trueswell, J. C. & Tanenhaus, M. K. Context and syntactic ambiguity resolution [J]. *Canadian Journal of Psychology*, 1993(47): 276-309.

Spivey-Knowlton, M. & Sedivy, J. Resolving attachment ambiguities with multiple constraints [J]. *Cognition*, 1995(55): 227-267.

Sternberg R. J. Increasing fluid intelligence is possible after all [J]. *Proceedings of the National Academy of Sciences of the United States of America*, 2008, *105*(19): 6791–6792.

Sternberg, S. *Science* [M]. New York: American Association for the Advancement of Science, 1966.

Sternberg, S. Memory-scanning: Mental processes revealed by reaction-time experiments [J]. *American Scientist*, 1969(4): 421–457.

Sturt, P. Semantic re-interpretation and garden path recovery [J]. *Cognition*, 2007(105): 477–488.

Sucuoglu, E. Analysis of motivational strategies used by English language teachers teaching at secondary schools [J]. *Procedia Computer Science*, 2017(6): 120–123.

Sugiura, L., Hata, M., Matsuba-Kurita, H., Uga, M., Tsuzuki, D., Dan, I., Hagiwara, H. & Homae, F. Explicit performance in girls and implicit processing in boys: A simultaneous fNIRS–ERP study on second language syntactic learning in young adolescents [J]. *Frontiers in Human Neuroscience*, 2018(12): 1–19.

Suh, S., Yoon, H.-W., Lee, S., Chung, J.-Y., Cho, Z.-H. & Park, H.-W. Effects of syntactic complexity in L1 and L2: An fMRI study of Korean-English bilinguals [J]. *Brain Research*, 2007(1136): 178–189.

Swaab, T. Y., Brown, C. & Hagoort, P. Understanding ambiguous words in sentence contexts: Electrophysiological evidence for delayed contextual selection in Broca's aphasia [J]. *Neuropsychologia*, 1998(36): 737–761.

Swaab, T. Y., Ledoux, K., Camblin, C. C. & Boudewyn, M. A. (in press). Electrophysiology of language [M]// Luck, S. J. & Kappenman, E. S. *Event-related Potential Components: The Ups and Downs of Brainwave Recordings*. Oxford: Oxford University Press.

Swain, M. & Lapkin, S. Interaction and second language learning: Two adolescent French immersion students working together [J]. *Modern Language Journal*, 1998(82): 320–337.

Swanson, H. L. & Beebe-Frankenberger, M. the relationship between working memory and mathematical problem solving in children at risk and not at risk for serious math difficulties [J]. *Journal of Educational Psychology*, 2004, *96*(3): 471–491.

Swets B., Desmet, T., Hambrick, D. Z. & Ferreira, F. The role of working memory in attachment preferences [C]. Poster presented at the 17th Annual CUNY Conference on Human Sentence Processing, University of Maryland, College Park, 2004.

Swets B. & Desmet, T. The role of working memory in syntactic ambiguity resolution: a psychometric approach [J]. *Journal of Experimental Psychology: General*, 2007, *136*(1): 64–81.

Swets, B., Desmet, T., Clifton, C. & Ferreira, F. Underspecification of syntactic ambiguities: Evidence from self-paced reading [J]. *Memory and Cognition*, 2008(36): 201–216.

Tabossi, P., Spivey-Knowlton, M. J., McRae, K. & Tanenhaus, M. K. Semantic effects on syntactic ambiguity resolution: Evidence for a constraint-based resolution process [M]// Umilta, C. & Moscovitch, M. *Attention and Performance XV*. Hillsdale: Erlbaum, 1994.

Tan, L. H., Spinks, J. A., Feng, C.-M., Siok, W. T., Perfetti, C. A., Xiong, J., Fox, P. T. & Gao, J.-H. Neural systems of second language reading are shaped by native language [J]. *Human Brain Mapping*, 2003(18): 158–166.

Terry, W. S. *Learning & Memory: Basic Principles, Processes, and Procedures, Fourth Edition* [M]. Hoboken: Pearson Education, Inc., 2009.

Tirre, W. C. & Pena, C. M. Investigation of functional working memory in the reading span test [J]. *Journal of Educational Psychology*, 1992(84): 462–472.

Towse, J. N., Hitch, G. J. & Hutton, U. On the interpretation of working memory span in adults [J]. *Memory & Cognition*, 2000, *28*(3): 341–348.

Traxler, M. J. Plausibility and subcategorization preference in children's processing of temporarily ambiguous sentences: Evidence from self-paced reading [J]. *The Quarterly Journal of Experimental Psychology Section A*, 2002, *55*(1): 75–96.

Traxler, M. J. Working memory contributions to relative clause attachment processing: A hierarchical linear modeling analysis [J]. *Memory and Cognition*, 2007(35): 1107–1121.

Traxler, M. J. A hierarchical linear modeling analysis of working memory and implicit prosody in the resolution of adjunct attachment ambiguity [J]. *Journal of Psycholinguistic Research*, 2009, *38*(5): 491–509.

Traxler, M. J., Pickering, M. J. & Clifton, C., Jr. Adjunct attachment is not a form of lexical ambiguity resolution [J]. *Journal of Memory and Language*, 1998(39): 558–592.

Trueswell, J. C. The role of lexical frequency in syntactic ambiguity resolution [J]. *Journal of Memory & Language*, 1996(35): 566–585.

Trueswell, J. C. & Tanenhaus, M. K. Tense, temporal context and syntactic ambiguity resolution [J]. *Language and Cognitive Processes*, 1991(6): 303–338.

Trueswell, J. C. & Tanenhaus, M. K. Toward a lexicalist framework for constraint-based syntactic ambiguity resolution [M] // Clifton, C., Rayner, K. & Frazier, L. *Perspectives on Sentence Processing*. Hillsdale: Lawrence Erlbaum Associates, 1994.

Trueswell, J. C., Tanenhaus, M. K. & Garnsey, S. M. Semantic influences on parsing: Use of thematic role information in syntactic ambiguity resolution [J]. *Journal of Memory and Language*, 1994(33): 285–318.

Tulving, E. Episodic memory: From mind to brain [J]. *Annual Review Psychology*, 2002(53): 1–25.

Turner, M. L. & Engle, R. W. Is working memory capacity task dependent? [J] *Journal of Memory and Language*, 1989(28): 127–154.

Ullman, M. A neurocognitive perspective on language: The declarative/perspective model [J]. *Nature Reviews Neuroscience*, 2001(2): 717–726.

Ullman, M. Contributions of memory circuits to language: the declarative/procedural model [J]. *Cognition*, 2004(92): 231–270.

Underwood B. J. Interference and forgetting [J]. *Psychological Review*, 1957(64):

49-60.

Unsworth, N. & Engle, R. W. Speed and accuracy of accessing information in working memory: An individual differences investigation of focus switching [J]. *Journal of Experimental Psychology: Learning, Memory, and Cognition,* 2008(34): 616-630.

Unsworth, N., Heitz, R. P., Schrock, J. C. & Engle, R. W. An automated version of the operation span task [J]. *Behavior Research Methods,* 2005, *37*(3): 498-505.

Unsworth, N., Redick, T. S., Heitz, R. P., Broadway, J. M. & Engle, R. W. Complex working memory span tasks and higher-order cognition: A latent-variable analysis of the relationship between processing and storage [J]. *Memory,* 2009(17): 635-654.

Ur, P. *Teaching of English as a Second or Foreign Language* [M]. Cambridge: Cambridge University Press, 1984.

Uylings H. B., Groenewegen H. J. & Kolb, B. Do rats have a prefrontal cortex? [J] *Behavioural Brain Research,* 2003, *146*(1-2): 3-17.

van Berkum, J. J. A. (in press). The neuropragmatics of "simple" utterance comprehension: An ERP review [M]// Sauerland, U. & Yatsushiro, K. *Semantics and Pragmatics: From Experiment to Theory.* Ontario: Palgrave.

van Dyke, J. A. & McElree, B. Retrieval interference in sentence comprehension [J]. *Journal of Memory and Language,* 2006(55): 157-166.

van Gompel, R. P. G., Pickering, M. J., Pearson, J. & Jacob, G. The activation of inappropriate analyses in garden-path sentences: Evidence from structural priming [J]. *Journal of Memory and Language,* 2006(55): 335-362.

van Herten, M., Chwilla, D. J. & Kolk, H. H. When heuristics clash with parsing routines: ERP evidence for conflict monitoring in sentence perception [J]. *Journal of Cognitive Neuroscience,* 2006, *18*(7): 1181-1197.

van Herten, M., Kolk, H. H. & Chwilla, D. J. An ERP study of P600 effects elicited by semantic anomalies [J]. *Cognitive Brain Research,* 2005(22): 241-255.

van Petten, C., Weckerly, C., McIsaac, H. K. & Kutas, M. Working memory capacity dissociates lexical and sentential context effects [J]. *Psychological Science*, 1997(8): 238-242.

Vos, S. H. & Friederici, A. D. Intersentential syntactic context effects on comprehension: The role of working memory [J]. *Cognitive Brain Research*, 2003(16): 111-122.

Vos, S. H., Gunter, T. C., Kolk, H. H. J. & Mulder, G. Working memory constraints on syntactic processing: An electrophysiological investigation [J]. *Psychophysiology*, 2001(38): 41-63.

Vuong, L. C. & Martin, R. C. Domain-specific executive control and the revision of misinterpretations in sentence comprehension [J]. *Language, Cognition and Neuroscience*, 2014, *29*(3): 312-325.

Wager, T. D. & Smith, E. E. Neuroimaging studies of working memory: a meta-analysis [J]. *Cognitive, Affective & Behavioral Neuroscience*, 2003, *3*(4): 255-274.

Walters, G. S., Caplan, D. & Hildebrandt, N. Working memory and written sentence comprehension [M]// Coltheart, M. *Attention and Performance XII: The Psychology of Reading*. Hove: Erlbaum, 1987: 531-555.

Wang, L., Schlesewsky, M., Bickel, B. & Bornkessel-Schlesewsky, I. Exploring the nature of the "subject" -preference: Evidence from the online comprehension of simple sentences in Mandarin Chinese [J]. *Language and Cognitive Processes*, 2009, *24*(7-8): 1180-1226.

Wang, Y., Xue, G., Chen, C., Xue, F. & Dong, Q. Neural bases of asymmetric language switching in second-language learners: An ER-fMRI study [J]. *NeuroImage*, 2007(35): 862-870.

Wang, Y. & Hamilton, A. F. de C. Anterior medial prefrontal cortex implements social priming of mimicry [J]. *Social Cognitive and Affective Neuroscience*, 2014, *10*(4): 486-493.

Wartenburger, I., Heekeren, H. R., Abutalebi, J., Cappa, S. F., Villringer, A. & Perani, D. Early setting of grammatical processing in the bilingual brain [J]. *Neuron*, 2003(37): 159-170.

Waters, G., Caplan, D. & Hildebrandt, N. On the structure of verbal short-term memory and its functional role in sentence comprehension: Evidence from neuropsychology [J]. *Cognitive Neuropsychology*, 1991(8): 81-126.

Waters, G. S. & Caplan, D. Working memory and online syntactic processing in Alzheimer's disease: Studies with auditory moving window presentation [J]. *Journal of Gerontology: Psychological Sciences*, 2002(57B): 298-311.

Waters, G. S. & Caplan, D. The capacity theory of sentence comprehension: Critique of just and Carpenter (1992) [J]. *Psychological Review*, 1996a(103): 761-772.

Waters, G. S. & Caplan, D. Processing resource capacity and the comprehension of garden path sentences [J]. *Memory and Cognition*, 1996b(24): 342-355.

Waters, G. S. & Caplan, D. The measurement of verbal working memory capacity and its relation to reading comprehension [J]. *The Quarterly Journal of Experimental Psychology*, 1996c(1): 51-79.

Waters, G. S. & Caplan, D. The reliability and stability of verbal working memory measures [J]. *Behavior Research Methods, Instruments, and Computers*, 2003(35): 550-564.

Waters, G. S. & Caplan, D. Verbal working memory and on-line syntactic processing: Evidence from self-paced listening [J]. *The Quarterly Journal of Experimental Psychology A: Human Experimental Psychology*, 2004(57A): 129-163.

Waters, G. S. & Caplan, D. Age, working memory, and on-line syntactic processing in sentence comprehension [J]. *Psychology and Aging*, 2001(16): 128-144.

Waugh, N. C. & Norman, D. A. Primary Memory [J]. *Psychological Review*, 1965, *72*(2): 89-104.

Weber, A. & Cutler, A. Lexical competition in non-native spoken-word recognition [J]. *Journal of Memory and Language*, 2004, *50*(1): 1-25.

Weber-Fox, C. & Neville, H. J. Sensitive periods differentiate processing of open- and closed-class words: An ERP study of bilinguals [J]. *Journal of Speech, Language, and Hearing Research*, 2001(44): 1338-1353.

Weckerly, J. & Kutas, M. An electrophysiological analysis of animacy effects in the processing of object relative sentences [J]. *Psychophysiology*, 1999(36): 559–570.

Weiten, W. *Variations in Psychology* [M]. 9 ed. Belmont: Wadsworth, 2013: 281–282.

Whitney, P., Arnett, P., Driver, A. & Budd, D. 2001. Measuring central executive functioning: What's in a reading span? [J] *Brain and Cognition*, 2001(45): 1–14.

Wickelgren, W. A. The long and the short of memory [J]. *Psychological Bulletin*, 1973, *80*(6): 425–438.

Wickens, D. D., Born, D. G. & Allen, C. K. Proactive inhibition and item similarity in short-term memory [J]. *Journal of Verbal Learning and Verbal Behavior*, 1963(2): 440–445.

Williams, J. N. & Lovatt, P. Phonological memory and rule learning [J]. *Language Learning*, 2005(55): 177–233.

Williams, J. N. Memory, attention, and inductive learning [J]. *Studies in Second Language Acquisition*, 1999(21): 1–48.

Williams, J. N. & Lovatt, P. Phonological memory and rule learning [J]. *Language Learning*, 2003(53): 67–121.

Withaar, R. G. & Stowe, L. A. Re-examining evidence for separate sentence processing resources [A]. A paper presented at AMLaP, Edinburgh, Scotland, 1999.

Wu, X., Chen, X., Li, Z., Han, S. & Zhang, D. Binding of verbal and spatial information in human working memory involves large-scale neural synchronization at theta frequency [J]. *NeuroImage*, 2007, *35*(4): 1654–1662.

Yang, Y. & Raine, A. Prefrontal structural and functional brain imaging findings in antisocial, violent, and psychopathic individuals: a meta-analysis [J]. *Psychiatry Research*, 2009, *174*(2): 81–88.

Yantis, S. & Jonides, J. Abrupt visual onsets and selective attention: voluntary versus automatic allocation [J]. *Journal of Experimental Psychology: Human Perception and Performance*, 1990, *16*(1): 121–134.

Ye, Z. & Zhou, X. Executive control in language processing [J]. *Neuroscience and Biobehavioral Reviews*, 2009, *33*(8): 1168-1177.

Yokoyama, S., Okamoto, H., Miyamoto, T., Yoshimoto, K., Kim, J., Iwata, K., Jeong, H., Uchida, S., Ikuta, N., Sassa, Y., Nakamura, W., Horie, K., Sato, S. & Kawashima, R. Cortical activation in the processing of passive sentences in L1 and L2: An fMRI study [J]. *NeuroImage*, 2006(30): 570-579.

Yoo, H. & Dickey, M. W. Aging effects and working memory in garden-path recovery [J]. *Clinical Archives of Communication Disorder*, 2017, *2*(2): 91-102.

Yuan, P. & Raz, N. Prefrontal cortex and executive functions in healthy adults: a meta-analysis of structural neuroimaging studies [J]. *Neuroscience and Biobehavioral Reviews*, 2014(42): 180-192.

Yuan, Y., Woltz, D. & Zheng, R. Cross-language priming of word meaning during second language sentence comprehension [J]. *Language Learning*, 2010, *60*(2): 446-469.

Zacks, R. T. & Hasher, L. Directed ignoring: Inhibitory regulation of working memory [M] // Dagenbach, D. & Carr, T. H. *Inhibitory Mechanisms in Attention, Memory, and Language*. New York: Academic Press, 1994: 241-264.

Zalbidea, J. One Task Fits All? The roles of task complexity, modality, and working memory capacity in L2 performance [J]. *Modern Language Journal*, 2017, *101*(2): 335-352.

Zanto, T. P. & Gazzaley, A. Neural suppression of irrelevant information underlies optimal working memory performance [J]. *The Journal of Neuroscience*, 2009, *29*(10): 3059-3066.

Zechmeister, E. B. & Nyberg, S. E. *Human Memory: An Introduction to Research and Theory* [M]. Monterey: Brooks/Cole, 1982.

陈宝国,徐慧卉. 工作记忆容量的差异对第二语言句法歧义句加工的影响 [J]. 心理学报,2010,42(2):185-192.

陈鸿标. 英语水平对中国学习者理解英语句法歧义句的制约作用 [J]. 现代外

语，1998（2）：5-18.

陈吉棠. 记忆与听力理解［J］. 外语界，1997（3）：43-48.

陈吉棠. 再论记忆与听力理解［J］. 外语界，2002（3）：36-40.

陈吉棠. 三论记忆与听力理解［J］. 外语界，2005（2）：38-44.

陈吉棠. 四论记忆与听力理解［J］. 外语电化教学，2009（128）：48-52.

陈吉棠. 五论记忆与听力理解［J］. 广西师范大学学报：哲学社会科学版，2012，48（4）：153-157.

陈平文. 基于工作记忆的语言理解［J］. 语文学刊，2007（6）：9-12.

陈士法，王邵馨，彭玉乐，崔馨元，杨连瑞. 英语二语"直接宾语／主语"类花园路径句加工的时间进程［J］. 现代外语，2022，45（1）：78-89.

顾琦一，程秀萍. 中国英语学习者的花园路径句理解——与工作记忆容量和二语水平的相关研究［J］. 现代外语，2010（3）：297-304.

桂诗春. 记忆和英语学习［J］. 外语界，2003（3）：2-8.

桂诗春. 新编心理语言学［M］. 上海：上海外语教育出版社，2000.

韩亚文，刘思. 任务复杂度和工作记忆容量对中国英语学习者书面语产出的影响［J］. 山东外语教学，2019，40（2）：66-75.

侯建东. 中国英语学习者"直接宾语／主语"类花园路径句的理解［J］. 浙江外国语学院学报，2014（6）：34-40.

金霞. 二语口语广度测试及其对口语流利度的预测能力［J］. 当代外语研究，2011（1）：36-40.

金霞. 工作记忆容量限制对二语学习者口语产出的影响［J］. 外语教学与研究，2012，44（7）：523-535.

靳红玉，王同顺. 任务复杂度、工作记忆容量与二语写作表现——学习者能动性的作用［J］. 外语与外语教学，2021（3）：102-113+150.

彭聃龄，张必隐. 认知心理学［M］. 杭州：浙江教育出版社，2004.

王初明. 应用心理语言学——外语学习心理研究［M］. 长沙：湖南教育出版社，1990.

王佩杰. 英语局部句法歧义理解［D］. 长春：吉林大学，2007.

王甦. 认知心理学［M］. 北京：北京大学出版社，1992.

温植胜. 对外语学能研究的重新思考［J］. 现代外语，2005，28（4）：383-392.

温植胜.外语学能研究新视角——工作记忆效应 [J].现代外语,2007,30(1):
　　87-95.

吴潜龙.关于第二语言习得过程的认知心理分析 [J].外语教学与研究,2000,
　　32(4):290-295.

徐方.短时记忆、外语听力理解与输入假设 [J].国外外语教学,2005(1):28-
　　35.

杨治良.记忆心理学 [M].上海:华东师范大学出版社,2011.

药盼盼,王瑞乐,陈宝国.工作记忆容量对二语句子加工中动词偏好信息利用
　　的影响 [J].外语教学理论与实践,2013(1):15-21.

张凯,杨嘉琪,陈凯泉.学习者情感因素对英语合作学习投入的作用机理 [J].
　　现代外语,2021,44(3):407-419.

朱智贤.心理学大词典 [M].北京:北京师范大学出版社,1989.